'OURS'

THE JERSEY PALS
IN THE
FIRST WORLD WAR

IAN RONAYNE

First published 2009

Reprinted 2011

The History Press
The Mill, Brimscombe Port
Stroud, Gloucestershire, GL5 2QG
www.thehistorypress.co.uk

British Library Cataloguing in Publication Data.
A catalogue record for this book is available from the British Library.

ISBN 978 0 7524 5145 9
Typesetting and origination by The History Press
Printed in Great Britain

Contents

To Christopher 'Jimmy' Scoones,
father, footballer, soldier, and the starting point for this book.

Foreword

His Excellency Lieutenant General Andrew Ridgway CB CBE
Lieutenant-Governor of Jersey

Each year the people of Jersey gather around the Cenotaph in The Parade on Remembrance Day and listen to the moving words of the Kohima Epitaph, and to the haunting sound of the Last Post played by a member of the Island of Jersey Band. They stand in silence and remember with pride the 6,000 Jerseymen who left the island to fight in the First World War, and especially the 862 who made the ultimate sacrifice and never returned to these shores. But how much do the people of Jersey really know of these brave young, and not so young, men who willingly answered the call and marched off to war; and especially of the 300 or so who volunteered, long before conscription was in force on the island, to join the Jersey Company, a company of Jersey pals, and thus to represent the island's most tangible contribution to the war effort.

In this excellent and well researched book, Ian Ronayne traces the story of the Jersey Company from its conception in 1914, through the heady day of the recruits' departure from the New North Quay on board SS *Ibex* with bands playing and flags waving in 1915, to their almost unnoticed return to the island in 1919. The lives of the young soldiers as they prepare for war with the 7th Battalion the Royal Irish Rifles in Ireland and subsequently in Aldershot are brought vividly to life and characterised by the impromptu Muratti football match played between the contingents from Jersey and Guernsey in Aldershot in October 1915, and which I am pleased to report that Jersey won with a single goal scored by Lance Corporal Mick McCarthy. Life for the Jerseymen in the trenches is also brought into sharp relief; the monotony of routine around Loos and the desperate battles against trench raiding parties, the awful slaughter of the offensives at the Somme and Ypres, and the desperate attempt to cling on to the ground gained at Cambrai after the major tank battle of November 1917. In each case the dramatic events are vividly brought to life by the accounts of the individuals who fought and died so gallantly there.

But this book is much more than just a series of connected war stories. It also highlights the political and constitutional battles that were going on behind the scenes. The initial reluctance of the War Office in London to accept a Jersey unit at all; the perceived failure of the island to support the Jersey Company by failing to generate the necessary reinforcements; the protracted debate on the island over the introduction of conscription; and the Company's eventual disbandment and incorporation into the

Hampshire Regiment – a relationship that continues through the Princess of Wales' Royal Regiment to this day.

It is a remarkable story of momentous events and how they affected a whole community, and a story of individual courage and devotion. On the very last pages of the book it is stated that the day the Jersey Company sailed from St Helier's harbour was the proudest day in the island's history, but goes to observe that, ninety years on, few on the island have ever heard of this unique little band. Well now there is no excuse. This book will ensure that the memory of the Jersey Company in the First World War and the bravery and devotion of this loyal band of 'Jersey Pals' will live on forever.

Introduction

I had not expected to have to write this book. When drawn to the subject some years ago by the passing comments of a colleague, I naturally assumed somebody must have done so already. It seemed inconceivable that the story of more than 300 young 'Jersey Pals' who left their island to fight in one of the most terrible of wars had not yet been written.

Yet a search of local history shelves in the public library revealed nothing published on the subject – or for that matter on any aspect of Jersey in the First World War. It was as though written history had skipped this period in a leap from the Victorian era to the dark days of the Second World War. Investigation of the archives and local history interest groups revealed much the same, although some tantalising glimpses did appear.

Undeterred, I sought people who may have known these 'Jersey Pals' – the men themselves having all passed away by then. Several names led to several meetings, but the response was almost universally the same: they had known the men, but never been invited to discuss their wartime experiences. The old soldiers, it seems, had been reluctant to share their memories with anyone but their own.

At this point, a growing sense of purposeful excitement began to take over. The story of the Jersey Company, its raising, training, wartime service and losses was missing, and growing dimmer by the year. Moreover, in the strands of information I had gathered, there seemed to be an underlying theme of alleged duplicity and broken promises. It was a story that demanded research, and to be told.

In the absence of primary sources of information, the task of research proved challenging. Fortunately, there was at least a wide selection of secondary information available from which to gain or decipher the facts. Most important were the newspapers of the period, by then stored on reels of microfiche at the public library. Endless hours of scrutiny brought forth both snippets and sometimes chunks of important information, albeit slanted in the understandably jingoistic style of the day. The war diaries and the records of military units with whom the Jersey Company served with directly, or fought alongside, contained key elements of the story, along with other relevant books on the First World War. Finally, the Jersey Archive, Commonwealth War Graves Commission, contemporary trench maps, servicemen's records, and even walking the old battlefields made important contributions.

In the end, like a jigsaw, the facts came together to complete a picture, although inevitably, there remain some pieces missing or distorted by time. On encountering them, I relied on interpretation, logical comparisons, and even some assumptions to fill the gaps and maintain continuity. This invariably must mean some (hopefully minor) errors and oversights on my account, for which I apologise unreservedly.

A number of people, either knowingly or not, have assisted in the production of this book, and to them I offer sincere thanks. Notable among them are friends and colleagues from the Channel Islands Great War Study Group (www.greatwarci.net), in particular my brother Paul, Ned Malet De Carteret, Warwick Blench, Mark Bougourd, Roger Frisby and Barrie Bertram. Thanks also to Gareth Syvret of the Société Jersiaise for his kind assistance with some of the photographs. Special thanks to the His Excellency the Lieutenant-Governor of Jersey, Lieutenant General Andrew Ridgway CBE CB, for taking an interest and contributing the Foreword, and to The History Press for agreeing to publish this book. Finally to those individuals and organisations who kindly allowed me to include quotations from their publications.

A last word of thanks must go to the men of the Jersey Company, that small band of 'pals' who volunteered more than ninety years ago to fight for king, country, and their island. Although all are long gone by now, it is their deeds, camaraderie and sufferings that are the inspiration for this book. I like to think they would have approved of it, though I may have had a hard time as they put me right on several things.

Ian Ronayne
August 2009

Prologue

The Proudest Day in Our History?

Cursing, Sergeant Charles Laugeard threw himself to the ground for the third time in as many minutes. With eyes tightly screwed shut, he held his breath and waited. The piercing whistle of a descending artillery shell grew louder, louder, and louder. It sounded frightening close; where would it land? The answer came almost instantaneously. Just moments after its approach had been detected, the shell buried itself into the earth twenty or so yards to his left and exploded – harmlessly.

That was close. Only when the last debris thrown up by the explosion settled did Laugeard feel secure enough to open his eyes and start breathing again. Slowly gulping air, he remained prone however, and waited for the wave of shock and anger to subside. Artillery was the great killer of the First World War. Anyone in the trenches for more than a few days understood the carnage it could inflict on vulnerable flesh and bone, and everyone at the front lived in fear of its impact. Particularly despised was the impersonal nature of shellfire. Artillery, remorselessly served day and night by nameless, faceless gunners, claimed its victims in a cold-hearted and indiscriminate fashion. Worse still, it might even be your own guns firing the shells. Sergeant Laugeard knew that British batteries were firing many of those landing around him that day, the confused fighting of recent days having left the gunners unclear over the new location of the front line. Despite urgent appeals to cease, British artillery had sporadically continued to shell its own side with so-called 'friendly fire'.

Bad enough being killed by a shell, thought Laugeard as he scrambled back to his feet and set off once more, but one fired by your own side. What a way to fight a war!

Minutes later, he found the rest of the Company – or rather, what was left of it – still huddled along both sides of the low trench they had dug the previous night. Despite being in the middle of an artillery battle, most were dozing, trying to snatch a few moments rest after five days of more or less continuous shellfire and five nights of labour. Only one or two had the energy or enthusiasm to look up and acknowledge his return.

One who did was the young Lieutenant that had sent him back to headquarters half an hour earlier for any changes to orders. He picked his way down the trench towards Laugeard, carefully stooping and ducking to avoid presenting a target to vigilant German snipers. 'Well Sergeant,' he enquired in a low voice when close enough, 'are we still due to go over the top as planned?'

'Over the top'. Such an innocent phrase, masking the terrifying reality of what it actually entailed. For a soldier in the First World War it was probably the most dangerous thing he would have to do. Climbing out of the trench and advancing across no man's land towards the enemy seemed innocuous enough; but take one or two well-sited machine guns, fired by a determined enemy, and the advance could falter in seconds. It was a fearful prospect. Yet it was exactly what Laugeard and the others in the Company would have to do that afternoon – for their very first time.

'Nothing changed, sir,' he confirmed with a nod, 'the attack will start at a quarter to five this afternoon as planned. Two hours from now.'

Leaving the Lieutenant to his thoughts, he sought a space in the trench and slumped down. Sprinkled around were the remnants of his platoon. Such familiar faces, such trusted faces, all etched now with the grime and trauma of their ordeal. Good friends, he thought. How many would still be alive tonight?

The sounds of laughter from somewhere in the trench shook him from his gloomy reflections. Remarkably, amid this folly, there were some men actually enjoying themselves! Straining to peer round a slight bend, Laugeard saw that the sound of merriment came from one small group playing cards crouched around an upturned ammunition box. Seemingly oblivious to the shells whistling overhead, the staccato crackle of machine gun fire and the dull crump of mortars landing nearby, the four members of the card school were focused only on winning the next hand. Laugeard knew them all of course. They had been with the Company since the beginning, and seemed to have led a charmed life ever since. During training in Ireland, while hanging around at Aldershot, when learning how to survive at Loos, these four always managed to land the best jobs – and miss the worst. Even in the last few days, during the toughest conditions yet encountered, fortune seemed to smile on them. Real characters, thought Laugeard leaning back and closing his eyes, but great to have around.

Minutes later, he awoke suddenly with a start. Something was wrong. The trench was heaving with commotion. Men were shouting and hurling themselves to the ground. Laugeard barely had time to move before the shell struck with a deafening crash and reverberating force.

For a few seconds, his world seemed to turn upside down. Everything went quiet; then as sound returned it was distant or muffled, like noises heard underwater. Had he been hit? Where was the pain? He waited – but it never came. Regaining his senses, to Laugeard's great relief a quick look down revealed no injuries, no blood, everything present. Just another near miss – or was it?

The shell had struck the lip of the trench just above the card school. Fortunately, this meant most of the explosive force dissipated away; unfortunately, those directly below had stood little chance. By the time Laugeard arrived, two players were already dead, their contorted and bloodied bodies sprawled face down in the dirt. A third was badly wounded, being held down, struggling and screaming in unnatural fashion as attempts were made to press iodine and dressings onto jagged wounds. The last of the players remained sitting beside the makeshift table, apparently unhurt. To everyone's horror, however, as he tried to stand the extent of his injuries became clear. A splinter from the shell had neatly severed his arm above the elbow and left it lying on his lap.

Medical help took some time to arrive, and longer to half-carry, half-drag the wounded men away. Passing by, the young man who had lost the arm turned a deathly pale face towards Sergeant Laugeard and tried to say something. Grimly noting the growing damp red stain that suggested the roughly applied tourniquet was not working, Laugeard smiled back, unconvincingly. 'You'll be alright son,' he mouthed, 'count yourself lucky to be getting out of it.' A few walking-wounded followed – the real lucky ones. What a time to pick up a 'Blighty Wound'. Looking both embarrassed and elated at the same time, they made their way through the trench, shaking a hand here, tweaking a cheek there. 'Good luck' they called back, disappearing from sight.

The commotion was over. All that remained was to heave the dead unceremoniously out of the trench and onto the ground behind. With luck, a Graves Registration Unit would recover the bodies later and deposit them in one of the many official burial grounds; without it, like thousands of others, the dead would eventually be swallowed by the battlefield and remain there forever. Job done, Laugeard settled down once more to await the order to attack.

Fifteen minutes to go. Still seated, Sergeant Laugeard stared incessantly down at his wristwatch. The second hand swept irresistibly round the face, relentlessly and unstoppably ticking off the minutes to zero-hour. By now, the bombardment of the German positions in front had increased noticeably in intensity. The air overhead seemed thick with flying shells, their explosions combining to make the very ground tremble. Could anyone survive that level of destruction? They would soon find out, he thought with a wry smile. Reinforcements arrived, filing into the trench and taking a place along the side. Everyone nervously focused on some task or another; tightening straps, checking weapons, scribbling a few last lines.

With five minutes to go, the men made final preparations. In the British trenches, officers took out whistles and stared at their watches, waiting for the moment to give the signal. 'Good luck mate', an unnamed man at Sergeant Laugeard's side said quietly, thrusting a hand out to shake. 'See you in Ginchy.'

It was Saturday 9 September 1916, in a small corner of the Battle of the Somme. The 16th (Irish) Division had orders to capture the German fortress village of Ginchy – a position that had resisted all previous assaults. The Irish were determined to do better.

At a quarter to five that afternoon, along a broad swathe, the 16th (Irish) Division's soldiers scrambled out of the trenches and lined up to face their objective. Ahead, at the top of a gentle slope, the smoking remains of the village brooded. Even now, shells continued to crash into the ruins, each explosion sending great plumes of dust and debris into the air. Suddenly, there was the order to advance. With a great shout, the wave of men surged forward.

Just for a moment, Sergeant Laugeard hesitated. Not through fear – the last nine months had proved he was no fugitive from danger – but to take in the significance of the moment. This, after all, was what it had been all for: why they had volunteered; why they had left their island; why they had spent so long training; why they had endured nine months in the trenches.

On that day, on a broken field in northern France, the 'Jersey Pals' would finally have the chance to truly prove their island's worth. Would it turn out to be the proudest in Jersey's history?

One

No Cause for Panic

It would be foolish to underestimate the gravity of a situation unparalleled in civilised history, yet, on the other hand, it would be equally unwise to rush to the other extreme, as so many of our people seem inclined to do.

Editorial, Evening Post, August 1914.

The outbreak of war in August 1914 came as something of a shock to the island of Jersey. Not just because its approach had been missed by most inhabitants, nor again because no one could possibly know how it would end. What really infuriated, at the very start at least, was that it interrupted what was turning out to be a first-class summer.

Lying only fifteen miles from the French coast, snug in the protective embrace of the Bay of St Malo, the largest of the British Channel Islands has always enjoyed a mild, if somewhat fickle, climate. With its surrounding waters gently warmed by the Gulf Stream, fine and dry summers are often the result. The summer of 1914 had certainly been following this trend. May, June and July had been mostly warm and settled, and Jersey's 52,000 inhabitants were looking forward to more of the same.

Proprietors in the up-and-coming tourism industry had been especially pleased with the fine weather. The island's charming aspect and appealing climate were first 'discovered' by the Victorians in the late nineteenth century, and a steady business been building ever since. Right up to the end of July that year, hotels and lodging houses were reporting healthy rates of occupancy, while advance bookings held the promise of more to come. Indeed, even in the last days of peace, the hardworking little steamers plying the seas between the Channel Islands, England and France continued to deliver boatloads of visitors. Many were eager to deposit what money they had in island tills; and most islanders were eager to take it.

Members of the island's foremost industry were also satisfied with the conditions. In 1914, agriculture dominated Jersey's forty-five square miles – from a geographical, financial and political perspective. This had become particularly so in the last fifty years when the industry had dramatically grown from a mainly local business into a powerful and successful exporter of produce. Strong overseas markets had been developed, firstly for the famous Jersey cow, and then, after its discovery in 1878, for the equally renowned Jersey Royal potato. By the start of the twentieth century, great shipments of

Jersey Royals were making their way to Britain, and the resulting profits making their way back. In a good season, everyone could do well, and the years leading up to the First World War were some of the best ever. Hopes were high that 1914 would exceed all previous records. Up until the end of July, the year showed every sign of doing just that.

Success in tourism and agriculture was a key factor shaping life in Jersey at this time. Success meant profits, and profits had helped fund a remarkable half-century of civic and commercial development. The summer of 1914 capped a period of impressive transformation. Schools, hospitals, railways and fine public buildings had all sprung up for the benefit of islanders. The general expectation was for more to come. Profits also trickled down, eventually reaching the pockets of most by one means or another, and that summer, with its long evenings and fine weekends, a little more money had been more than welcome. Leisure time was becoming increasingly important – there were fêtes, fairs and open-air concerts to enjoy, or strolls along coastal promenades and walks through leafy inland lanes. In those final days of peace, the annual Battle of Flowers spectacle – fast becoming the highlight of the summer – was approaching. With only weeks to go, tickets were fast selling out.

Business success, fine weather and personal enjoyment had all contributed to a general sense of wellbeing. 'There was no doubt about it,' claimed a senior government figure at the time, 'the tide of prosperity in Jersey has reached high water mark, and I hope it will remain so.'[1] There appeared no obvious reason why this should not continue to be the case. The traditionally resourceful and hard-working islanders were enjoying the fruits of a well-established and successful economy, and looking forward to the future with confidence.

Yet events elsewhere, and far beyond the control of this small community, were conspiring to bring this halcyon summer to a dramatic end. A startling series of unprecedented shocks were set to herald the end of an era, and the beginning of one of the most testing periods on the island's history. And it had all started in St Helier on the warm evening of 29 July 1914.

Jersey's capital and chief port is the town of St Helier, in 1914 the bustling heart of island life. As the beneficiary of much of the previous half-century's development, it had grown tremendously in recent years. From an original modest settlement centred on the historic Royal Square and Town Church, an expanding population had pushed out its boundaries until most of the land surrounding Mont De La Ville with its imposing Fort Regent was filled with houses and businesses. By the eve of war, St Helier was home to 27,000 people, or just over half of the island's population. It was also home to a number of popular theatres and playhouses. One was the iconic and imposing West's Picture House that filled the corner made by Peter Street and Bath Street. In recent years, along with others, it had been adapted to accommodate the latest and most exciting form of public entertainment, cinema. On the evening of 29 July, a packed auditorium was enjoying a programme that included a film starring that up-and-coming young comedian, Charlie Chaplin.

Located in nearby Charles Street were the offices of the *Evening Post*, then one of the island's foremost newspapers. In those days before television or radio broadcasting, it dominated local media together with fierce rival the *Morning News*. The offices of the *Evening Post* also happened to host the local telegraph bureau, making them the central location for the latest overseas news. As the cinemagoers left West's that evening, some had noticed a large and excited crowd gathered in Charles Street. Going over to find out what the fuss was about, they found the focus of attention was a notice posted in the *Evening Post* office window. In impassive type, it spelled out the astonishing news that was about to stop Jersey in its tracks.

As of the following day, 30 July 1914, the Jersey Militia was being mobilised for war.

War itself was nothing new for Jersey. In centuries past, islanders had been accustomed to its threat as frequent conflicts between England and France placed them in a front-line position. The last French invasion, however, was in 1781, and since the defeat of Napoleon in 1815, relations between the old enemies had steadily improved. In 1914, the chance of an attack from France was all but unthinkable. Yet 133 years after its last battle, the Jersey Militia was to be mobilised once more.

The Royal Militia of the Island of Jersey, to give its full and proper title, was a distinguished and historic corps that dated back to the fourteenth century at least. At that time, English monarchs anxious to retain their southern bulwark had ordered the island fortified against the French. Castles had been built, military garrisons installed, and island's men ordered to form a military force to be mobilised against the threat of invasion. Down the centuries, with this threat never far away, the principle of a local Militia had become enshrined in Jersey's traditions and laws. By the start of the twentieth century, although the threat had diminished, the Jersey Militia remained one of the pillars of island life.

Although its organisation had changed over the years, in 1914 the principle of Militia service remained the same. By law, all able-bodied Jerseymen between the ages of sixteen and forty-five were liable for Militia service. Once enrolled, they trained to be soldiers, giving up a number of evenings and weekends for drill, instruction and rifle practice. For those between the ages of eighteen and twenty-eight, there was also mandatory attendance at a two-week summer military camp. The most important expectation, however, was that if the island was ever threatened, the men had to fight in its defence.

Remarkably, it was an arrangement unique to Jersey (and the other Channel Islands of Guernsey and Alderney). In no other part of the British Empire did such a compulsory military service exist. There were militias in the Dominions and Colonies, and in England, Scotland and Wales an equivalent force called the Territorial Army existed, but service in all these was on a voluntary basis only. Outside of the Channel Islands, no one was compelled to join by law.

In 1914, this local law established that Jersey should have a Militia force capable of defending its shores. The backbone of this force was its three infantry battalions, recruited on a parochial basis from an allocated number of the island's twelve parishes. The 1st, or West Battalion, represented the parishes of St Lawrence, St Brelade, St Peter,

St Ouen, St Mary and St John. The 2nd, or East Battalion, took men from St Saviour, St Clement, St Martin, Grouville and Trinity. The 3rd, or Town Battalion, was raised exclusively from a single parish, St Helier. In addition to the infantry, there existed an artillery regiment with two batteries of field artillery and two companies of garrison artillery, a medical company and a company of engineers. The mobilisation order of 29 July 1914 demanded that all these units turn out for service.

The news that the Militia was being mobilised once again had spread through the island like a shock wave. On the streets of St Helier, there was lively and heated discussion over what exactly was going on. Was it just an exercise, or the real thing? How long was the Militia expected to be mobilised? And what was it expected to do? With no information forthcoming that night, in the end there could only be speculation as to the answers. Everyone would have to wait until 2.00 p.m. on 30 July, the time at which the men of the Militia had orders to report for duty.

On the following day, the men of the 3rd Battalion mustered at the Town Arsenal. Throughout the morning, an excited crowd of onlookers had built up outside cheering and waving as the men went in. Their presence, it was reported, lent the occasion a Sunday school outing atmosphere rather than that of a serious military mobilisation. Once inside the Arsenal, the excited mood persisted. The mobilisation order had dramatically interrupted everyday life and there were plenty of stories swapped on the sacrifices made to make the deadline. One man had apparently even missed his wedding to be there. Yet the chief topic of conversation remained why exactly were they there, and how long would they have to stay. At 2.00 p.m., the men at last started to receive some firm answers.

With the Battalion paraded, their Commanding Officer, Lieutenant Colonel Gerald McKenzie, stepped up to address the now hushed ranks. In ringing tones, he explained the reason for the mobilisation, and the strict expectations on the men from now on:

> At the outset I wish you to realise that this was not merely a test mobilisation, as supposed by some, but a serious mobilisation ordered by the War Office. I repeat that this is not a joke, but a serious mobilisation ordered by the War Office in view of the state of feeling amongst the European Powers.
>
> You have been called up as soldiers, and I expect and know that you will behave as such. How long it would last, I cannot say, but all ranks must understand that they are under Military Law until demobilisation takes place.[2]

In a more subdued mood, the men had filed away after the speech to collect weapons and supplies. Clearly, this was no exercise. As they formed up behind their officers and marched out of the Arsenal, questions nevertheless remained in many minds. What exactly was this 'state of feeling amongst the European Powers'? And for that matter, how could it possibly affect Jersey?

Europe's slide to war in July 1914 had not been widely reported in Jersey. Apart from local news, the attention of island newspapers had been on events closer to home.

With divisive national issues such as the struggle for women's rights and Home Rule for Ireland grabbing headlines, European news found comparatively limited space among the columns. Yet one story that had managed to receive a few terse paragraphs was that of the assassination of Archduke Franz Ferdinand.

On 28 June 1914, the heir to the throne of the Austro-Hungarian Empire was visiting the city of Sarajevo. In 1914, as now, Sarajevo lay at the heart of a troubled Balkans, a region of mixed nationalities and religions held together and apart by poorly defined borders. Waiting among the crowd that day were a number of people determined to take a stand against the presence of the Austro-Hungarians in the Balkans. One was a young Serbian nationalist called Gavrilo Princip. Encountering the car carrying the Archduke and his wife Sophie, he had gone over and shot them both dead.

Austro-Hungary and Serbia were rivals in the region. With the killings, the former had seized upon the chance to humble its small Serbian neighbour. Uncovering tenuous evidence linking the actions of Princip to the Serbian government in Belgrade, the Austro-Hungarians decided to act. On 28 July, after the Serbians had understandably declined to meet a series of humiliating demands, Austro-Hungary declared war. Suddenly, the Balkan incident was becoming more serious – and not just because of the looming regional conflict. The Serbians had a powerful friend.

The sprawling Russian Empire was Serbia's traditional supporter and protector. Faced with the prospect of fellow Slavs being crushed in a one sided war, Russia decided to become involved. It demanded the Austro-Hungarians back down, and threatened to mobilise part of the Russian Army if they refused. Given the delicate state of affairs in Europe at this time, this was a decision with far-reaching and potentially explosive consequences.

In 1914, a complex web of alliances and treaties divided Europe into two powerful opposing camps. On one side lay the Triple Alliance of Germany, Austro-Hungary and Italy, and on the other, the Triple Entente of Russia, France and Great Britain. Like the nuclear deterrents of a later age, in theory these alliances had existed to minimise the risk of war breaking out. In reality, however, all of the countries involved expected conflict sooner or later, and each had detailed plans for just such an eventuality. In the case of Germany, this was the famous, or more correctly perhaps the infamous, Schlieffen Plan.

Of all the European powers, Germany's position had been one of the most precarious at this time. Confronted by Russia on one side and France on the other, it needed a plan to deal with both at the same time. The answer was the Schlieffen Plan. Devised by the military, the plan assumed that because of its immense size and limited infrastructure, Russia would take at least six weeks to mobilise its army and launch an attack on Germany. During this period, the plan directed that virtually the whole German Army could attack France and win a decisive victory there. Then, with the French defeated in the west, Germany could turn to face its lumbering eastern neighbour.

It was a risky but audacious proposal, with one obvious and major flaw. The plan assumed war would start with both Russia and France at the same time. In late July 1914, however, with Russia then mobilising unilaterally against the Austro-Hungarians, this flaw suddenly became critically obvious. Trapped by its own strategy, Germany was forced to weigh up its options. In the end, the decision was to follow the provisions of the Schlieffen Plan – regardless of the consequences. If Russia did continue to mobilise in the east, Germany would just have to attack in the west.

The murders in Sarajevo had unexpectedly started the countdown to a general European war. Within a month, and virtually without warning, the incident in the Balkans had escalated to the point where communities across Europe found themselves unexpectedly on the verge of conflict. This included the tiny Channel Island of Jersey, for which even the threat of war had immediate and far-reaching consequences.

During the years leading up to the First World War, Britain had maintained a garrison in Jersey for the island's defence. In 1914, around 1,000 men were present, the majority from the 1st Battalion of the Devonshire Regiment. Under the terms of its alliance with France, however, these men would join the army sent to the Continent as part of Britain's contribution to a war. On 29 July 1914, with tension between Germany and Russia rising, the British War Office ordered the men of the Devonshire Regiment to start preparations to leave Jersey. To take their place, an order had arrived at the same time to mobilise the island's Militia. Although war might still be avoided, the War Office clearly reasoned it was better to be safe than sorry.

So although it may not have been necessarily clear on 30 July as the Militia left their barracks, war was expected and Jersey needed to be prepared. On that night – and in the days and nights that followed – the men had stood guard around the island's coast and kept watch over key installations. On the morning of 31 July, islanders woke to find themselves in the midst of an army camp, as the *Evening Post* reported:

> It must surely be many years since the island was so well guarded as it was last evening. Patrols and pickets practically surrounded the coasts, and many amusing tales are told of country folk arriving home to find militiamen camping out in their fields and hedges.[3]

Despite the depravations of now having to sleep rough, and the unexpected interruption to their normal lives, spirits were high among the men of the Militia. Absenteeism, even in the country parishes where busy farms needed every hand, was negligible. How long this spirit remained would of course depend on how long the mobilisation lasted – few held out any illusions that what seemed enjoyable in July would be anything but come winter. Hopefully, things would be back to normal long before that time.

From the Continent, however, the news was not good. On 1 August 1914, Germany had declared war on Russia. That same day, France ordered its army to mobilise for war – with further dramatic consequences for Jersey.

To service its booming agricultural industry, Jersey had needed a labour force larger that the island was capable – or perhaps willing – to provide. The solution lay in the nearby French region of Brittany. From the end of the nineteenth century, Breton labourers were coming to the island in large numbers to work on farms, and later in hotels and boarding houses. By 1914, they represented a considerable portion of the population – around 20 per cent according to the 1911 census. Virtually all, however, had remained French nationals, with the men liable for military service and recall in the event of a general mobilisation.

At that time, France relied on massive armies of conscripts for its defence. This meant that upon reaching a certain age, all suitable men received a call-up to the armed forces. Following a number of years service, they returned to civilian life, but remained liable for recall in the event of war. This recall, together with a movement of men and material from their peacetime stations towards the frontier, was termed mobilisation. It extended to national subjects outside of the country, including those men working at the time in Jersey. Late on the evening of 1 August 1914, the widely expected French mobilisation order had arrived in the telegraph office of the *Evening Post.*

By mid-morning of the next day, the French Consulate building in St Helier's Church Street was crowded with men applying for passports and arranging transport to France. Outside in the street, hundreds more awaited their turn. The French mobilisation order left little room for delay; war was imminent and men were to report for duty in the shortest possible time. With the necessary documents secured, they had made the short journey to St Helier's harbour in order to catch one of the specially chartered ships to France. As it was a Sunday, a large crowd of curious onlookers had gathered at the harbour to watch the unfolding spectacle. Yet little preparation had been made for these extra numbers, and soon the situation became somewhat chaotic as departing French reservists jostled their way through the crowd to reach the quayside. A reporter later described the scene, and some of the emotional farewells that ensued:

> Naturally several pathetic incidents were witnessed just prior to the vessel's departure, wives separating from their husbands and girls from their sweethearts. In short, yesterday's scenes were such as have rarely if ever been witnessed before in Jersey. So ended our first acute touch with this great European tragedy.[4]

In all, more than 2,400 Frenchmen would leave the island to fight in the First World War, most in the days immediately following the mobilisation order. For the island's farmers in particular, it was a devastating blow. Coming hard on the heels of the Militia mobilisation, many wondered how they would manage to keep up any kind of production.

It was, of course, also a devastating blow for the families of the departing men, many of whom had accompanied their husbands and fathers to Jersey and settled there. On 3 August, even as many French reservists were still leaving, Germany had declared war on France, ending the last slim chance of avoiding conflict in Western Europe. It was a fateful moment for France and its people. During the course of the war, of all nations, it was one of those to suffer most in respect of material damage and casualties. Indeed, within weeks of leaving Jersey, many of the Frenchmen would find themselves fighting and dying in the first desperate clashes of the war.

There was one more wave of departures for Jersey to witness in those first few days of August as a number of British reserve soldiers and sailors had also left to rejoin their units. Despite ordering preparations for war to begin, Britain hesitated for a moment when it came to actually joining in. There were hopes that it could remain out of the unfolding conflict. A German invasion of neutral Belgium, however, had forced the matter. On 4 August 1914, Britain declared war on Germany.

Britain's declaration of war brought to a close one of the most dramatic weeks in Jersey's history. It was hard to comprehend that just seven days earlier, the island had been enjoying a normal, peaceful and successful summer season. Now, through a series of unprecedented events, the situation had changed beyond all recognition and few, if anyone, knew what might happen next.

There were many, however, prepared to speculate. It was an anxious time. In the absence of any real news, rumour and hearsay understandably filled the gaps. Fanciful reports quickly circulated regarding the enemy's intentions. A German warship had been apprehended in local waters; a fleet of German airships were heading towards Jersey; a gang of German spies were on the island with plans to put poison in the reservoirs. On 5 August, with rumours reaching fever pitch, the *Evening Post* had called for calm:

> The suspense of the last few days has, we admit, been difficult to endure in serenity, and in addition other causes have contributed to the feverish excitement that prevails … but while our hearts are moved we must see to it that we keep our heads, remembering that under the circumstances patience and self control are the first essentials.
>
> Had the German fleet been anchored in St Aubin's Bay yesterday one could have understood the pitiable nervousness to which many women were reduced, but under the circumstances it was as unwarranted as it was inexplicable.[5]

Potentially the most serious rumour circulating was that food and other vital goods were about to run out, and in truth there was a genuine ground for concern. The island relied on imports of many necessities, including all of its fuel. Any disruption to supplies could be serious, although given that the war was only a few days old the situation had been far from critical. Yet that did not stop an immediate run on food shops as people rushed to stock up. It also did not stop merchants from swiftly raising the price of goods in response. To ensure the continuation of supply was the justification; to everyone else, however, it was just plain profiteering. Tensions rose with the prices and the situation threatened to spiral out of control. It was time for the island's government to intervene.

Jersey was then, and is now, a self-governing Crown Dependency of Britain. This status dated back to the time of William the Conqueror and his invasion of England in 1066. As one of William's original possessions, Jersey (and the other Channel Islands) had become part of his enlarged realm following the Norman victory at the Battle of Hastings. This situation persisted until 1204, when one of William's less successful heirs managed to lose control of their lands on the French side of the Channel. Faced with a choice, Jersey had decided to remain with the English Crown, rather than side with the new French rulers. It was a far-reaching decision. In return for their loyalty, the English monarch had granted the islanders certain entitlements and privileges, including the right to self-government.

Understandably, however, Britain had retained responsibility for the island's defence because almost overnight, Jersey had changed from a sleepy community in the middle of the realm to an exposed and vulnerable outpost pressed against the enemy's border. To ensure security from outside attack (and to persuade against any change of heart by the people) the king had appointed a trusted lieutenant to govern the island and watch over his affairs. This turned out to be a long-lasting arrangement. In 1914, as the war started, the man holding the post of Lieutenant-Governor was Major General Sir Alexander Rochfort, KCB, CMG.

History showed that the relationship between the often independently-minded islanders and their Lieutenant-Governor was not always harmonious. Fortunately, sixty-six-year-old Rochfort was well suited to the position. After arriving in 1910, he endeared himself with a friendly and welcoming nature. In dealing with issues of government, he had adopted an even-handed approach and managed to maintain a good working balance between Jersey's interests and those of Britain. This was just as well as the war was going to put considerable stress on this balance. Indeed Rochfort's first act as conflict threatened had been to call out the Militia on 30 July following instruction from the War Office. The second was summoning the States of Jersey for an Extraordinary Session on 5 August 1914.

The States of Jersey, or simply the States as they were called, was the island's long-standing and time-honoured parliament. Its membership in 1914 was an interesting blend of elected and appointed members, drawn mainly from the island's traditional ruling classes. Unsurprisingly, it was an all-male affair – women on the island being unable to stand or even vote. There were no political parties; technically, members represented the people's interests as independents. Presiding over the States was the island's Bailiff.

The role of Bailiff is a hard one to describe easily. At various times, they had to play the role of States president, the island's mayor, and its senior judge. In essence, however, if the Lieutenant-Governor was responsible for all military matters, then the Bailiff was responsible for everything of a civil nature. As in the case of the Lieutenant-Governor, the British monarch appointed the Bailiff to the position – although this was usually based on the advice of senior figures on the island. Once selected, they held the post until they retired at the age of seventy. As the island's most senior figure, only men (there has never been a female Bailiff) of impeccable experience, character and integrity were chosen. In 1914, the man deemed to possess these traits was Sir William Henry Vernon.

When the First World War broke out, Vernon had been Bailiff for fifteen years. His appointment had followed a distinguished career as a lawyer, judge, cattle breeder and high-ranking Militia officer. Despite this background, he remained a private and quiet man, somewhat introverted and maintaining only a small circle of friends and acquaintances. Publicly, however, he was a gifted speaker and a shrewd judge of character and circumstances. He was also a dogged advocate of Jersey's independent rights, often in the face of British pressure to change. This was a just as well – testing times lay ahead. At the start of August 1914, Jersey needed a strong guiding hand to restore calm.

Mindful of the growing level of anxiety, the States met in a special session on 5 August. It was an understandably excitable and noisy affair. The Lieutenant-Governor led off the proceedings. In the uncertain times that lay immediately ahead, he had explained, there may be difficulties securing sufficient quantities of food and other necessities for the island. Given these circumstances, it was the duty of the States to impose the required firm measures to limit the risk to the civilian population and the military forces of the island. Powerful new legislation, he concluded, was needed immediately. Firstly, he announced, he wanted to prohibit the export of food and goods from the island. Secondly, to manage the import of food and fuel, and to establish price controls to prevent profiteering. Finally – and most draconian – he demanded that any undesirables be removed from the island to limit the number of unnecessary mouths to be fed, and steps to be taken to prevent the arrival of any more. Anxious to comply, the States overwhelmingly agreed to act as suggested.

Within days, the new regulations had begun to have effect. With measures in place to control both the supply of food and its price, the population quickly calmed down. As day-to-day life slowly resumed an air of normality, attention turned to events on the Continent.

As Jersey settled down, in Belgium and France the war was soon beginning in earnest. Within weeks, millions of men were locked in bitter conflict as both sides embarked on their plans for war. Britain, alone among European powers, had fielded only a relatively small army of regular soldiers, all of whom were volunteers. The British Expeditionary Force, or BEF, fought its first battle on 23 August 1914 in and around the Belgian mining town of Mons. On the following day, despite performing well against the enemy, the BEF began to retreat. Alongside, French armies were doing the same.

Germany had won the Battle of the Frontiers and gained the upper hand; the Schlieffen Plan appeared to be working. As August drew to a close, in a seemingly unstoppable advance, its armies closed on Paris while the British and French continued to fall back before them. To the great consternation of the Allies and their populations, after only five weeks of fighting, it looked like they might lose the war.

By the start of September, German armies were within a few miles of the French capital. Yet 200 miles of advance had taken its toll on the soldiers, leading to the forces available becoming increasingly tired and stretched. At last, in positions along the Marne River, the Allies began to fight back. For a few days, the world had held its breath while the outcome of the battle was in the balance. Finally, on 9 September, struggling to make progress and beset by uncertainties, the Germans gave way and began to retreat. The Allies had won the Battle of the Marne and saved Paris.

It had been a very close thing, but the war was destined to continue. Communities everywhere breathed again, and wondered what would happen next.

Two

Are We Roused?

The youth of the island now had a glorious opportunity to show that they as Jerseymen
neither feared death nor the enemies of the country.

William Vernon, Bailiff of Jersey, December 1914

On 13 September 1914, the Dean of Jersey stepped into the pulpit of St Helier's Town
Church and glowered down on the upturned faces of his parishioners. Not a man
known for holding back, the Very Reverend Samuel Falle had chosen an increasingly
topical subject for his sermon that day, 'England was calling today as she had never called
before and yet Jersey, the oldest part of the Empire, was not represented by a unit', he
announced. He appealed to the congregation, 'Oh, young men of St Helier, and of the
country parishes of the island, the call has come to you!'[1]
The sermon echoed a popular and growing sentiment. With the British Expeditionary
Force engaged at this time in a life or death struggle in France, should the young
men of Jersey stay on the island, or volunteer to help the mother country at its
hour of greatest need. Most of them, after all, had already trained to be soldiers with
the Militia. Would it not be better to employ their skills in France? It was not as
straightforward a question as it seemed. Complex matters lay at stake, but the issue at
the heart of this question was one that was set to overshadow the island for the next
six months – and indeed for rest of the war. Before the Dean had raised it publicly,
however, the subject was one that had been discussed in hushed tones only. Now, with
the Germans apparently defeated and in retreat, surely there was no longer a reason to
keep it quiet. It was time to face the overriding question. Should Jersey send its men
to fight in the war?

The Allied victory on the Marne had ended any immediate threat to the Channel
Islands. With the Germans in retreat, the likelihood of hostile forces appearing on the
nearby French coast had diminished daily. Any perceived threat from the German fleet
was also declining and they had yet to come out from their ports and challenge Royal
Navy supremacy in the North Sea. It seemed safe to conclude therefore that Jersey,
for the near future at least, was unlikely to come under direct attack. If this was the
case, some questioned, why was it necessary to keep the island on such a high state of
defence?

Since mobilisation on 30 July 1914, the Jersey Militia had remained on guard over the island's coasts. Indeed, when the British Army garrison finally left on 21 August, the local troops became the sole defenders. Yet were they really required for that task – or at least in such numbers? With the war apparently being won or lost in France, was it then time to reconsider? It was a controversial question; and it would come into stark focus during the early days of September as the famous Kitchener appeal had begun.

Lord Herbert Kitchener was the British Secretary of State for War. In these early days of the conflict, the famous old soldier, conqueror of the Sudan and South Africa, was one of the few to really grasp that this was going to be a long war – and understand the implications of this for Britain. To win would require men – and men in their millions at that, but with Britain's army raised exclusively from volunteers, there was no legislation – or indeed resolve – to compel men to serve. Kitchener would have to rely on the power of persuasion, and, in one of the most famous (and successful) poster campaigns in history, he did just that.

Across Britain, his face and pointing finger appeared everywhere with the clear message, 'Your Country Needs You'. The campaign worked, and to an extent not envisaged even by Kitchener himself. Up and down the country, hundreds of thousands flocked to join the army. From all walks of life, men responded in a great patriotic outpouring, rushing to do their bit for king and country. At the time, many of these volunteers had banded together to join up as a group. Coming from the same region, town, profession or college, these units quickly became known as the 'Pals Battalions', and through media interest, captured the nation's imagination. The enthusiasm and comradeship of these tight-knit bodies of men seemed to embody the nation's desire to see the war through to the end.

It was not only the communities of Britain that were rallying to the cause. In Australia, Canada, New Zealand and South Africa, thousands more were also coming forward to volunteer. Even in India, as the Dean had told his congregation on 13 September, the people had risen as one to support their King-Emperor. The whole country it seemed, and the wider empire beyond, was lining behind Britain at this critical moment in its history, with one apparent exception – there were no plans to form a 'Jersey Pals' unit.

In the days that followed the Dean's provocative sermon, popular interest in Jersey forming a military unit of its own had swiftly gained momentum. If communities across Britain could raise Pals Battalions, then what was stopping Jersey? Among the Militia too, there were strong feelings on the subject. Many were keen to take part in this epic conflict, rather than sit out the war at home. At the start of September, there had at least been a concession granted by the War Office. Although it continued to insist that the Militia as whole remain on the island, it would allow individual militiamen to enlist in the British Army. Yet many were holding back in the prospect of joining a Jersey unit – if one ever appeared.

The uncertainty over the matter had led to confusion. The *Morning News* was uncompromising in its views about who was to blame. Since the start, it contended, the whole matter of forming a Jersey unit had been mishandled. Between them, it claimed, the civil and military authorities had set a 'beautiful example of how not to do things!'[2]

Unknown to the newspapers, however, behind the scenes the island's authorities were considering the matter very seriously. In view of the apparently improving situation in France, a decision had been taken to challenge the War Office's order to keep the Jersey Militia on the island. On 18 September, the Lieutenant-Governor had raised the subject of a Jersey unit in a letter to the War Office:

> I have the honour to report that a desire has been expressed here to furnish a small contingent from the Militia of the island, for service with the Expeditionary Force, during the present war.
>
> Recruiting for the Regular Army is open to all militiamen, but it is believed that the formation of a Jersey Unit would attract men not otherwise desirous of serving on the continent.[3]

Given the chance, Major General Rochfort estimated at least 500 men would volunteer. With some special training, he went on, within a month they would prove very useful. It took until 25 September for a reply to arrive. 'It would be inadvisable at the present juncture to reduce the military strength now available for the defence of Jersey,' the War Office had stated, 'by withdrawing any of the trained personnel from the Royal Jersey Militia.'[4] The offer of a Jersey Pals unit had been turned down.

Two factors may have influenced the War Office when making this decision. The first was that although the threat to the island appeared to have diminished because of the German retreat, the military situation in France remained fluid. With the British Army relying on strong lines of communication to the ports landing their supplies, should the Germans advance again, these ports would end up being in Brittany, or even further south. In this situation, the Channel Islands would find themselves strategically positioned close to important shipping routes. Better therefore, that they remained firmly in British hands.

The second factor may have related to Kitchener himself. The Secretary of State for War had an inherent mistrust of part-time soldiers. This was underlined when he chose to form the recently raised volunteers into a 'New Army', rather than expand using the existing part-time Territorial Army structure. It could well be the case – although it is not certain – that he passed judgement on the offer of a group of part-time soldiers from Jersey by the same standards.

Either way, it was with disappointment that the States, and the wider island, learned on 28 September about the War Office's decision. With the fighting continuing to rage on the nearby Continent, for some the lack of a Jersey unit was becoming nothing less than deplorable. 'One cannot but ask oneself what is Jersey doing, or is likely to do, as regards sending men into the fighting line,' fumed one commentator in November, 'where each day sees fresh examples of the most practical patriotism on the part of communities often far smaller than our own.'[5]

With the matter closed – for the time being at least – most people had turned their attention to events closer to home. Following the dramatic events in early August, and although the situation may have settled down, the war continued to affect everyday island life. One of the most noticeable changes was the presence of a growing army of khaki-clad foreigners.

From the start of September, the number of men under arms on the island began to rise considerably. Supplementing the Militia, who of course remained mobilised, on 9 September, the 4th Battalion of the South Staffordshire Regiment had arrived on the island. Its role was twofold: assume garrison duties and continue its normal peacetime role of training new recruits for the regiment's active service battalions. With Kitchener's drive for volunteers in full swing, there was certainly no shortage of men pouring into recruitment offices across Britain. It meant that within weeks, nearly 2,000 eager young men from the West Midlands had arrived on the island, with the prospect of more to come.

From the start, the new arrivals set out to foster good relations. With one important resident at least, they seem to have succeeded. 'The cheerful way the men had settled down,' claimed Major General Rochfort in early October, 'has won the hearts of all classes on the island.'[6] Others were less impressed. Years of isolation and close community living had led many inhabitants to hold a deep-rooted sense of misgiving towards anyone deemed an outsider. Towards the end of October, the more cynical might have claimed their fears were justified. To protect the newly arrived and apparently easily-led young soldiers, the States had agreed to an Army request to reduce licensing hours. From then on, public bars, hotels and clubs would need to close at 8p.m. For an island with a healthy appetite for beer and spirits, it was a black day.

With the outbreak of war, drinking establishments were not the only places of public entertainment under curfew. People were soon dismayed to find the opening hours of local picture houses and theatres were similarly restricted, or in some cases, the venue closed altogether. Frivolous entertainment, it seemed, needed restricting at this hour of national struggle. Other more significant (but apparently less resented) measures were also coming into place. In September, these included adopting a limited form of martial law that introduced restrictions on freedom of speech. In December, the first charges would be brought under it when a local man was accused of spreading malicious rumours.

Yet not every development was unfavourable. For instance, the South Staffordshires brought numerous army contracts with them, meaning lucrative deals for the supply of goods and services to local businesses. In addition, some of the restrictions originally established when war broke out were being lifted. This included easing the limitations on travel and the export of goods. To the delight of the farming community, this meant that from late September 1914, shipments of cattle and potatoes could start again.

The island was also generally getting into its stride in supporting the war effort. If they could not send their men, the people of Jersey could certainly demonstrate their loyalty in other ways. Whether it was helping Belgian refugees, raising funds for military ambulances or opening canteens for soldiers, islanders had responded with generosity. With winter approaching, socks, scarves and blankets were asked for and given in great quantities. Particularly popular was a *Morning News* campaign to collect 'Smokes for Our Troops'. Thousands of cigarettes were donated and dispatched to the front.

Yet during this period of goodwill, it seems ironic that one war-related cause closer to home was being increasingly overlooked. The Militia (who after all had never asked to be mobilised) were becoming sidelined in a rush to support overseas troops. With the arrival of the South Staffordshires, and diminishing threat of invasion, the role of the local force had become progressively less clear, its contribution less obvious. Nonetheless, with winter fast approaching, it was a role and contribution about to get increasingly challenging, as one militiaman wrote in November:

> I had a pretty bad week on Outpost Duty, for I had four nights of it as against three at headquarters. This outpost business is naturally very trying at first, but they tell me that after two or three years one gets used to it. When you are on Outpost you need not expect much sleep, but you get some fine night scenery and plenty of wind dodging practice.[7]

To ease the burden of Militia service, some concessions had at least been made. Without them, the island would have undoubtedly come to a halt. Most important was the introduction of a rotation system dividing the militiamen's time between military and civilian roles. It meant they could return to their families and places of work on a regular basis. In addition, the number of militiamen available was increased by scraping together every available man – in some cases regardless of suitability to be a soldier. These changes had made Militia duty bearable, although still onerous. Nevertheless, bearable or not, the prospect of a cold and wet winter watching over deserted beaches and cliffs clearly did not appeal to everyone. From October onwards, there would be a steady stream of men leaving the Militia.

The concession of allowing individual men to join the British Army had been the trigger. With seemingly little prospect of a Jersey unit, some did not want to remain aside from the thrilling events reportedly taking place on the field of battle. With a widely held belief at the time that the war was going to be over by Christmas, failure to get involved now would mean missing out. Others, perhaps no less patriotic, but more practical, were enticed by the prospect of advancement or personal gain. In the now rapidly expanding British Army, there were plenty of openings for a man with some previous military training. Indeed, many departing militiamen at that time had their pick of the regiments, and an offer of an enhanced rank.

In total, perhaps 250 individuals chose to leave from the Militia during October and November 1914 and enlist in the British Army. This, as it turned out, would have consequences. As November drew to a close, a surprise announcement was being prepared on the subject of a Jersey unit. In the weeks that followed, those already departed militiamen would be sorely missed.

On 4 December 1914, with little warning or fanfare, a small, innocuous notice appeared in the columns of Jersey's newspapers:

> The War Office have reconsidered a decision made at the commencement of the war, that it was undesirable to reduce the military strength available for the Defence of the Island.
>
> They have now consented to meet the desire of the inhabitants to be represented overseas by a contingent raised from the island Militia.
>
> Volunteers from the Militia Units are accordingly called for, and should report to their Commanding Officers on or before Wednesday, 9th Instant.

It was an about-face. September's unequivocal decision to keep the Militia at home had been overturned. Perhaps the fact men were leaving anyway – albeit in ones and twos – had caused the War Office to change its mind. Alternatively, the continued lobbying for a Jersey unit by key figures on the island's administration had made a difference. Yet most likely, however, was that contrary to popular opinion, the war was certainly not going to be over by Christmas after all. The Allied victory in early September may have saved Paris, but it certainly did not end the war. Swiftly regrouping, the German Army was soon on the move again. This time its target was the Channel coast, and the open left-flank of the Allied forces.

The Allies had the same idea, and were soon moving forces towards the coast themselves in an attempt to outflank the Germans. This phase of the war, later known as 'The Race to the Sea', had ended in November in a series of bitterly contested and close-run battles around the small Belgian town of Ypres. Here the British Army tenaciously held its ground against repeated attacks, while on either side French and Belgian forces had done likewise. Germany's attempt to win the war in 1914 had been thwarted.

The cost of doing so was a high one. The small professional army Britain had gone to war with had been virtually destroyed in the five months of fighting. To continue the war, it needed not just replacing, but expanding on a previously unimagined scale – men were going to be required from across the British Empire. With local threat of invasion removed, some at least could come from Jersey.

The requirements for a Jersey contingent were clearly set out in the War Office's notice. Men between the ages of nineteen and thirty-eight, with a minimum height of five feet and three inches and a chest that measured at least thirty-four and half inches could volunteer. Standard rates of army pay were on offer, plus normal separation allowances and pensions. A Private would earn 1s a day, a Sergeant 2s and 4d. The wife of a man killed in action could expect to receive 5½s a week, with an extra 1½s added for each child (excluding stepchildren). Food and lodgings, the notice added, were free. Volunteers should expect to serve for the duration of the war.

What form this contingent would take, the notice continued, all depended on the numbers coming forward. With 500 or more volunteers, the men could form half of a Channel Island infantry battalion, with Guernsey providing the other. Less than that, and an infantry company could be formed, for incorporation into one of Kitchener's 'New Army' battalions. It had all seemed very straightforward. Advocates of a Jersey unit were elated. 'Jersey has at last been given the opportunity of practically demonstrating that loyalty and patriotism which forms part of her traditional heritage,' the *Morning News* asserted, 'If Jersey, with a male population trained to arms, cannot offer 500 men to serve ... she will cut a very ignoble figure.'[8]

Yet awkward rumours were soon circulating. Contrary to expectations, it seemed many of the Militia that remained on the island were in no hurry to demonstrate the newspaper's particular brand of loyalty or patriotism. The number of volunteers was reportedly growing – but only slowly. One explanation given was that many men were still making up their mind, so to give them more time the deadline was moved quietly back three days to 12 December. Even by then, however, the total remained stubbornly low – with most of those who had volunteered coming from the Town Battalion. If Jersey was going to avoid the potential embarrassment of failing to meet even the minimum requirements, something more had to be done. The time for government intervention was ripe.

With news that recruiting in Guernsey was apparently going well and criticism in the newspapers over its failure to act sooner, the States met in a special sitting on 15 December 1914. The session had started with a stirring resolution:

> Proud of its traditions and of its past steady and loyal attachment to the Throne of England, and determined to bequeath to generations to come the glorious heritage of British patrimony; confident in the patriotism of Jerseymen, and resolved to incur any sacrifices to help the Mother Country and her Allies to throw back and conquer the common enemy on foreign soil; The States have unanimously decided to appeal to the Island, and especially the Royal Jersey Militia, in order to be able to provide forthwith a contingent of trained Jersey volunteers for the service of the Crown...[9]

What had been missing up to then, the Bailiff had announced to the animated assembly, was a direct appeal. 'The youth of the island now had a glorious opportunity,' he reasoned, 'to show that they as Jerseymen feared neither death nor the enemies of the country.'[10] And it was the duty of the States to put the case to them. Quietly, the deadline for volunteering was put back once more, this time until the end of the year.

The campaign for hearts and minds had begun almost immediately. Two days after the passing of the resolution, the audience of West's Picture House were surprised to find that evening's film interrupted for an address. The Constable of St Helier, Mr John Pinel, climbed onto the stage for a ten-minute slot. Patriotism, he reminded the audience, was not just a word on people lips. The time has come for every true Jerseymen to do his duty; surely Jersey would respond to the call? It was an appeal to be repeated in venues across St Helier and the wider island that night. In the days that followed, there was more of the same. The newspapers too added their voice. The names of volunteers were published, along with patriotic comments and – perhaps strongest of all – anonymous letters allegedly written by young Jersey women:

> The time has come when Jerseymen are required to show their loyalty to the Mother Country. Will you respond to the call? Will you show your true patriotism? This is no time for idle talk. It is be up and doing. Show the women of Jersey that they need not be ashamed of you. Do not let them brand you as cowards when then meet you in the street.[11]

The campaign finally wound down as the year came to an end. If nothing else, it had certainly succeeded in stirring public excitement. As the *Evening Post* noted on 20 December, the subject was 'all you hear around the island'[12]. Some young women were so enthused that they had decided to take direct action on the matter. Prowling the streets outside some of the Militia barracks armed with white feathers, they handed them out as a mark of cowardice to men who had not yet volunteered.

Others, however, fought back on behalf of those not coming forward, arguing that the defence of Jersey and its people's wellbeing should come first. Eventually, both sides of the argument – and everyone else – could do nothing more to influence the outcome. With the deadline reached, in the final days of December those men who had volunteered attended army medicals to have their health and fitness checked. Apprehensively, the island waited for the result.

On 3 January 1915, the official number of volunteers was released. Some 330 men in total had come forward by the end of December – a considerable improvement on that reported at the expiry of the first deadline. Yet it was a number still well short of that required to form half a battalion. Then there was further disappointment when it was revealed that only 75 per cent of volunteers had been passed as medically fit – leaving the actual number available at only 250.

Fortunately, given that an infantry company only required 230 men, this total was enough to meet the army's minimum requirement. Only just, it seemed, Jersey was to have its own 'Pals' unit after all. As the dust settled on December's bruising recruitment campaign, there had been some disappointment in civil and military circles at the final number of volunteers. Expectations had been high; the Dean of Jersey had set the tone in early December when he had prayed earnestly for 'not 500, but 1,000 volunteers', and posed the question 'Are we roused, or only turning in our sleep?'[13] Yet was the disappointment justified?

One possible way to answer is by comparing the response of Jersey to that of other communities. This in itself poses a problem however. In contrast with the mainland UK, or perhaps most British overseas colonies, Jersey is an island, with its population and boundaries strictly defined by the sea. While it possible to show that the town of Accrington, with a population of just over 45,000 at the time of the First World War, raised a 1,000 volunteers to form the Accrington Pals, the comparison is misleading. Further scrutiny reveals that recruitment was not limited to the town itself, but extended to the surrounding communities. Technically, men could have travelled from across the country to join; this was simply not possible in the case of Jersey. It seems sensible to conclude this could be the case with virtually all mainland units, and therefore not a valid comparison.

A better approach would therefore be to compare with a more representative community. The obvious choice is Guernsey. Although smaller in size and population (the 1911 Census showed Guernsey having a male population of 20,661 compared to Jersey's 24,022), in terms of demographics, the population background and composition was broadly similar. Guernsey was included in the War Office's appeal for a contingent, and like Jersey, had set about raising volunteers. By the end of 1914, it had managed to find 319 volunteers, of whom 285 were accepted.[14] As a representative portion of the male population, this number represented 1.5 per cent, a figure only slightly higher than that of Jersey, which stood at 1.4 per cent. This would indicate, broadly speaking, that Jersey's effort was at least on a par with its principal counterpart.

Could it be, therefore, that the Channel Islands as a whole performed poorly when it came to volunteering? It is possible to find other suitable comparisons. One is the British Dominion of Newfoundland, famous for having raised and sent overseas its own battalion of infantry during the First World War. Its 1911 census showed a male population of 121,632 – considerably larger than either of the Channel Islands. During the same period of volunteering, it managed to raise some 1,000 recruits – hailed widely as an excellent effort. Yet by comparison, it was rather less than 1 per cent of the male population: lower than either Jersey or Guernsey, suggesting that both could have exceeded expectations.

Of course, these comparisons have to be accepted as being only superficial. Truly accurate analysis could only come with detailed consideration of a host of local factors and conditions. These would include at least the relative effort made by each community to find recruits, the likelihood of individual elements of the male population responding, the general sense of responsibility to fight in someone else's war. However, in general it seems fair to conclude that Jersey (and Guernsey for that matter) were probably no better or worse at raising volunteers than other communities at this time. In the eyes of some, it appears, they just could have done better.

Whatever the individual views on the success or otherwise in getting men to volunteer, by the start of January, Jersey had its contingent. The next issue to be decided was when it would leave, and where it would go.

On 2 January 1915, Major General Rochfort sat down at his desk to compose a formal letter to the War Office. The subject of the Lieutenant-Governor's communication was Jersey's contribution to the nation's struggle. In response to the request of 27 November 1914, he wrote, it was his pleasure to offer a military contingent from Jersey for overseas service. Admittedly, the numbers were not as many as hoped for, but the volunteers were of the highest calibre. After due training and familiarisation they would be ready for whatever role the War Office saw fit to allocate. As originally proposed, they would ideally be attached to one of General Kitchener's newly formed battalions, preferably in a regiment with which the island had an association. Yet understandably, he conceded, the final decision on the matter rested with others. Whatever it was, however, it would be splendid if the volunteers were permitted to maintain a sense of identity and a link to their island by being accorded the title 'The Jersey Company'.

Outside the Lieutenant-Governor's warm office, the island was shivering in the grip of a cold and stormy spell of winter weather. They were gloomy conditions to match a widespread gloomy mood. With the arrival of a new year, people were coming to terms with the fact that – contrary to popular belief – the war had not been over by Christmas after all. Indeed, the end then seemed further away that ever. There was a growing realisation also that the cost was going to be far higher than anyone had actually realised, in terms of lives alone. At least forty-five Jerseymen lost their lives in the first five months of the war, and many more were wounded. Understandably, something was needed to lift the islands spirits, and divert attention from the bleak weather and demoralising news. The spotlight had fallen on the newly-raised Jersey contingent.

'In its way the departure of the contingent will make an epoch in our history', the *Evening Post* enthused in early January 1915, 'good luck and a safe return to our lads.'[15] It was a marked change in tone from the challenging leaders of December when the recruiting campaign had been in full swing. Almost overnight, the divisive arguments over numbers were put aside, while the focus shifted to those who had actually volunteered. Everyone, it seemed, now wanted to do his or her bit to support 'Ours'.

The term 'Ours' to describe the volunteers appears to have first been used by the newspapers in January 1915 when shortening the phrase 'our contingent'. As a concept, it had soon found support among the public, who latched on to its sentimental overtones. It was a very suitable name, because for next few months at least, the island would take these Jersey Pals to its heart.

The volunteers were in popular demand. They were by now marked out from other militiamen by prominent red 'V's on their sleeves (presumably to help avoid the attentions of the feather wielding young women), and fêted wherever they went. Schools opened their doors for visits, theatres laid on gala performances, and dignitaries lined up to wish them well. Behind the scenes, a send-off committee was busy preparing for the contingent's departure by collecting hats, scarves and other practical items of warm clothing. Additionally, to ensure that each volunteer's spiritual well-being was not forgotten, Christian organisations prepared to present each man with a Bible, to ensure that the word of God went overseas with him.

Meanwhile, on 3 February, the public had finally learned where exactly it was that their contingent was destined to go. The delay in receiving this news had led some to conclude that the War Office had rejected the offer of a Jersey unit altogether. A few went as far as to start malicious rumours claiming the volunteers would remain in Jersey, or end up on garrison duty in some far-flung part of the Empire. So there was some relief at the announcement stating the War Office had finally accepted the offer.

Furthermore, and as requested, the communiqué revealed that the volunteers were to be attached as a company to one of the 'New Army' battalions being raised at that time. The unit selected was the 7th Battalion of the Royal Irish Rifles, at that time training in southern Ireland. Finally, the War Office had been pleased to confirm that from that time forward, the contingent would be officially entitled The Jersey Company, Royal Irish Rifles. Although the choice of regiment was somewhat surprising because the Royal Irish Rifles had no recent connections to Jersey, nobody really minded. It was at least a clear decision – and one to silence any detractors. All that remained outstanding was a date for departure, but that, the War Office assured, was to be in the very near future.

In the time remaining in Jersey, there were final preparations made for the departure. The most significant had come during the second week in February when the volunteers paraded for special ceremonies in which they officially left the Militia and joined the British Army. Although the uniforms, equipment and badges remained the same – for the time being at least – from that time forward, they were members of the Royal Irish Rifles.

A less pleasant ceremony took place four days later at the Military Hospital in St Helier's Brighton Road. It had been time for inoculations – and the first to step up was the Jersey Company's new Commanding Officer.

Prior to volunteering in December 1914, Lieutenant Colonel Walter Stocker had been serving as the second-in-command of the Militia's East Battalion. He was a popular choice, despite not actually being a Jerseyman. Stocker had been born and raised in Yorkshire, and had come to Jersey at a young age. This early start on the island did mean, however, that he could thoroughly integrate with his adopted community. Stocker was a natural leader, well suited to command with his strong sense of discipline and order tempered by a genuinely outgoing and humorous nature. Charismatic and caring, the only potential shortcoming was his age. At forty-seven, he was far older than average for a Company Commander – especially in wartime.

This, however, was a future problem. For the present, Lieutenant Colonel Stocker's age would lend him the reassuring aura of a father figure, something particularly important to many of the younger volunteers about to embark on the journey to war.

By the end of February 1915, despite efforts to keep the date of departure secret, it was common knowledge the volunteers would shortly leave. There had been a very public round of send-off engagements and functions, while in the barracks final preparations had been obviously under way. Furthermore, with just a few days to go, all of the volunteers had learned they were about to depart. Despite a request for discretion, they had understandably passed it on to close friends and family, and the news had spread like wildfire. There was little surprise, therefore, when on 2 March the volunteers from the Town Battalion marched into St Helier's Royal Square at 6.00 a.m. to find it already half-full with a noisy crowd of well-wishers.

Despite dreary conditions that morning, the atmosphere in the square had been heavy with an excited sense of anticipation. Nothing like this had happened since the heady days of the previous August when the French and British reservists had left. Moreover, this day was even more special; this time it was Jersey's own who were leaving for war, and the island had turned out to mark the occasion. It was 'a red letter day in Jersey annals,' proclaimed the *Morning News*, 'never since the outbreak of hostilities has the community been so deeply stirred.'[16]

While waiting for the volunteers from the East and West Battalions to arrive, the men from the Town Battalion in the Square were permitted to mingle with the crowd, by then being marshalled by a cordon of Military Police. It led to scenes of mixed emotions. Some volunteers, such as local butcher and well-known footballer Christopher 'Jimmy' Scoones were clearly enjoying the moment, proclaiming loudly that he was looking forward to the next match against the Germans. Others, however, were in a more reflective mood. Seeking mothers, wives and sweethearts for a final few moments together, many were reportedly on the verge of breaking down. There were tearful scenes as the men, stuffing last minute gifts of chocolate and cigarettes into their packs, eventually rejoined the ranks following the arrival of the remaining volunteers.

At 7.00 a.m., it was time to leave. Appropriately, the rain had at last stopped, and, as the clouds cleared, the grey square sparkled under the first rays of a winter sun. Rations were distributed for the journey – bread, jam, beef, cheese and biscuits – and the volunteers were called to order. With Lieutenant Colonel Stocker leading the way, they had turned and marched off the square.

On their short journey that morning to the nearby harbour, a mass of cheering and flag-waving well-wishers lined the route. Led by a military band of pipes and drums, the column was joined by both the Bailiff and Lieutenant-Governor as they passed the Town Church. Flanking Stocker, the island's leaders had marched with the men across the broad sweep of the Weighbridge and on to the New North Quay beyond. It was an unmistakable message of support - to both the volunteers and the assembled crowds – and a remarkable scene.

In a fenced off area alongside the waiting ship, further dignitaries had assembled, everyone anxious to shake the hand of each man as he stepped up to the gangplank. At last, with everyone safely on board, the mooring ropes were slipped at 7.30a.m., and the SS *Ibex* slowly pulled away from the quay. The *Ibex* was one of the best known and most favoured of the Great Western Railways ships working the route between the Channel Islands and mainland Britain. That morning, as seemed befitting, the vessel had looked particularly splendid sitting high up on the early morning tide. 'A magnificent spectacle as she floated majestically above the quay,' one commentator observed, 'the whole length of her decks being crammed with khaki-clad warriors.'[17]

Amid a throng of cheers and calls from the crowd, bands struck up sentimental tunes that were sung with great passion by those on the ship and back on shore. The water was as calm as a millpond, and the *Ibex* had slid easily across the expanse of the harbour before departing between the pier heads to the blasts of saluting cannon fire. It was, the *Evening Post* later claimed, 'The proudest day in our history'.[18]

As the *Ibex* rounded Corbière point on Jersey's south-west coast and headed north, Jersey began to fade from view. It had been a magnificent send off, and one that made a great impression on the volunteers, then watching their island disappear over the horizon. In their minds at least, a bond existed from that time forward between them and their community. The show of support from both the island's authorities and people could mean nothing less. The volunteers were determined not to let their side of the bargain down – they expected that their island would do the same.

It must also have occurred to some that they might never see Jersey again. Despite the wonderful send-off, they were after all leaving for war. Somewhere in their future, they may have to face death in some foreign battlefield, fighting an enemy of whom they knew little. Fortunately, if it had to happen, it was some way off. For now, they were heading in the opposite direction. At the end of this particular journey there lay only the unknown prospect of Ireland, and the green hills of County Cork.

Three

Not so far from Tipperary

All the lads are well and in the best of spirits. We are about twenty miles from Tipperary, so can't sing 'it's a long way to Tipperary' but sing instead 'it's a long way to sunny Jersey'.

Lance Corporal Oscar Williams, Jersey Company RIR, March 1915

'It would take an artist or a poet with very exquisite taste and expression to adequately picture the present beauties of the Munster hillside', wrote Sergeant Harry Ross of the Jersey Company, Royal Irish Rifles in May 1915. 'At Ballyvonare, we stand and look on one of the most beautiful scenes Dame Nature has ever painted'.[1]

The Sergeant was not the only one captivated by the charm of the Irish countryside. To the volunteers from Jersey after they arrived in March 1915, it must have seemed they had exchanged one beautiful island for another. For most, the six months spent there would remain forever the highpoint of their time and experiences in the army. In Ireland, under clear and sunny skies, they would learn to be soldiers. In smoke-filled bars and halls, many would begin to experience something of life in the wider world for the first time. Overall, it would be fair to say that if this was the introduction to one of the most terrible wars the world had ever seen, it certainly was not the worst.

Yet these outward appearances disguised a land harbouring a troubled past, present and future. For beneath this green and pleasant veneer, Ireland in 1915 was in the process of being split apart by deep-rooted and bitter tensions. The cause was the so-called 'Irish Problem'; and the 'Irish Problem' – indirectly at least – was why the Jersey volunteers were here in the first place.

In bestowing its fortunes, history has often overlooked the land of Ireland. Down the centuries, misfortune in the guise of religious war, exploitation, and famine had been far more commonplace. After years of suppression, at the beginning of the twentieth century the complicated legacy of these events had bubbled to the surface. At the core of the problem lay the vexing issue of how Ireland should be governed.

For more than 100 years, the British Parliament at Westminster had directly governed Ireland, along with England, Wales and Scotland. While many in Britain considered this a perfectly acceptable state of affairs, for many of those who actually lived in Ireland, the arrangement was an intolerable one.

For generations, the predominantly Catholic working classes of Ireland had been treated as second-class citizens in their own land. Denied fundamental rights and often exploited by unscrupulous English landowners, their resentment had built up. Galvanised by a growing Nationalist movement, many were demanding looser ties with Britain, or even outright independence. Yet there was also a population of staunch opponents to the nationalist cause inhabiting Ireland. The largely Protestant Unionist, or Loyalist, community lived mainly in the north of Ireland. Despite being blatantly in the minority, they strongly opposed any change to the status quo, fearing it would lead to a loss of historic wealth, power and influence. The British government invariably came down on their side.

So strongly did both sides of the divide believe in their cause, many were openly prepared defend it by taking up arms. In the years leading up to the First World War, the simmering Irish Problem had threatened to boil over into open civil war. Fanning the flames of discontent was the passage through Westminster of the Irish Home Rule Bill.

In 1912, a British government had at last conceded to the Nationalist demands and proposed a devolved Irish government based in Dublin. It was not full independence, but a halfway-house compromise. For two years, however, the proposal had been the subject of prolonged and acrimonious debate, and the cause of considerable unrest in Ireland. Finally, in September 1914, the Irish Home Rule Bill had at last passed into law. By that time, however, Britain was at war. As a gesture of solidarity, the Nationalists agreed that the law's implementation was suspended until the conflict was over, and to support the British cause wholeheartedly. The Unionists naturally agreed to the same. Throughout Ireland, politicians and community leaders had zealously set about demonstrating their loyalty by raising men for the army.

Among the Unionist communities in the north of Ireland, recruiting had been brisk and quotas soon filled. In the Nationalist south, however, the going proved tougher. Many of those living there simply did not see this as their war – enlisting and dying for a Britain that had oppressed them for years was far from an appealing prospect. Many Irish regiments were soon struggling to find the volunteers needed to meet overly optimistic army expansion plans. To the dismay of Lord Kitchener, at the start of 1915 many newly-formed Irish battalions remained woefully short of men.

One was the 7th Battalion of the Royal Irish Rifles. Like other infantry regiments of the British Army, the Royal Irish Rifles recruited men territorially and formed them into battalions for military service. When war began, the regiment had embarked on an ambitious growth programme as part of Kitchener's drive to create a 'New Army'. One of the first units formed was the 7th (Service) Battalion. Initially raised in Belfast, it had been despatched to County Cork in the south-west of Ireland to recruit from the communities there. Problems finding volunteers meant that by February 1915, only 350 men had come forward to join the ranks. With 1,000 men needed for the battalion to reach full complement, the future of 7th RIR (as it will be called from here on) had looked bleak. It was one of the poorest recruitment records in Ireland – if things did not improve, 7th RIR faced the axe, and its men the prospect of redistribution to other units.

Yet early in 1915 a glimmer of hope had appeared. Lying on some War Office desk in London was a letter from the Channel Island of Jersey offering 250 trained militiamen for overseas service. The logical course of action was to send them to a battalion in Ireland, and 7th RIR had a greater need than most. Accepting the offer, all that had remained was to get the Jersey volunteers to Ireland.

The weather during the Jersey Company's crossing to England on 2 March 1915 had remained excellent throughout. The *Ibex* made easy work of the unseasonably calm sea conditions, and, after a brief stop at Guernsey, the south coast of England was in sight by early afternoon.

With the ship tied up in Weymouth harbour, at just after 3.00p.m. the volunteers disembarked and clambered excitedly onto the specially arranged train waiting near the docks. For most it was the first time they had ever left Jersey, meaning all of the sights, sounds and experiences were new. Soon the train was clattering through southern England, its occupants catching glimpses of Yeovil, Bath and Bristol as they slipped by. By the time darkness fell, they had passed into southern Wales *en route* to the small port of Fishguard for the second sea-crossing of the journey. It turned out to be a very different affair from the one earlier that day.

In place of the comfortable *Ibex*, the transport for the crossing to Ireland that night turned out to be far from choice. In fact, one of the volunteers complained, the SS *Innisfallen* was a 'dirty sea boat', built for transporting cattle and 'with bunks and cushions of sawdust'.[2] Furthermore, in place of a calm English Channel, a far more seasonal Celtic Sea had pitched and tossed the ship and its unfortunate passengers until most were green with sea-sickness.

The ordeal lasted until noon 3 March when the *Innisfallen* finally entered into the shelter of Cork Harbour. Staggering off the ship, the volunteers were welcomed to Ireland with tea and sandwiches before boarding another train to continue their journey. After two hours, the train had come to a halt alongside the platform of Buttevant station. They had arrived.

For generations, the small town of Buttevant in rural County Cork had played host to a military garrison. Given this background, logically it was picked as one of the locations for assembling and training some of Kitchener's newly formed Irish battalions, including 7th RIR. The Battalion had sent a small welcoming party to greet the Jersey Company, and a band that played cheery tunes as the weary volunteers climbed down onto the platform. Under a steady drizzle, belongings were gathered and then loaded onto waiting carts. Hoisting packs and rifles, they had set off to march the six miles to 7th RIR's camp.

At last, wet through and exhausted, the volunteers arrived at their destination. At the camp's gate a crowd of curious Irish soldiers waited to greet the newcomers. As the Jersey Company entered, the band struck up a familiar but puzzling song, as one volunteer later recalled:

When we arrived the Royal Irish band completely surprised us by playing the 'Marseillaise' as they thought we were Frenchmen! The [Royal Irish] men said to us: 'You're a smart lot of Frenchmen, smarter than our chaps', and they were surprised when we answered them in English. They have now found out we speak English better than them, so they have dropped the idea us being French.[3]

That evening, over a welcoming meal followed by a traditional 'smoker', there was the opportunity to address the confusion over language and identity. The Irish volunteers, with little understanding of the location and history of Jersey, had naturally assumed it was a company of French soldiers joining them. The confusion showed it was obvious that time would be needed for both groups to get to know each other. Fortunately, there would be plenty of this. Compared to the ex-militiamen, most of the Irish volunteers had little or no military experience. 'It will be a long time before they go to the front,' commented one of the Jersey volunteers about his new Irish comrades, 'as they are only raw material yet.'[4]

A long summer of training in Ireland beckoned. It was clearly going to take time, and a lot of hard work, to wield these disparate groups into a single, effective infantry battalion. The man who had been given that task of achieving this was Lieutenant Colonel Desmond Hartley.

At nearly sixty years old, Hartley was far from an ideal age for a battalion commander. Like many others at the time, however, he had been recalled to help with the formation and training of Kitchener's 'New Army'. Despite his advancing years, Hartley remained a tall and upright figure, reportedly physically fit for a man of his age, and in possession of a stern sense of military discipline. He was going to need it. Turning this group of ex-civilians into a battalion ready for active service would be a challenging task. The arrival of the partially-trained Jerseymen must have been very welcome then; and Hartley would be quick to recognise their value. 'They are a very good lot of officers and men,' he was soon writing, 'and quickly becoming part of the Battalion.'[5]

Then as now, infantry battalions were the backbone of the British Army. They were the most numerous of all the various supporting arms, and, with 1,000 men at full complement, possessed considerable firepower. Each was divided into a headquarters and four companies, in the case of 7th RIR, the latter designated, A, B, C and D. On joining the Battalion, the Jersey Company was allocated the role of 'D' Company.

The new designation would lead to some confusion. Within 7th RIR, the Jerseymen now fully assumed the identity of 'D' Company, particularly in respect of all formal orders and instructions. Among the Jerseymen themselves, the use of 'Jersey Company' and 'D' Company seems to have been interchangeable; certainly, there was pride in the nickname 'The Fighting D', which later developed. Back home in Jersey, however, the use of the 'Jersey Company' continued, along with the term 'Jersey contingent'. All were, of course, correct and acceptable, but for the sake of continuity within this book, the term Jersey Company will be used for as long as it is appropriate.

Ultimately, the name was only of passing consequence. It was the actions and accomplishments of the individuals who constituted the unit that really mattered. So who then were the officers and men comprising this unique little band?

The Jersey Company remained under the command of Lieutenant Colonel Stocker. By the time Ireland was reached, however, he had been given the temporary rank of Major, a level more appropriate for an officer leading an infantry company. By contrast, the man appointed his second-in-command had been elevated a rank on taking on his new role.

Like Stocker, George Johnson was not a native of Jersey. Before the war, this quiet and serious-minded Scotsman had come to the island from Aberdeen to take up a senior position at the local agricultural school. Joining the Militia's East Battalion, he had reached the rank of Lieutenant by the time war broke out, and gained the reputation of being a capable officer. In February 1915, this reputation – together presumably with a recommendation from Stocker – had led to him being offered the post of second-in-command of the Jersey Company, together with a promotion to Captain. Johnson had accepted both.

To command the Jersey Company's four platoons, there were also four junior officers selected. Second Lieutenant Thomas Dickson joined from the Militia's West Battalion, while Second Lieutenant Lawrence Hibbs, Lieutenant Cyril Nicolle, and Lieutenant Cyril Ogier all came from the Town Battalion. Each was in charge of a platoon formed from a mix of Sergeants, Corporals and Riflemen (Within the Royal Irish Rifles, and other Rifle Regiments, the rank of Private was changed to Rifleman).

In addition to the officers, the Jersey Company also had two senior non-commissioned officers, or SNCOs. The first, Adolphus Crocker, as Company Quartermaster Sergeant, or CQMS, had responsibility for ensuring everyone was equipped, housed and fed. The second was Company Sergeant Major, or CSM, John Dournald Le Breton.

More commonly known as Jack, thirty-two-year-old Le Breton came from St Helier where he worked for a grocery business. Ironically, like Major Stocker and Captain Johnson, he too had been born outside the island, although in his case to Jersey born parents. The Le Breton family had been living on Canada's Gaspé coast, a location with strong Jersey connections through the cod fishing industry. Yet while Jack was still a boy, they had decided to return home to Jersey, and there he completed his education. After leaving school, Le Breton had quickly gained a reputation as an energetic, thoughtful and capable organiser – someone well suited to leadership. By the outbreak of war, these qualities had helped propel him to the rank of CSM in the Militia's Town Battalion. There was little surprise then at the offer of the same role in the newly-formed Jersey Company. It turned out to be a providential decision nonetheless.

Jack Le Breton set about his new role in a characteristically calm and unassuming fashion. Seizing the cause of the Jersey Company and its men, he began working tirelessly to ensure 'his boys', as he called them, were trained, prepared and, wherever possible, kept from danger. He never relented, and in the years that followed, this devotion would earn him the accolade 'Father of the Jersey Company'.

Just who were CSM Le Breton's boys?[6] Firstly – and understandably – the mass of men making up the so-called 'Other Ranks' were mostly young. In 1915, when they left Jersey, 77 per cent were below the age of thirty, with some 31 per cent of these younger than twenty years old. The average age for all the volunteers was twenty-four, although there were, of course, extremes on either side. At fifteen years old, Riflemen Clarence Dorkins and Alfred Hingston appear to have been the youngest members, while at forty-four, Rifleman Charles Pallot appears the oldest. Technically, at least, in view of their ages, these three men, along with quite a few others, should never have been accepted. Yet in the spirit of the time, recruiting officers had clearly turned a blind eye.

In respect of religion, the volunteers were mainly Protestant, citing either Church of England or Wesleyan on their attestment papers. For the most part, they were also unmarried when joining up, although a few did wed while serving. About one-third had wives, with perhaps half of these men having children, in at least one case as many as five.

Unsurprisingly, given the size of the community from which they came, many of the volunteers were related to each other. There were at least nineteen pairs of brothers in the ranks, and, in the case of Riflemen Arthur, Frank and George Dobin, a set of three. Numerous cousins were also present, several in-laws, and a rather complex combination of nephews and uncles. Perhaps most remarkably, father and son Riflemen Thomas and Richard Finch had joined and served together. Additionally, of course, there were numerous old friends, ex-work colleagues, former schoolyard chums, devoted church congregation members, and so on.

From the start, this closely interdependent characteristic appears to have helped the Jersey Company to bond, and quickly lent it a sense of camaraderie. Yet it could become less desirable when the men reached the front. Having close relatives and life-long friends present in the same military unit would only serve to magnify the effects of casualties when they inevitably came. And there was a further factor to potentially magnify the effect of battlefield losses. Despite the all-island appeal, the majority of the volunteers came from St Helier. While the town parish contributed 73 per cent of the total, no other individual parish contributed more than 6 per cent. The lowest were St Lawrence and St Mary, both of which had contributed fewer than five members each. Demographics, of course, can partly explain this bias, but given that St Helier did not contain 73 per cent of the population at the time (the figure was just over 50 percent), the explanation, therefore, must be that other factors were at play.

Much of St Helier's workforce in 1914 earned its living on the island's service industry. They had worked in the town's shops, stores, offices, hotels and public bars, or they served across the island as tradesmen, deliverymen, gardeners and the like. Inevitably, one early impact of the war was a general decline in the demand for the services they sold, provided or delivered. By contrast, the loss of the French labour force at the start of the war would have increased the demands on the men living in the country parishes to continue working on the farms. It is obvious, therefore, that from Jersey's perspective, the town-dwellers were the ideal ones to go.

Furthermore, for lots of town-dwelling volunteers, the prospect of army life – even in wartime – would have been appealing. Many came from the poorer parts of St Helier, brought up in the densely populated working class streets, in living conditions that were far from choice. While not strictly slums, life there in the early years of the twentieth century would have been tough, with only limited prospects for advancement and improvement. For a young man with this background, the chance to get out and do something different must have seemed an attractive proposition.

That said, for all of the volunteers the chance of joining the army and fighting in a war was clearly appealing. War in the early years of the twentieth century still managed to conjure up notions of patriotism and romance; at the end of 1914 the caustic effects of life and death in the trenches had yet to filter through. Additionally, army life had offered security, pay, food and lodgings, while for those who had never left Jersey before, there was a chance to see something of the world. In March 1915 the Jersey volunteers were about to see a lot more of County Cork's green hills.

Ballyvonare Camp lay a few miles to the north-east of the town of Buttevant, built on fields in the wide valley of the meandering River Awbeg. Although not intended as a permanent installation, the camp was a solid enough construction. The fact that most of its buildings were made of wood rather than canvas had certainly been appreciated during the period of wet weather that marked the Jersey Company's arrival. These were mostly single-storey accommodation huts, although there were others used as dining halls, offices, latrines, wash-blocks and stores. The open spaces in between were given over for parade grounds and training fields. These fared less well in the rain – one of the volunteers reported on arrival that instead of grass, there was mud everywhere. Despite this, it seems there had been little to complain about. While not luxurious, Ballyvonare Camp was a satisfactory enough establishment.

The Jerseymen had soon settled in. In no time at all, a large Jersey flag floated above the hut serving as Jersey Company headquarters to mark their presence. It had been a gift from the readers of the *Evening Post*, commissioned only days after the departure from Jersey. 'It is very good of you and your readers to send along a flag to remind us of Jersey,' Major Stocker had telegraphed back when he received the gift, 'The men, I'm sure, will be delighted.'[7] Later the flag would accompany the men to the front. For now, however, they were here to train as soldiers in the modern British Army; and training in this army (like most others) started early.

At Ballyvonare, a trainee soldier's day began at 6.30a.m. when reveille sounded. A frantic thirty minutes followed; time for the men to dress, wash, shave and brush-up. They had to be on parade by 7.00a.m. when, regardless of weather, there was a session of physical exercise. This continued until 8.00a.m., at which time everyone stopped for a much-welcomed breakfast.

The venue for this first meal of the day, together with dinner and tea, was one of the camp's large dining huts. Breakfast and the other meals appear to have been remarkably hearty affairs. 'It's not all burnt bacon for breakfast and stew for dinner,' explained Sergeant Harry Ross in a letter home:

> One morning it is kippers; another ham and tomatoes; another boiled eggs; another sausages; another herrings, and so on. The dinners are also varied with haricots or green peas, and there is always soup. There is only one word for the Irish bread, butter and eggs – superb.[8]

Training recommenced at 9.00a.m. At Ballyvonare, the Jerseymen would follow the largely tried and tested routine of the time.

Initially, the focus was on teaching new recruits the basics of soldiering, and instilling the unquestioning sense of discipline demanded by the army. Monotonous hours drilling on the parade ground, route marches and practice trench digging served both purposes well. Breaks from this routine had come with lectures or demonstrations, on first aid and field craft for example, or time spent using the British Army's fearsome seventeen-inch bayonet to attack stuffed dummies.

In time, however, training would progress onto more specialised skills. There was instruction on stretcher-bearing, cooking, care and preservation of water, medical skills and physical training. Most of this took place at Ballyvonare, although some men had gone elsewhere to complete courses away from the camp. In the months that followed, the Jersey Company's junior officers spent time in London and the south of England, while a number of NCOs went off to Dublin to qualify as shooting instructors.

The British Army placed great emphasis on a soldier's ability to shoot well. On many days after lunch, the training activity had moved to the rifle ranges near the camp. In this discipline, the Jerseymen excelled as the years of pre-war shooting practice in the Militia clearly paid off.

In general, this previous military experience had greatly assisted with most aspects of the Jerseymen's training. In the early days, it showed itself as a marked superiority over the far less experienced Irish volunteers, as one 7th RIR officer acknowledged at the time. 'They were marvellous,' he later recalled when talking about the Jersey Company, 'all were trained far superior to us.'[9] Regardless of superiority, however, there was no let up in the training routine, which on occasions continued until late in the night, as Harry Ross also recalled:

> Night operations are held on average twice weekly and very interesting they prove especially if you find yourself lost in the forest and surrounded by donkeys, squirrels, rabbits and crows. Such specimens infest the place. These operations are rare fun, more particularly when you find yourself up to the knees in the bog or up to your thigh in a ditch you didn't bargain for. It's a good training though. No lights, or smoking, or talking are allowed. When you get back to the camp at ten, eleven, or later, you find your cot jolly 'comfy', I can assure you![10]

Night exercises aside, training only took place during weekdays at Ballyvonare, leaving most evenings and weekends free. Apart from some lectures to attend and obligatory church parade on Sunday mornings, the men still needed to be kept occupied. For the army, one way to achieve this was with sport and music.

From the start, the Jerseymen fully involved themselves. Boxing, athletics, tug-of-war and later cricket were all popular. Yet it was football that really attracted most attention. Among the ranks of the Jersey Company, there was a fair sprinkling of men who had played football for the island side, and plenty of others who played competitively at a decent level. With all this talent available, it was not long before a team was assembled to take part in a league of inter-company matches. There was a hitch, however, as no one had thought to bring football strips to Ireland, while decent boots were in very short supply. A hurried appeal home ensued, with an urgent request to send football kit. It worked, and in the first match the Jersey Company, clad on the island's traditional red and white, showed its credentials by thrashing a combined team from A and B Companies by 6–0.

For those less inclined to physical pursuits, the band of 7th RIR offered an outlet for talent. The Battalion had possessed a traditional Irish military band and some of the newly-arrived Jerseymen soon joined its ranks. A number seem to have excelled in playing the bugle, drum or bagpipes. One, Rifleman Frank Vautier, even became the personal bugler of Lieutenant Colonel Hartley, accompanying him on formal parades and ceremonies. Another, Rifleman Wilfred Journeaux, showed an aptitude for the bagpipes, and, after a month's course in Buttevant, became the Jersey Company's official piper.

Apart from sport and music, the army, ever keen to keep its young men from mischief, had laid on other events and attractions to fill the off-duty hours at Ballyvonare. The large dining halls doubled as theatres and cinemas, the canteen as a socialising area complete with newspapers, gramophone and a piano. On one occasion, a circus had even turned up to put on a performance for the men. Understandably, however, many of the men were anxious to seek out distractions of a different nature. Most of these only existed outside the confines of the camp.

The town of Buttevant, and the smaller village of Doneraile to the east, were easily reached by wagon, or by walking if necessary. Soon after their arrival, the Jerseymen had found their way to both, and into the bars and public houses scattered among their streets. There seems to have been no shortage of place to find a drink, even if they were a bit different to those at home. In Buttevant, one Jersey volunteer recalled that 'practically every shop is a general store where you can purchase almost anything, and in many there is a department for the sale of liquor.'[11] And with little else to spend their money on, these establishments soon became magnets for most soldiers in the area – despite the price and apparently low quality of the product on offer there. Alcohol was noted as generally expensive, with the beer frothy, and whiskey and brandy almost as 'pale as water'. 'I can't get boozed over here,' one man complained, 'either I can't get enough, or the stuff here is much weaker than in Jersey.'[12] Nevertheless, with so many young men around, the army tried to limit the opportunities for drunkenness. Bars could only serve alcohol to a man in uniform after 5.00p.m. in the evening and then had to shut completely by 8.00p.m.

In general, it appears the Jerseymen abided by the rules and caused no significant problems for either the army or the locals. Harry Ross, writing home in April claimed in fact that by then:

> Our lads are popular with everybody – officers, NCOs, their Irish comrades and with all the civilians they come into contact with. There is no shopkeeper in Buttevant or Doneraile – the closest villages – who would not put himself out for our boys, and who does not look forward to their weekly visit on a Saturday afternoons.[13]

Having made such a good impression, the Jersey Company had clearly settled into its new community.

By the time May arrived, that community was certainly getting to see a good deal of their Jersey visitors. Training was progressing well, with many of the fundamental skills already learned. The emphasis had progressively shifted onto new skills and activities, including more and more stamina-building route-marches through the County Cork countryside. Many of these took the Jersey Company into the nearby Ballyhoura Mountains. This low range of hills with its forest and moorland was fine walking country – although those wearing full uniform and equipment at that time may not have regarded it as such. By May the weather had also settled into a gloriously fine spell. With blue skies overhead, and a warm sun beating down, most found time to appreciate the splendour of surrounding countryside, despite the hard work. 'Even we Jerseymen, in spite of the fact that Jersey offers many pleasing scenes to the eye,' wrote Harry Ross, 'were struck with the glory of the land through which we marched'.[14]

The men were encouraged to sing as they marched along. There were many favourite tunes, both old and new. One of the most popular had been the well-known 'It's a Long Way to Tipperary', although by then the Jerseymen had reworked the lyrics to the more appropriate 'It's a Long Way to Sunny Jersey'. With many able to speak French as a second language, the marchers also broke into that tongue for the occasional song, much to the astonishment of the locals who often turned out to watch the soldiers pass by.

In view of this positive start in Ireland, the first brush with death came as a great shock. Rifleman Albert Richards had fallen ill within weeks of the arrival in Ireland, and been taken to a hospital in the town of Kanturk for treatment. To everyone's great concern, the diagnosis was typhoid, and for some weeks, the twenty-five-year-old had remained gravely ill. By the end of April, however, news had come through that Richards was improving, and there were genuine hopes that he would soon return to Ballyvonare. It would have been an even greater shock when news arrived that he had died on 11 May.

A few days later, the entire Jersey Company somberly turned out for the funeral at Buttevant churchyard and pensively watched the first of their company being laid to rest.

Throughout April, May and June, the number of Jersey volunteers present at Ballyvonare had been increasing. Illness and withdrawals had reduced the number who left Jersey on 2 March to only 230, but by the end of June, it had increased again to 250. Some of the newcomers were men who had volunteered in December 1914, but for one reason or another had not made the original departure date. Others, however, had been more recent volunteers. Having missed the original intake, these men decided that joining the Jersey Company was the right thing to do, and one of the reasons for this had been the activities of Sergeant Harold Ross.

Harry Ross was one of the Jersey Company's larger-than-life characters. The former police officer, editor and renowned newspaper reporter already had a colourful and somewhat controversial background when he volunteered in December 1914. Declaring that he was putting 'patriotism before commercialism', Ross announced that for 'every able-bodied young man there should now be no civil occupation'[15], and he had made it his cause to see this was the case. In April 1915, he had returned from Ireland to Jersey. On this occasion, he had the job of collecting some of those who had been unable to travel with the main contingent at the start of March. While there, however, Ross had taken the opportunity to encourage others to come forward. Writing a long article for the *Morning News* detailing the Jersey Company's experiences in Ireland to date, he embellished it with plenty of reasons why others should consider joining them. The article had soon turned into a regular column. Every couple of weeks the people of Jersey were able to read about the exploits of 'Ours' while Sergeant Ross continued to beat the recruitment drum.

From the start, the motivation for finding additional volunteers was not simply Ross's enthusiasm for the cause. Even though the original group of volunteers had been sufficient to form the infantry company requested, it was obvious they would be insufficient to sustain the unit in wartime. Not only would non-battle losses like Albert Richards need replacing, but once the Jersey Company reached the front, significant losses had to be expected. The problem would be replacing them. With no mechanism left behind in Jersey for this purpose, the task fell on those already in Ireland.

Recognising the success of the initial small-scale efforts, Sergeant Ross received permission to again return to Jersey in July and conduct a full-scale recruitment campaign. In a series of public meetings and lectures, he had extolled the benefits of life in the army, and the virtues of serving as part of the Jersey Company. A temporary recruitment office had also been opened on St Helier's King Street to encourage men passing by to sign up.

The campaign was a great success. When Sergeant Ross returned to Ireland in mid-July, he took with him no less than forty-eight new recruits. Others had promised to follow on soon. The Jersey Company was now really growing in number.

By the time this latest batch of recruits arrived, however, there had been a significant change to the arrangements in Ireland. In mid-June, 7th RIR had departed Ballyvonare for a new training camp near the village of Ballyhooley, around twenty miles to the east, and it was to be the Battalion's home for the next eight weeks.

This move had started early on the morning of 18 June. With baggage and belongings stowed for transport by train, the entire Battalion set out on its longest route march to date. Once more, the weather was perfect, and once more the countryside all around was breathtaking, as Harry Ross recalled in his column:

> Leaving Doneraile we passed through the usual class of country around Buttevant, but as we progressed the scene changed considerably. For a time we lost sight of the mountains and marched with the forest on our right, and the country stretching to our left, the land under grain showing sharply against grazing grounds even in the distance. Up hill and down dale we seemed to travel; the roads appeared to wind through the hills, and each incline or decline brought us face to face with a fresh panorama of beauty.[16]

By nightfall, Ballyhooley had remained some way off, so the march was broken at the tiny hamlet of Scart. Bedding down nearby, that night was the first the Jersey Company spent sleeping out under open skies. The next morning, after a wash and shave in a nearby river, they set out on the final leg of the journey.

Convamore Camp was less permanent than the one left behind at Ballyvonare. It lay in the grounds of Convamore House, the ancestral home of the Earl of Listowel, among the expansive woodlands and meadows lining the banks of the River Blackwater. A mass of tents pitched among the trees on a gentle slope leading down to the river served as accommodation. Here, with eleven men to each tent, the Battalion made itself at home.

On first impression, Convamore Camp had appeared to be another idyllic location. Before pressed into army service, the picturesque river valley and surrounding countryside had been renowned for its beauty, and the abundance of fish and game. Even with the presence of large numbers of soldiers, wildlife still frequented the area of the camp, while the thick canopy of trees overhead created a cool living and working space beneath. Yet appearances — as the men soon found out — could be deceptive. When the temperature climbed, so too did the swarms of flies and wasps frequenting the woods and river bank. Furthermore, when the weather broke, the valley revealed itself as a natural rain trap. In wet conditions, the sides dissolved to muddy slopes, scored by numerous small streams that managed to find their way into the tents on too many occasions. Wringing out wet clothes, someone had gloomily pointed out that at least conditions at the front would be no more challenging.

Perhaps these conditions were beneficial because one of the reasons for coming to Convamore Camp was to undertake simulated battlefield training. This took place on the surrounding hills and among some local villages pressed into service as temporary army training grounds. For authenticity, the entire 48th Infantry Brigade, of which 7th RIR was just one part, was present. With the 8th and 9th Battalions of the Royal Dublin Fusiliers and the 9th Battalion of the Royal Munster Fusiliers also assembled here, the Brigade was approaching its full war-time strength of nearly 5,000 men.

All these soldiers at Convamore Camp had stretched the on-site recreation facilities, which mainly consisted of a large YMCA canteen. In the men's spare time swimming in the River Blackwater was therefore popular. The sluggish river seemed safe enough, with plenty of sheltered spots to enter the water and to get out again. Yet appearances proved tragically deceptive. On 23 July, nineteen-year-old Rifleman Charlie Blampied went swimming alone after tea. Shortly afterwards a group coming down for a bathe had spotted his lifeless body under the water. Despite everyone's best efforts, it took a while to pull him out. Frantic attempts at resuscitation proved fruitless, and the young man was pronounced dead at the scene. Two days later the entire Jersey Company attended its second unexpected funeral. Blampied was laid to rest nearby in the estate's private cemetery.

The tragedy left a cloud over the remaining time at Convamore. Spirits were not helped by days of pouring rain turning the camp and much of the estate into a quagmire. 'Lord Listowel is back from London this weekend,' remarked Harry Ross on 7 August as the Jersey Company prepared to depart, 'we are wondering what he will say when he surveys his park – or rather what the army has left of it.'[17]

Three days later, on 10 August, it had been time to journey back to Ballyvonare camp. In contrast with the outward march in June, miserable weather blighted the return journey. Struggling through wind and rain, and led by Major Stocker, the Jersey Company brought up the rear of the Battalion with the CSM marching behind looking out for any stragglers. There were none. In spite of the trying conditions, everyone had pulled together as a team, ensuring that nobody was left behind. The achievement highlighted the advances made since the Jersey Company had come to Ireland. It had been six months since the men first stepped down from the train at Buttevant station, and nine since most of them had first stepped up to join the Jersey contingent. Now, as the march demonstrated, their training in Ireland was almost over. In the words of the their commander in Ireland, the Jersey Company had 'won golden opinions from their Brigadier and Commanding Officer.'[18]

From a mass of individuals with a common purpose, the Jersey volunteers had come together as a group and become a company of infantry fit for war. The only question that remained was when and where exactly they would join the conflict.

On 9 September 1915, the Jersey Company boarded a ship in the port of Dublin and prepared to leave Ireland for good. Once more, the sounds of bands and a cheering crowd marked their departure, and crowding the rails, the Jerseymen watched as Ireland slipped slowly from sight.

One man was however absent. Sergeant Harry Ross was back in Jersey once more – this time on a mission to find a second Jersey Company.

Four

Autumn in Aldershot

I am often driven to think that not sufficient is made of the 'Jersey contingent'... We ask only to be kindly remembered...

Sergeant Harry Ross, Jersey Company RIR, December 1915

Even as final preparations for the Jersey Company's departure from Ireland were underway, the campaign to drum up more volunteers had gone on. Hard on the heels of his success in July, Harry Ross, the jocular ex-newspaper editor and semi-official recruiting Sergeant, was back on the island.

For the visit at the end of August, however, he had an even more ambitious target. Noting that the last effort netted more than forty volunteers, the men's overall commanding officer, Major General Sir Lawrence Parsons, wondered if Jersey could do even better. In a letter to the island's Lieutenant-Governor, Parsons had raised the subject of recruiting another company of infantry. Describing the existing Jersey Company as clean, smart, well-trained and very well conducted soldiers who had become 'quite a part of the Battalion', pertinently, he concluded, 'now, like Oliver Twist, I write because I want more!'[1]

The campaign to find more had kicked off optimistically enough on 31 August 1915. In reportedly inspiring form, Sergeant Ross addressed the packed assembly room at St Martin's Parish Hall. Using glowing terms, he described life in the modern British Army, and the development and achievements of Jersey Company since joining. It would difficult to find a body of men more united, Ross concluded emphatically. Now, who was ready to join them?

As the crowd drifted away at the end of the evening, the Sergeant collected the names of those who had expressed an interest. It turned out to be a disappointingly low number. Despite the apparent enthusiasm, he was left with a couple of definite candidates; one or two possible volunteers, and plenty of excuses. Even more disconcerting was that the next rally ended with the same depressing outcome - and the next and the next. There were very few men who were prepared to enlist. By mid-September, when the campaign concluded, it was possible to count the number of new volunteers on the fingers of one hand.

It certainly meant one thing, reflected a troubled Ross as he departed the island; there would not be a second Jersey Company in 1915.

The lack of volunteers also troubled the island's newspapers. From the start, the *Evening Post* and *Morning News* had strongly advocated the creation of an identifiable Jersey unit, and both had remained staunch supporters of 'Ours' ever since. The *Morning News* in particular - partly though its connection with Harry Ross - had forged and maintained strong links with the volunteers throughout their time in Ireland. In the late summer of 1915, there was open irritation at the apparent lack of enthusiasm for the Jersey Company – particularly when it seemed that men were still willing to join other regiments:

> [The] Jersey Company represents in tangible form the Island's direct response to the call to arms. It is by far the largest body of Jerseymen gathered together in a single fighting unit, and as such has a greater share of the public attention centred upon it. That being so, it is somewhat regrettable, and not a little surprising, that as many Jerseymen who have enlisted since its formation have elected to join other units rather than 'Ours'[2]

'There can surely be no serious reason,' challenged the editor of the *Morning News*, 'for what seems, on the face of it, to advocate a certain prejudice against Major Stocker and his men.'[3]

Prejudice or not, it was clear that by September 1915 volunteering for the Jersey Company had all but dried up. Less than five names on Sergeant Ross's list was evidence of that. Yet why was this case, since in July he had managed to attract over forty new recruits? Then again, did it really matter? By this time the Jersey Company had enough men to meet its immediate commitments, and indeed, more to spare. Both questions were very important in the history of the Jersey Company. The answers to them were interrelated, and, in the longer term, would have profound implications for this small unit and the men serving in it. Yet neither answer was straightforward. The starting point for both is to consider the broader situation with the war at this time, and its impact on recruitment in general.

By September 1915, it was not just in Jersey that volunteers were becoming harder to find. Across Britain generally, the story was the same. The country, by this time, had been at war for over a year, and it was starting to grow weary. After a dramatic and fast-moving start, for the Allies, the conflict had settled into a depressing stalemate marked only by failed campaigns and heavy casualties. There seemed little prospect of it ending soon.

By the close of 1914, the Allies had managed to halt the German advance into France and Belgium. Germany, however, had not intended to relinquish the territory it had captured without a fight. Along a 400 mile stretch of front, its army had begun digging-in on the line reached when the war of movement had come to a halt. At first, the fortifications were just rudimentary in nature, a single trench or series of earthworks to maximise defence and minimise casualties during the winter months. Yet soon, as the benefit of these defences were realised, the trenches began to take on a more permanent character.

The Allies had little choice but to follow. By the spring of 1915, the armies faced each other from trenches laced with barbed wire across a deadly strip of earth known as no man's land. Despite efforts by the Germans at Ypres in April, and the Allies for much of the rest of that year, neither side could find a way to penetrate the other's defences and return to a war of movement. With deadlock on the so-called Western Front that now stretched from the Swiss border to the English Channel, both sides turned their attention elsewhere in the search for a decisive victory. For the Germans, it was fighting in the east against the Russians that dominated most of that year. For the Allies, France and Belgium remained the primary place of conflict, but there were offensives against Germany's ally Turkey at Gallipoli and in Mesopotamia. Unfortunately, both would become costly and largely ineffective sideshows.

At sea, despite British success in keeping the German surface fleet largely in port, enemy submarines were at large and starting to take a toll on British shipping. Everywhere, it seemed, Allied efforts to win the war were being thwarted, with an ever-increasing list of casualties as the only tangible result. Understandably, these circumstances did little to increase the appeal of volunteering. Yet the military still required men. Losses in battle needed replacing while the growth of Kitchener's 'New Army' had continued. It was becoming increasingly obvious, however, that it was no longer enough to rely on the innocent patriotism that drove hundreds of thousands to volunteer in the early months of the war. For Britain to continue the fight into 1916 – and almost certainly beyond – something more would be needed. In July 1915, the British Parliament took the first steps by passing a National Registration Act.

Under the terms of the new law, men and women between the ages of fifteen and sixty-five were required to register and provide the government with their full name, age and occupation. At a stroke, this list had presented for the first time a comprehensive picture of the country's manpower potential – for both military and essential civil purposes. It also identified those men most suitable for the armed forces, but not yet in uniform. In due course, this group could become the natural focus of a more draconian compulsory military service policy. At the time, however, compulsory conscription had been placed on hold. The British government decided instead to conduct one final campaign to encourage continued voluntary enlistment.

Under some pressure from the British government, Jersey had followed suit. In August 1915, the States passed a similar registration law. Then, at the start of October, a sweeping campaign commenced to persuade more island men to come forward and volunteer for overseas service. As in the previous campaign in December 1914, the prime targets were the men of the Militia.

For much of 1915, the island's defences had remained fully manned. A battalion of the South Staffordshire Regiment still served as the island's army garrison, and the Militia – although diminished in number – remained mobilised and on guard over the coast. Their retention on the island, however, continued to be controversial – and increasingly so in view of the fact that island taxpayers were footing the bill. To some it seemed incredulous that so many young men should be kept on the island when the war was clearly being fought elsewhere. One newspaper correspondent had summed up the feelings:

> A visit to any local picture house or band performance any evening of the week will reveal … hundreds of able-bodied young fellows in jackets of the latest cut, hair plastered down the middle, accompanied by their favourite 'flapper,' absolutely unmoved by the momentous doings in Belgium and France.[4]

Officially, the island's authorities remained staunch supporters of the Militia, and its role on the island's defence. Behind the scenes, however, there was some unquiet. Certainly, when the latest campaign to persuade militiamen to volunteer commenced, the States and other government figures were firmly behind the appeal.

In a series of rallies and addresses, Major General Rochfort and other island leaders had worked their way through the Militia units, starting with the West Battalion on 5 October 1915. The Lieutenant-Governor's stirring rhetoric left little doubt what was expected:

> We know now that if we are to continue to rely on voluntary recruiting to bring this war to a speedy and successful issue the time for a supreme effort has arrived… You all know where the recruiting office is, and I say to you that any man who without good reason now holds back is evading his duty to his county.[5]

The campaign worked. After slumping in August and September, the rate of volunteering picked up again in October. Stirred by a new-found sense of patriotism, or perhaps resigned to the fact compulsory military service was just round the corner anyway, more than 100 men came forward. In November, the response was similar. Once more, the recruitment offices filled with men signing up for overseas service. The difference at this time, however, was where they would end up. With the army desperate for recruits, these latest volunteers had the pick of regiments and corps from which to choose. Most, understandably, chose an option that would hopefully keep them out of the trenches. The Royal Artillery, Army Service Corps or Royal Army Medical Corps for example, offered better training and pay, and potentially lessened exposure to German shells and bullets. An analysis of recruiting statistics show that more than three-quarters of Jerseymen who volunteered at this time chose a non-infantry role.[6]

Yet even with this trend, it still meant some twenty-five men joining the infantry per month for October and November 1915. Yet all of these chose to join a regiment other than the Royal Irish Rifles, meaning that none found their way into the ranks of the Jersey Company. As suggested by the *Morning News*, it did indeed appear that some kind of prejudice existed against the island's own military unit.

In August 1915, the *Evening Post* suggested a possible answer for the lack of enthusiasm. 'Letters received [from the Jersey Company] make it plain that there is practically no hope of promotion and no talk of going to the front.' What's more, the editorial noted, given these circumstances it was hardly 'encouraging to others at present on the island who might wish to offer their services.'[7]

The claim appears to have some validity. When offering a contingent for overseas service, Jersey's government had insisted its men remain together as a unit. For a volunteer to receive promotion to a higher rank (and consequently higher pay) he had to wait until one appeared within the Jersey Company. For the ambitious, or those with a family to consider, this was potentially a long wait given the unit was at full strength from the beginning. And there was no denying the Jersey Company appeared to be taking a long time to reach the front. By the start of September 1915, after all, it had been six months since it left Jersey, and nine since most of the men first volunteered. In that same time, men joining other regiments had completed their training and reached the front by now. For the patriotic, anxious to take part in the fighting, the delay in the Jersey Company joining the fray could have been off-putting.

These two issues may have conspired to limit the chance of success for Sergeant Ross's September campaign. When coupled with the overall slowdown in volunteering, this would certainly go some way to explain the lack of success. Yet on their own, the restrictions do not fully explain the lack of volunteers for the Jersey Company in October and November, especially as Ross had gone deliberately out of his way to downplay both these problems at the recruiting rallies and his regular *Morning News* updates. In September, for example, there was extensive reporting on a number of recent internal promotions. Additionally, the Jersey Company *had* finally left Ireland that month, with a clear understanding it was moving towards the front. Were further factors conspiring to prevent additional recruits for the Jersey Company? One of the most likely was the attitude of the island's government and arrangements that it had made.

In offering and raising a contingent for overseas service, the Jersey authorities must have felt they had done their bit. They had hit the quota needed for an infantry company, and had sent their men off with due ceremony to join the British Army. Yet following this, there seems to have subsequently been little formal contact between the island and its contingent. Once in the army, the Jersey Company, despite a desire to retain an independent identity, invariably would progressively become lost as part of the far larger organisation. Ties with its island, in all but name, were bound to be lost unless the Jersey authorities made stringent efforts to retain them. By choice or by design, Jersey's authorities do not appear to have made any such effort.

For a community to maintain strong bonds with its military unit some part of that unit needs ideally to remain within that community. Typically, this would be a local recruiting station and an army depot for the reception and training of new and existing members. In wartime, these men could then replace losses within the active service element of the unit – a vital requirement if that unit is going to remain effective. For the Jersey Company, however, no such recruiting station, depot or any other supporting arrangement existed. While the self-generated efforts of Sergeant Ross had served the purpose for a time, these could only ever be interim arrangements. Yet the island established nothing longer-term to fill their place.

By the end of September 1915, the Jersey Company had all but received its last recruits – for the immediate future at least. Not that it was a pressing problem at the time, for by then some 326 men had joined the Jersey Company, a number far in excess of that needed to form the requested infantry company.[8] The problem of replacements, if it came about, was for the future. At that time, the immediate challenge facing the men was the prospect of an autumn in Aldershot.

For generations the town of Aldershot has been known as the 'Home of the British Army'. In September 1915, its barracks, camps and training facilities expanded beyond recognition to meet the demands of a world war, and the title was never more deserved. The town, and its surrounding communities, had become one vast military camp. Men arrived, were trained, and left for the front without a pause. Among those arriving in the autumn of 1915 were the volunteers of the Jersey Company.

The journey by ship and rail after leaving the port of Dublin on 9 September had been slow and remarkably uneventful. After its arrival in Aldershot 7th RIR, along with the rest of 48th Brigade, had gone on to Deepcut a few miles to the north. Here, in the Marne Barracks at the sprawling Blackdown Camp, the Jerseymen made themselves at home. It was certainly quite a home. Compared to the draughty huts of Ballyvonare, or a damp tent under the trees at Ballyhooley, the new camp seemed nothing less than luxurious. In fact, claimed one man, the barracks were so good they seemed more like a convalescent home.[9] Sergeant Harry Ross, now back with the Company, elaborated on the facilities available:

> In Blackdown Camp itself we have a football field, institutes, homes, fives courts, 'rests' galore. First and foremost the Garrison institute, a building the size of Olympia (Jersey), furnished with capital billiards tables by Burroughes and Watts, newspapers, bar, a magnificent organ, etc. The building has a spacious gallery, fitted with a cinematographie operating box, and a continuous picture show goes on nightly. All the London papers are provided within an hour of their publication. Billiards are 2d per 100 only! There are institutes run by the Church Army, the Y.M.C.A., the Salvation Army, the Wesleyans and others that I have not yet discovered because you can keep walking round in this place and discovering pastures new every time.[10]

It was soon realised moreover that outside the camp's boundaries lay an even more alluring prospect. London was just fifty or so miles away to the north-east, less than an hour away by train. Armed with a weekend pass, and a ticket costing only 2s 6d, the more adventurous could easily reach Waterloo Station, and the brighter lights of the West End beyond. In no time, a steady stream of Jerseymen had been heading in that direction.

Unfortunately for the more adventurous, and others, the reason for coming to Aldershot that autumn was not simply to enjoy its amenities or location. This was a place for military units to complete their final preparations before going overseas. It was also, of course, a centre for military training, with extensive on-site facilities and plenty of nearby open spaces for army exercises. There, within a few days of arriving, the daily routine had picked up where it left off in Ireland a few weeks before.

Not long after their arrival, Harry Ross recounted a typical week for the Jersey Company:

> We have had an exceptionally busy week. Musketry has re-commenced on Pirbright ranges, but up to now A and B Companies only have fired and have not yet completed their course by any means. These two companies are temporarily struck off all other duties, which means that much extra work devolves on C and D, the latter our Company. Daily guards, picquets and fatigues have to be found by C and D alternately and when not employed, we are hard at it in the trenches, situated at Tunnel Hill about two miles from the camp. Here we have done some very fine work in the way of dugouts and underground passages. Our field kitchens accompany us daily and we have dinner out. Tomorrow, each man has to cook his own grub in his mess-tin.[11]

What Ross had failed to mention was that training now took place in progressively deteriorating conditions. As September gave way to October, the weather turned for the worse. The heady days of Ireland soon became a distant memory. Instead of glorious marches under cloudless skies across a lush County Cork, it was grim hikes in the driving rain through muddy Surrey. Shooting practice at nearby Bisley and Pirbright had left the men numb with cold.

There were some new skills to focus on. 'One portion of the Jerseys are being trained as bomb-throwers,' continued Harry Ross, 'and some of our best shots have been selected as snipers.'[12] Yet mostly it was a repetitive and by then largely unchallenging routine. The days dragged into weeks, firing on the ranges, undertaking the same manoeuvres and exercises. With no escape from the monotony in sight, attention naturally turned to other distractions. Some of these arrived in the form of visitors seeking out the Jersey Company.

News of the Jersey Company's arrival seems to have gotten round Aldershot quickly, leading to a steady stream of visits by other Jerseymen serving in the area. Reunions with family, friends and old acquaintances soon became commonplace. Some had turned up with welcome news from home while others came with lurid tales of life at the front, having already served in the trenches by now. The greatest distraction, however, had been the arrival of another group of Channel Islanders.

Like its Jersey counterpart, a Guernsey company had been formed late in 1914 and sent in March 1915 to reinforce an Irish battalion. In its case, this was the 6th Battalion of the Royal Irish Regiment, part of the 47th Infantry Brigade. Unlike Jersey, however, sufficient volunteers had come forward to form a second Guernsey company, which in September 1915 was attached to the 7th Battalion of the Royal Irish Fusiliers. In Ireland, the Jerseymen and Guernseymen had been mostly apart, but here in Aldershot the first Guernsey company was also in Blackdown Camp, while the second was in nearby Woking. It did not take long for the longstanding and (mostly) good-humoured rivalry that existed between the two islands to resurface. Invariably, the only way to settle differences had been on the football field.

The 'Muratti' is the local name given to a traditional and longstanding annual football match between Jersey and Guernsey. On 23 October 1915, an extraordinary version took place on a windswept playing field at Aldershot. The cream of both contingents took the field in the presence of a large and very partisan crowd. Harry Ross later recounted the outcome:

> Last Saturday afternoon a great event was brought off in Blackdown Camp. It took the form of an inter-insular football match which vividly recalled Muratti days. Jersey and Guernsey again met in deadly combat and a hard-fought encounter resulted in a win for Jersey by one goal to nil, scored by Lance Corporal Michael McCarthy early in the first half … There was a goodly crowd along the touch-lines and much good humoured banter was engaged in on both sides, many old Channel Island gags and catcalls being exchanged … The return match will be eagerly looked forward to.[13]

It appeared there would be plenty of time for a return match. Despite training for both contingents proceeding apace, there was no news yet when they would be leaving Aldershot for the front. While other units came and went, the Irish battalions remained. To some it seemed Aldershot was more about marking time than any serious training. Unfortunately, in some respects they had been right. In the autumn of 1915, the 16th (Irish) Division was far from ready to go to war.

During the First World War, infantry divisions were the British Army's major independent formations. When fully established, they controlled three infantry brigades, four artillery brigades and numerous smaller supporting units, including engineers and field ambulances; in total a force of around 19,000 men. During the course of the war, there were sixty-seven formed by the army and sent for service overseas. One of the most problematical, and controversial, was the 16th (Irish) Division.

Initially, this division's problems had centred on its struggle to find sufficient men to fill out its ranks. With recruiting grounds among the Nationalist-leaning communities in the south of Ireland, it had been a challenge to meet quotas. Even by September 1915, the month it had moved from Ireland to Aldershot, many of its units remained under strength. Controversy came with the question of its men's loyalty, as from the start the 16th (Irish) Division was strongly linked with the Irish Nationalist cause, and especially to the political parties demanding Home Rule from Britain. This had led some senior army officers and politicians to question the competence and reliability of its officers and men.

Finally – and especially significant in the autumn of 1915 – there was the transfer of 16th (Irish) Division's units to other divisions. In order to build up other formations, the army had successively ordered 16th (Irish) Division to give up its artillery brigades, supporting units and even some infantry. This meant that by the time of arrival in Aldershot, only two of its infantry brigades, the 47th and 48th, were anywhere near strength. The 49th Brigade remained woefully short of men while the divisional artillery and supporting units were all just reforming. These changes left it far from ready for active service.

Ultimately, it meant that while many other 'New Army' divisions were already serving at the front, 16th (Irish) Division remained mired in Aldershot. It was a sensitive state of affairs. The delay allowed detractors to further question the value of the Division, while supporters regarded the delay as some kind of political plot to prevent the Nationalist community proving its worth. The arguments had filtered down to the men biding their time at Aldershot. For them it had become a period of increasing uncertainty and frustration, especially for those units now fully trained and up to strength. One of these was definitely the Jersey Company.

By the end of September 1915, the Jersey Company had attracted far more volunteers than the 230 needed to form a standard infantry company. Not all, however, had travelled to Aldershot. Some of the men had struggled during the training in Ireland. Despite passing the original army medical, underlying physical or medical problems had subsequently emerged. The army had discharged some of the volunteers quickly, their health or condition such that there was no role for them. Others had been designated as fit for 'Home Service' only, meaning they could serve in a garrison but not travel to the front on active service. Some fifteen of the Jersey volunteers had fallen into this category, and had left 7th RIR in August 1915 to join the 3rd Battalion of the Royal Irish Rifles, the Regiment's Depot Battalion serving at that time in Dublin.

For some, this transfer to the Depot Battalion was to become a permanent arrangement; they were destined to see out the remainder of the war in Ireland or elsewhere in the British Isles. For others, however, there remained an expectation that it was only a temporary move and once their condition improved, or their training completed, they could return to duty with the Jersey Company. Rifleman William Hervé was one those moved to the Depot Battalion. While in training at Ballyhooley, the twenty-three-year-old had caught a chill that prevented him travelling to Aldershot with the others. Despite expectations that the delay would only be short-lived, his condition worsened as pneumonia took hold. On 14 November he died, the sad news reaching Aldershot the following day.

Despite the loss of Hervé, and the other Home Service men, the Jersey Company had still arrived in Aldershot with more than 300 officers and other ranks. It was a surplus welcomed by 7th RIR, which had been able to second the additional Jerseymen to fill many of the specialist roles in the Battalion. For example a group of twenty-six, including Sergeant Chris D'Authreau as senior NCO, formed 7th RIR's Machine Gun Section. Another group of fifteen men, led by Corporal Oscar Williams, had become specialist signallers attached to the Battalion headquarters. Other individuals were allocated all manner of duties, including cooks, butchers, officer's servants, medical orderlies, drivers and military policemen.

Yet whatever the role, there remained a question over when exactly they would be leaving Aldershot for the front. It took until the end of November for the answer to finally to arrive. Despite its lack of readiness, 16th (Irish) Division was to go to the front by the end of the year with those of its formations then trained and ready. The rest of the Division would catch-up in the new year. Political lobbying and a pragmatic approach appear to have won the day.

With the decision to depart, the mood at Aldershot changed dramatically. The remaining weeks there became a whirlwind of preparations and parades. 'Never shall we forget the last days at good old Blackdown,' remarked Harry Ross, 'the hurry, scurry and excitement everywhere.'[14] All of the Battalion's equipment had needed inspection, with a general exchange of old for new prior to departure. There was also a final comb-out of Home Service men to leave only those suitable for active service.

On 2 December, a grand royal review had taken place. Queen Mary arrived to inspect the 16th (Irish) Division and take the salute from the massed ranks proudly marching past. One of the leading units was the Jersey Company, which reportedly presented a splendid sight. Major General Sir Lawrence Parsons, the commander of 16th (Irish) Division, leaned over to the Queen as the Jerseymen went by and singled them out for special comment. 'This is the Jersey Company', he announced with a wave, 'and that is Major Stocker'.[15] It was, by all accounts, a memorable day.

Perhaps most exciting of all, however, had been the prospect of some home leave. As was tradition, soldiers about to leave for overseas service were granted a few days off. Understandably, most of the Jerseymen decided to travel home. Journeying down to Weymouth by train, they caught the first ship bound for the island. An emotional few days with friends and family had followed. Yet it seems that not everyone was that pleased to see them. On returning to Blackdown, some of the men reported disappointing comments from a few cynics convinced that they were having an easy time. 'I am often driven to think that not sufficient is made of the Jersey contingent,' reflected Harry Ross on hearing the news, 'We ask only to be kindly remembered...'[16]

Fortunately, it was just a small minority. In the island as a whole, a public campaign was underway to collect and send 'Christmas Gifts' to Jerseymen serving in the forces. Championed by the *Morning News*, it was heartening for those at Aldershot to see that its initial priority remained the men of 'Ours.' The island responded to the appeal with generosity; there was soon enough money and goods donated to send each member of the Jersey Company an individually wrapped parcel. They had arrived at Aldershot on 16 December and Major Stocker wrote back immediately to thank the campaign organisers:

> This afternoon every man of the Jersey Company received his gift of woollen articles so kindly and generously given by the '*Morning News*' readers, the extras in the way of cakes, sweets, pipes, notepaper, apples, etc., etc., adding an extra width to the beaming smiles of the contented recipients as they went off with their own particular gifts.[17]

This was to be the final communication from Aldershot. Three days after the gifts arrived, the Jersey Company departed for the front.

The roads of Deepcut had still been in darkness on the morning of 19 December 1915 as 7th RIR marched out Blackdown Camp. Nonetheless, some locals turned out to see off the departing soldiers, calling hushed goodbyes and best wishes from their open windows and doors. The early morning was a bitterly cold one, and many of the Jerseymen had swaddled themselves in the recently arrived woollens. It presented an amusing spectacle, the circles of bright colours, someone remarked, gave the men the appearance of Christmas trees.

A slow train that morning had carried the Battalion down to Southampton docks. The great port city had become one of the major south coast gateways for the war on the Continent. From it in one direction flowed fresh men and supplies; coming back in the other was a steady stream of tired and wounded soldiers. On that day, the docks thronged with men waiting to travel to France. The threat of German submarines, however, meant a crossing had to wait until the hours of darkness. A monotonous afternoon followed, lightened only by the presence of a band, and the amusing antics of the kitten that had been brought along as a mascot by the men of Number 2 Platoon. The creature's ultimate fate is not known, but the men were determined to take it to the front. That evening, it was smuggled onto the ship under the jacket of Rifleman George Le Lievre, and presumably crossed to France with everyone else.

After dark, the ship slipped away from the quayside and nosed out into the Channel. Being one of the largest vessels on the route, its commodious decks could easily accommodate hundreds of soldiers in relative comfort. Finding space, the Jerseymen had settled down for the night. It was December, however, and true to form, a storm was whipping up the English Channel. In darkness, the great ship lurched towards France with understandable consequences for its passengers. 'The sea was very rough and the boat was rolling and pitching all of the way across,' wrote home Rifleman Frank Sorel, 'nearly all of the men were sick.'[18] The storm only abated when the French coast was reached, and the ship dropped anchor outside the port of Le Havre.

As the grey dawn broke, the ship had finally entered the port and tied up against one of its quays. It was a quiet Monday morning and few people were around yet. There was certainly no welcoming party to mark the arrival of Jersey's official contribution to the war. Yet the newly arrived Jerseymen still managed to attract some curious stares and remarks however. In keeping with their origin, they had retained Militia style shoulder badges on their uniforms sporting the name 'Jersey' and these stood them out from their Irish comrades and other soldiers. The fact that these newcomers had also called out to them in French furthered the local's interest.

Most of that day was spent in a nearby rest camp where, after a cursory wash and shave, there was little to do save brew tea and eat something from their rations. In the afternoon, there had been an issue of field service postcards and most took the opportunity to scribble a few lines home. These ubiquitous little items came pre-formatted; a man could only write an address on one side, and add the scantest of details to the other. Nevertheless, the arrival of scores of them in Jersey a week or so later was the first indication the island had that the men of 'Ours' had crossed to France.

Later that afternoon, the Battalion marched back through the port and on to the railway station. On the platform, there was some consternation to discover that the train's carriages consisted mainly of former cattle trucks, emblazoned on their sides the words '40 Hommes, 8 Chevaux' to indicate the type and number of passengers to be carried at any one time. In time, the Jerseymen were to become very familiar with this principle means of transporting soldiers across the overstretched French railway network. On this occasion, however, they climbed on board grumbling.

The train had soon pulled away. Settling down for the long journey, even the usually upbeat Harry Ross struggled to remain positive:

> ...it wasn't too bad for we spread our water-proof sheets and blankets and experienced the delight of being able to stretch our legs out, which was what we required badly. There was however, comparatively little sleep, as the carriage rocked so.[19]

A long twenty-four hours followed as the train clattered slowly across northern France. Finally, as the light was fading on the afternoon of 21 December, the journey ended in a complex of platforms and sidings on the southern outskirts of the town of Bethune. Fading on a nearby wall was the name of the place, Fouquerueil. As they stiffly climbed down, however, most were too tired to notice. The smell of the first hot meal since leaving Le Harve had been far more important.

At around 6.00 p.m., with everyone fed and assembled, the Jersey Company marched off. Ahead that evening lay a six-mile trek through the dark to a camp outside the village of Houchin. Tired and disorientated, the men stumbled down country lanes. Increasingly, they became conscious of a distant rumbling sound away to their right, while in that direction, frequent flashes lit up the sky. Everyone had known what it was.

After nine months of training, they were almost at the front finally. A few miles away to the east, in front of the village of Loos, lay the British trenches, and, beyond them, those of the enemy.

Five

Caveland

I wonder if all of us, safe and snug in this tight little Island, really realise that the men of 'Ours' have now been at the front for weeks, and that at this very moment they may actually be in the firing line.

Editorial, Morning News, January 1916

In the years leading up to the First World War, coal mining had been the dominant industry in the countryside around the small French village of Loos. Beneath the gently undulating landscape, there lay rich seams of this most essential of fuels, and a host of industrious miners had laboured for its extraction. With the arrival of warring armies in the autumn of 1914, production had quickly fallen away, and, with the miners gone, new forces laboured there – only this time with a far more deadly purpose.

As the front line solidified during that first winter of the war, at Loos both sides had dug their trenches round and through the former mine workings. Wherever practical, the abandoned infrastructure was turned to military use. Mining villages, with their sturdy rows of brick-built cottages, became billets for the troops. Grimy clusters of mine buildings became fortified strongpoints, their pithead winding towers turned into excellent observation platforms. Finally, the huge heaps of mining spoil, locally called '*crassiers*', served as artificial areas of high ground. Soon, Loos was as strong a position as could be found anywhere on the Western Front.

Yet this had not stopped the British Army launching its largest offensive to date there in September 1915. The Battle of Loos was that year's final attempt by the British to break through the German lines and return to a war of movement once more. After some initial promise, like earlier attempts it had ended in yet another bloody failure. The war was destined to go on into 1916 at least.

In the meantime, a cold winter had descended over the battlefield. The Loos sector became what was termed a 'quiet one' – well suited for resting worn out divisions and introducing those just arriving in France. In December 1915, the 16th (Irish) Division had begun to assemble in the area. In due course, the plan was for the Division to take over full responsibility for part of the front there. Before then, however, there was to be a period of induction; a three month spell alternating between further training and instruction behind the front and time spent gaining first-hand experience in the trenches. For the Jersey Company, the first experience of trench duty came on the very last day of that year.

It had been ten days since the Jersey Company first clambered off the train at Fouquereuil, and set off through the dark to Houchin. There, in a camp next to the village, the men had spent Christmas – the first most of them had experienced away from home. Then, on 30 December, came the order they had been expecting since arrival. Everyone was to pack up and prepare to move out; the next day, the Jersey Company would be going into the trenches.

Under a darkening sky, the volunteers had picked their way quietly across the old September battlefield to take up positions in a trench near the village of Loos itself. The journey up had been nervy enough: scattered all around were small white crosses marking the final resting place of fallen British soldiers. As night fell, the tension increased. In the darkness, every strange sound had become amplified, every unexpected movement magnified. Everyone knew that only a few hundred yards of ground now separated them from the enemy, and the Germans certainly made their presence known. All night long, periodic bursts of machine fire had ripped across no man's land, while overhead parachute flares hung in the sky, their eerie light casting long shadows over British lines. Spread out along the trench, the Jerseymen could only listen, watch and wonder. 'It was a weird experience for those of us who saw the Old Year out and the New Year in the trenches,' recalled Harry Ross later, 'and our thoughts can be more easily imagined than described.'[1] Yet the welcome grey light of morning had found everyone still present and unharmed. They had survived their first night in the trenches.

Watching over the Jerseymen on that first night, and for the next eight days, was a battalion of experienced Scottish soldiers. In line with army policy, newly arriving battalions could expect to be under the wing of a veteran unit during their first few spells in the trenches. They provided practical experience of how to go about living – and hopefully surviving – in this most unforgiving of environments.

When the Jersey Company arrived at the front, the routine of life in the trenches had become firmly established. Twelve months of static warfare had seen to that. The lack of movement had also allowed the trenches themselves to develop; in layout and complexity, they had evolved enormously from the thin line of defences scraped out during the first winter of the war. Those at Loos occupied by the Jersey Company were typical of what existed along the whole of the Western Front.

By the end of 1915, trench systems had increased considerably in both depth and complexity. There were by then two parallel lines of deep trenches, or in many places even three. The first one, known as the front line or 'firing line', directly faced the enemy's trenches. A few hundred yards behind, a second line called the 'support line' acted as insurance against an enemy breakthrough. Behind it there was often constructed a third or 'reserve line'. To allow movement back and forth, and to gain access into and out of the trenches, a labyrinth of smaller communication trenches ran between them all, and back into the relative safety of the area known as 'the rear'. The layout meant a man could enter this strange sunken world and travel for miles without having to ever directly expose himself to enemy fire.

The speed by which a man could travel through the trenches was, however, somewhat restricted by their design. The fighting trenches, and wherever practical the communication trenches, were constructed to minimise the effect of a direct artillery hit and to prevent attackers firing along the length. This was achieved by a pattern of right-angled traverses that divided the trench into sections, or 'firebays', each roughly ten feet wide. From the air, this gave them a characteristic zigzag appearance, rather like the crenellated top of a castle wall. While eminently sensible, this shape did make movement through the trench difficult – particularly in the heat of a battle.

A good fighting trench could expect to be roughly 8ft in depth and 6ft wide. Inside, timber, corrugated iron, sandbags and wicker panels held its walls in place and strengthened the sides against collapse. Along the floor ran slated wooden duckboards, which attempted to keep men's feet out of the water in the inevitable wet periods. Tunnelled into the sides of the trench were holes and dugouts to offer some protection from both the elements and enemy fire. In the bottom of the trench, the side facing the enemy featured a raised platform called the firestep. Climbing up on it, the occupants of the trench could see and fire over the top, or parapet. In quieter moments, the firestep also served a more mundane role as a place for men to sit, work, cook, eat and sleep.

As the Jerseymen soon discovered, life in the trenches revolved about these quieter moments. Major battles, involving one side leaving their trenches to attack the other side, were infrequent. So for the most part, the daily routine was a monotonous affair interspersed with sudden violence when an enemy shell struck, or a sniper spotted some careless movement. Every day it started just before dawn in the same fashion. First light was a notorious time for surprise attacks, and so for half an hour before and after dawn everyone in the trench 'stood-to', ready to repel the enemy. If there was no attack (which was usually the case), the men were 'stood down' and the day's routine would begin. After a wash and shave, weapons and personal kit underwent vigorous cleaning in preparation for the officer's inspection that preceded breakfast. Following breakfast, there was a mix of sentry duties on the firestep or some minor working-party activity. The afternoons for all except those remaining on watch were the time for sleep. This was the only chance they would get; in this curiously inverted environment, there was precious little time to rest during the hours of darkness.

Under cover of the night, the trenches came alive with activity. Work considered too risky to carry out in daylight now needed completing before dawn arose. Yet night-time was also when the enemy was most active – everyone needed to be doubly on their guard. After another round of 'stand-to' and 'stand-down' at dusk, an exhausting routine commenced. In the trenches at Loos, the Jersey Company soon fell into it, as Harry Ross reported:

> There is no sleep at nights for anybody, be his rank what it may … In each fire-bay so many men are stationed, and the duty per man runs as follows: One hour's sentry, one hour's work, one hour's rest.

For the first hour he is on the fire-step, taking an occasional cautious peep over undercover, firing a shot now and then, or giving warnings such as: 'Trench Mortar to the right', etc., etc. Then after an hour of this arduous duty, he joins a fatigue party, and takes part in some form of work, such as repairing a parapet that a shell may have hit, and caused to crumble away, or digging a pit. This work is given to him for two reasons: to keep him awake, and to take his mind off 'Johnny German'.

The third hour the man has to himself and in it he is supposed to brew himself a tin of tea or cook a bit of something hot. He doesn't have time to get down, have a 'doss', and wake up again within the hour, and the wise people who originally drew up Tommy's trench timetable knew it. So the night wears on.[2]

A night's activity also frequently extended out of the trenches and into no man's land. There, one of the most loathed duties was to be detailed to work on the belts of barbed wire defences positioned in front of the trench. They had needed constant attention: there were repairs to carry out and new layers of wire to be added from time to time. In small working parties, men laboured to roll out coils and attach them to supports driven into the ground. At best, it could be a night of painful, frustrating and exhausting work. At worst, when the enemy detected movement in no man's land, there was the threat of machine gun fire, shells and mortars, or the sudden crack of a sniper's rifle. Day or night, snipers were a constant threat at Loos. They would often creep out under the cover of darkness to take up a hidden position in no man's land. Undetected, they would wait all day for the one chance to get a shot at someone careless or unfortunate enough to expose himself to view. In early January 1916, one of these hidden marksman were to cause the Jersey Company's first casualty in action.

In common with his fellow musicians, Bugler Sam Trenchard served as a stretcher-bearer when at the front. For the sniper who spotted him hurrying through the trench on duty, however, he had represented as good a target as anyone else. The shot struck Trenchard on the side of the head, having passed clean through a sandbag first. Fortunately, it seems that this barrier served to minimise the impact of the bullet, and to everyone's surprise and great relief the result had been a nasty, but not fatal wound. After an operation, and a period of convalescence, Bugler Trenchard would return to the trenches.

In the end, Trenchard was the only casualty of this first spell of in the trenches. On 8 January, the Jerseymen left the front to march to a rest camp some miles to the rear. On the way there, there was time to reflect. 'We have all heard and read a great deal of life in Caveland,' admitted Harry Ross at the time, 'I am afraid I have to admit that some of our chaps have still to appreciate what active service really means…'[3]

The village of Ames lies to south-west of Bethune, and in 1916 was some fifteen miles behind the front line. Like others in the area, it was host then to one of the many camps established by the British Army for resting and training troops outside of the fighting zone. There, on 10 January 1916, the Jersey Company had arrived to do both. Their first priority, however, was a much welcome bath.

In the trenches, fresh water was one of the most precious commodities. What was available had often been carried miles from the rear overnight, leaving it almost exclusively reserved for drinking and cooking purposes. There was little, if any, to spare for personal hygiene. This meant the underclothes and uniform that a man wore going into the trenches were the same ones in which he marched out again. Cleaning, other than a cursory wash and shave, was out of the question. For this reason, the army established an extensive range of communal bathing and washing facilities behind the lines. At Ames, these facilities were at the showers of a nearby coal mine. Although the march there was a long one, the experience made it more than worthwhile. 'How we revelled in the water,' wrote Harry Ross, 'each man has a cabin to himself and twenty minutes are allowed for the operation – five to disrobe, ten in water, and five to dress. The hot spray revived us wonderfully.'[4]

Bathed and in an issue of clean clothes, the next eighteen days at Ames were to be a mixture of training, instruction and fatigue duties. Training and instruction during this first three-month period in France mainly focused on a range of specialised skills to be used in the trenches. In groups, the Jerseymen enthusiastically took on barbed wire erecting, tunnelling, observing, learning how to fire trench mortars and advanced sniping skills. Less welcome were the fatigues.

One of the features of a First World War soldier's life was the constant engagement in manual activities of one sort or another. At the front, or immediately behind, there was a continuing requirement for men to carry out construction work, road building and repair, stores loading and unloading, and so forth. This work, collectively known as 'fatigues', could be exhausting. In a letter home, Rifleman Harold Gulliford complained that he had been made to work on a road repair machine known as the 'rack' because 'it gives you a racking headache when you've have been pulling it all day long'[5].

Fortunately, it was not all training and fatigues at Ames. In common with most locations frequented by the army during the war, the village contained a number of cafe-cum-bars known as '*estaminets*'. Some had existed before the war, while others had opened to take advantage of the mass of hungry and thirsty soldiers then in their midst. Menus reflected what the average British soldier wanted to eat, egg and chips being one of the most popular dishes. To drink, the estaminets had served a variety of weak local beers and rough table wine, but nothing stronger as the army forbid the sale of spirits to anyone not an officer.

Estaminets would become a staple of life for the men when not serving in the trenches. In their smoke-filled rooms, there was a chance to relax and forget about the war for a short while at least. The only real issue was the prices charged by some less scrupulous proprietors. 'We get five francs a fortnight,' complained Harold Gulliford about the prices charged in Ames, 'and as everything is very dear the money does not go far.'[6]

If any money remained – after the estaminets had taken their share – a priority was for writing material. Now they were at the front, with all its associated dangers, correspondence back home took on a new significance for the Jerseymen. Apart from the occasional period of home leave, letters would be the only means of communication with friends and loved ones. Understandably, the men wanted to hear about life in Jersey – even the most trivial of events. There was always great disappointment for anyone not receiving a letter when the post arrived.

In Jersey, letters home, together with Harry Ross's newspaper column, kept people abreast of the Jersey Company's progress. Yet with the war now dragging on towards its third year, and no end in sight, there were growing and recognisable signs of indifference towards the fate of this one small unit. With increasing numbers of Jerseymen now serving throughout the armed forces, and in all theatres, keeping the spotlight on this particular group of islanders had become increasingly difficult. The *Morning News*, which had remained a staunch supporter, did its bit to remind the people of Jersey about their contingent. 'I wonder if all of us, safe and snug in this tight little island, really realise that the men of "Ours" have now been at the front for weeks,' chastised one editorial early in 1916, 'and that at this very moment they may actually be in the firing line.'[7]

By the middle of February, the Jersey Company had indeed returned to the firing line. The period of training at Ames had ended on 28 January with a move to the village of Hesdigneul just behind the front. From there, 7th RIR sent parties into the trenches. On 19 February, it had been the turn of the Jersey Company.

The location for this second spell in the trenches was to the north of Loos near the German-held village of Auchy Les Mines. Yet although the location was different, the arrangements and routine were much the same as the previous time. For support and guidance, an experienced battalion had been on hand once more, although by now the Jersey Company was expected to be more independent. Once more, the casualties were mercifully small, with only a few minor injuries from enemy fire. There was, however, one significant change from January; the weather had taken a turn for the worse.

In February, the full force of winter had howled across northern France. Icy winds brought freezing rain, sleet and finally heavy snow to Loos:

> Never shall the memory of that one week be effaced, a week spent in the vicinity of slag-heaps, transformed into pure-white pyramids; a week of blizzard, and a week in which rifles were held in frozen fingers, and in which sandbags on the parapets resembled white fleecy pillows.[8]

Exposed in the trenches, the men could do little but endure the miserable conditions. 'No one will ever appreciate to any extent what the boys endured.' Harry Ross wrote at the time, 'They have proved what stuff they are made of.'[9] The impact of weather was soon to become evident, however, as increasing numbers of men began reporting ill.

On 28 February, to everyone's great relief, the Jersey Company left the trenches for another period of rest and training. Initially, the location for this was the hamlet of Guarbecque, but on 9 March, the men moved to the larger village of Lapugnoy. The army had transformed this formerly quiet community south of Bethune into a bustling centre of military activity with the addition of hospitals, stores and extensive training facilities. There the routine of training and labouring duties had been resumed, although on 17 March there was a break in the schedule to mark a special day in the calendar of 16th (Irish) Division.

For St Patrick's Day, normal training was suspended. After church services in the morning, everyone had gathered at a nearby field for a grand festival of sports and dancing. The Jerseymen played their part, competing in the running and cycling races, entering a team in the tug-of-war, and sending a man to ride in the donkey derby. Considering competition came from the entire 48th Infantry Brigade, the Jersey Company did remarkably well. Pride of place went to Sergeant Francis McDermott who easily won the quarter-mile race and Rifleman John Luce who triumphed in the signaller's three-mile cycle race. Buoyed up by this success, celebrations had gone on into the evening with impromptu music and singing in the billets, and even an extra tot of rum as a treat.

The only thing casting a shadow over the day was the news that Second Lieutenant Laurence Hibbs was unwell. The popular young officer, then in command of 7th RIR's Machine Gun Section, appeared to be suffering from a heavy cold. Admitted to hospital when there was no improvement, his condition had quickly worsened despite the best efforts of medical staff. Much to the shock of everyone, on 21 March he died of suspected blood poisoning. 'Your son was very dear to me,' Major Stocker wrote the following day to Hibb's father, 'we all turned out yesterday at his burial and I can assure you it was very sad for all of us who knew him. It has cast a gloom over the whole company.'[10]

The gloom was compounded a few days later with an order to return to the trenches. For the Jersey Company, the induction to the Western Front was complete. Now they were to be committed to the trenches on a more or less continuous basis. By the start of April 1916, the 16th (Irish) Division had assumed full control of the front line between the villages of Hulluch and Loos, a distance of about three miles as the crow flies. For its soldiers, the pattern of life soon began to follow a set and well-rehearsed routine. Typically, they would spend four days serving immediately opposite the enemy in the front-line trenches. Next, they would move back to the support line trenches for a further four days as their battalion took on a role called 'Brigade Reserve'. Another four days in the front line followed, before leaving the trenches altogether and moving back to spend four days behind the lines in 'Divisional Reserve'. Once complete, it was back to the front line again, and the whole routine would start over once more.

Although four days in each position was typical, in practice the time spent varied depending on prevailing circumstances. On average, however, each man could expect to spend about twelve days of every sixteen in the trenches, and four days out.

Following the routine meant the whole area around Loos would become very familiar for the men of the Jersey Company. Front line duty would be in the trenches before Hulluch or those in front of Loos itself. Brigade Reserve would usually be among the ruins of Loos, or in the badly damaged villages of Philosophe or Vermelles further to the north. The much longed for periods in Divisional Reserve were invariably at

Mazingarbe which lay about three miles behind the front line, or the less damaged Noeux-Les-Mines some six miles back. Yet even in the latter location, German long-range shells would periodically strike, leaving the men never completely clear of danger.

At the start of April the first tour of front-line duty was in the trenches before the German-held village of Hulluch. Despite the weather starting to show improvement, recent heavy rain had left these trenches in a terrible state. Collapsed in places, partly flooded and full of chalky mud that clung to men's uniforms, they were a grim reminder of how bad conditions could be. Within days, there had been an impact.

Trench foot was a debilitating condition brought on by standing in water for prolonged periods. Through bitter experience, the army had become particularly alert to the danger it presented, and by 1916 went to considerable lengths to prevent its occurrence. Men were required to rub whale oil regularly into their skin to act as a sealant while officers would check feet every morning for signs of neglect. Despite these precautions, within days of arriving in the trenches at Hulluch a number of men, including Sergeant Harry Ross, had gone down with the condition and needed evacuation to hospital.

Yet trench foot was not the only hazard to a man's health. Even during the best of weather, trenches were invariably unsanitary, with dirt, vermin, rudimentary latrines and the presence of unburied corpses threatening a potentially lethal cocktail of diseases. When coupled with a period of cold and wet conditions the rates of illness among the soldiers soared. By early April, the full effect of these conditions coming on top of February's severe weather was becoming obvious as scores of Jerseymen reported sick, with more than thirty needing hospitalisation for chills, fever and pneumonia. Although most members of the Jersey Company who fell ill at this time eventually recovered, some were so severely effected they would never return to active service. For two at least, the illnesses contracted would prove fatal. Rifleman Arthur De La Lande had been one of the first to fall ill when he contracted a bronchial condition in February. Despite treatment, the twenty-year-old would pass away at a hospital in Kent on 19 May 1916. Another, Rifleman Clarence Gregory, left the trenches in April 1916 suffering from trench foot. He never fully recovered, and eventually died of illness brought on by his condition in December 1917, seven months after being discharged from the army.

Fortunately, with the start of April, spring had begun to make a welcome appearance at Loos. As the weather warmed, the level of illness among the Jersey Company steadily declined. Unfortunately, spring's arrival also heralded the start of a period of even greater danger, as the warring armies stirred themselves after the long winter.

Even in quiet sectors such as Loos, the British Army expected its formations to maintain a level of aggressive activity. A general belief persisted that without it, men's fighting spirit would be lost, and a natural reluctance to leave the trenches would prevail. Yet the options to get at the enemy, aside from advancing directly across no man's land, were limited. The alternative was to resort to age-old tactics employed during centuries of siege warfare.

At Loos, the 16th (Irish) Division took up the challenge with gusto. Anxious to demonstrate its commitment to the cause, there was increased shelling of enemy trenches, night-time raids across no man's land, and constant mine-warfare activity. This last activity was one particularly loathed by the men in the trenches. Hidden from view, one side would quietly tunnel from its trenches under no man's land to a position in front of, or under, the enemy's defences. Once there, an explosive mine would be fired, destroying whatever was above and blowing a crater that both sides would often struggle to occupy. In late March 1916, during one of these sudden bursts of fighting, Rifleman Frederick Gibbons would win a Military Medal, the first bravery decoration for the Jersey Company.

For their part, the Germans responded to the intensified British activity in kind. They too had increased the level of shelling, raids and mining activity. On 27 April, they even launched a massive gas attack and infantry assault on 16th (Irish) Division's front that caused more than 400 casualties. Two days later, another similar attack caused several hundred more. Fortunately for the Jersey volunteers, on both of these occasions, 7th RIR was not in the trenches, and thereby suffered comparatively little as a result. Yet clearly, given the escalating fighting, it was only a matter for time before the Jersey Company would begin to suffer losses.

The first death to enemy action had, in fact, occurred only a few days after going into the trenches following the time at Lapugnoy. On 1 April, a German shell had landed in a support line trench occupied by a group of Jerseymen. A number of men had been wounded, including the Jersey Company's second-in-command, Captain George Johnson. Over the previous few months, the normally quiet and unassuming Scotsman had gained the reputation of being fearless in the face of danger. He seemed to have led a charmed life, although some had muttered that his luck was bound to run out eventually. On that day it did. There in the trench, or on the way back to a medical facility in the Vermelles, he died of his wounds and was buried in the village's British cemetery. Yet the death of Captain Johnson was only the start of a bitter period of loss and suffering.

On 16 April, twenty-two-year-old Rifleman Arthur Bree was killed in action, while four days later, Rifleman Ernest Vallois died of wounds at a hospital in Bethune. A few weeks later, on the night of 13 May, came the worst single incident of the period. A group of men working in no man's land on the barbed wire defences had been caught by a sudden burst of German machine gun fire. Rifleman William West died instantly. Several others, including Sergeant Francis Turner and Rifleman Charles Mallet, fell wounded and were carried back to the British trenches. That night Rifleman Mallet died of wounds to the abdomen and legs in a nearby dressing station, tragically in the presence of his brother. Sergeant Turner lived long enough to be evacuated to Bethune, but the twenty-eight-year-old died there on 18 May, a day after Rifleman Arthur Rogers was killed in an unrelated incident.

In June, the losses continued. Rifleman William Warren, who was serving with 7th RIR's Machine Gun Section, died on 12 June, apparently in an accidental fire incident. Four days later, on 16 June, Lance Corporal Charles Bartlett died while collecting rations. The Jersey

Company had suffered eight men killed in action in less than three months. Significantly, during the same period, more than thirty others had also been wounded, many seriously. In a letter home, Major Stocker was disconsolate at the losses. Writing to the *Morning News* to express thanks for another consignment of gifts, he noted 'We've just been through a strenuous time, especially some of us, and these gifts tend to bring home thoughts to them, and helps them forget the disagreeable things that must occur in the field.'[11]

By the end of June, it was not only the increasing number of casualties with which Major Stocker was struggling. The rigorous challenge of active service in the trenches had been steadily catching up with the forty-nine-year-old. In May, a short spell of home leave had brought some respite, but after his return to France, conditions remained challenging. At the start of July, he suffered a collapse while in the trenches. Pneumonia was diagnosed, and it was of such severity that his condition was regarded as life threatening. For a number of weeks, the outlook was bleak; it was only at end of July that news came through that the Major had recovered sufficiently enough to allow his transfer from a hospital in France to one in England. Ahead, however, lay weeks of convalescence.

The loss of Major Stocker presented a dilemma for the Jersey Company and 7th RIR. Lieutenant Colonel Sidney Francis, who had recently replaced Lieutenant Colonel Hartley as the Battalion's Commanding Officer, clearly had to replace Stocker, but with whom? Of the six original officers from Jersey, none remained in France; Captain Johnson and Lieutenant Hibbs were dead and Lieutenant's Dickson and Ogier were among the recently wounded. With Stocker ill, it left only one other, Lieutenant Cyril Nicolle, but he too was unwell and would soon leave the trenches because of a heart complaint. Therefore, alternatives needed to be considered.

One option had been to send another officer out from Jersey. When Lieutenant Hibbs had died in March, there had been effort made to replace him with another officer from the Jersey Militia. Things had gone as far a choosing and announcing a candidate, but when that individual had failed a medical, it led to the idea being dropped. In July, it appears that this option was not even contemplated – there was no action to replace any of the Jersey officers, not least Major Stocker. This left Lieutenant Colonel Francis with only one choice – a non-Jersey officer would have to take over command of the Jersey Company. The man chosen was a twenty-year-old Irishman, Captain James Steele. The decision, as he later admitted, came as a great surprise to him; the reaction of the Jerseymen is unknown. What is clear, however, is that having been with 7th RIR since its formation, Captain Steele knew the men well, and equally, they knew and apparently liked him. This bond, and CSM Le Breton's strong assistance, helped him carry out the job of steadying the Jersey Company after three difficult and painful months.

For the remainder of July, and most of August, the Jersey Company continued its routine of movement in and out of the trenches at Loos. Despite considerable losses in the previous three months, 16th (Irish) Division remained under orders to keep the Germans opposite engaged, and so the low-level aggressive warfare continued. The importance of doing so increased when a massive Allied offensive opened at the start of July further south, in the region of the River Somme. More than ever, the

British high command wanted the Germans at Loos kept fully occupied. Invariably, this meant more and more night-time patrols and trench raids.

Trench raids were a risky business. They involved groups of varying size setting off under the cover of darkness to cross no man's land and attack or enter the enemy's trenches. The goal could be to gather intelligence, to take prisoners – or just to kill as many Germans as possible. All too often, however, things went awry and there would frequently be more losses among the attackers than those being attacked. For this reason, the men in the trenches would have preferred the raids kept to a minimum. Unfortunately, the decision had not been theirs to make. At Loos, in the summer of 1916, this meant raiding parties setting out almost every night.

The Jersey Company were involved in their fair share, which inevitably led to more losses. On the night of 27 July, one small group under the command of Corporal Charles Laugeard set out to attack an advanced German position, or sap. It was to end tragically, as Laugeard later explained in his report:

> We made for the right side of crater and worked round to the centre of the far lip where we could see a sap leading towards the crater but about 30 yards from the lip. It was 'T' headed and had a machine gun facing west towards Wings Way. A party was working on the right of sap … about 30 yards from sap. I threw three bombs into the sap and two men threw one each from the lip of the crater. The three bombs fell in the sap and I think that the two men who were in the sap must have been killed. We then returned making our way through the wire.
>
> Rifleman Pennel [sic] – one of our men – was killed by a bomb which he must have been carrying in his hand and dropped, letting it off.[12]

The other members of the raiding party had carried the body of Rifleman Alfred Pennec back to the British trenches. He was buried in a small war cemetery just behind the support line trenches that already contained the graves of three other Jersey Company men killed earlier in the year. Three days later, Corporal Ernest Jeffreys had joined them, the twenty-one-year-old possibly killed in a retaliatory German trench raid on 1 August.

Jeffreys' death was to be the last suffered by the Jersey Company while at Loos. Just over three weeks later on 25 August, the Jersey Company left the trenches there for the last time. After eight months, the 16th (Irish) Division was transferring to a new sector.

For the Division as a whole, and its Jersey Company, they had been eight months of hard lessons and painful losses. In total, the 16th (Irish) Division had suffered 6,000 casualties during this period, including around 100 of its attached Jerseymen. Of the latter, fourteen had died – twelve at Loos itself, one in England of illness, and one, Rifleman Walter Martin, further south on 30 July while serving in a detachment sent to another part of the front. On the positive side, those who remained had greatly benefited from their time in the trenches. Arriving as novices, they had left as experienced soldiers well-versed in the art of warfare. They would be skills greatly needed in the weeks that lay ahead.

Six

Guillemont and Ginchy

The list of casualties in the Jersey Contingent which we have given in the last few days and from which the names continue to come proves that the gallant Jerseys were in the thick of the fighting in the great push....

Editorial, Evening Post, 18 September 1916

At 4.00 p.m. on the wet afternoon of 30 August 1916, the train carrying the Jersey Company slowed and then juddered to a final halt. They had reached the end of the line. Peering out from gaps in the wagon's sides, the men surveyed the grimy collection of platforms, sidings and sheds that constituted Longueau station. Through the rain, this nondescript railway halt to the south-east of Amiens was certainly not much to look at. Yet in the summer and autumn of 1916, it would become a familiar location for thousands of British soldiers. The station was one of the gateways for the Battle of the Somme.

On that afternoon, there was little time to consider the view – or the implications. With the train stopped, the air had soon filled with the all too familiar raucous shouts of the Battalion's NCOs. Striding up and down the platform, they threw open wagon doors and ordered the occupants out. Yawning and stretching, the men of the Jersey Company clambered down. Soon, with numbers counted, kit checked, and orders given, they were marching out of the station along with the rest of 7th RIR. Storms during the last few days had left the winding roads of the normally picturesque River Somme valley strewn with mud, leaves and other debris. This, together with a continuing deluge, had done nothing to make that evening's ten mile march any less arduous. Depressingly, the route took them east, towards the ominous rumble of a major battle being waged somewhere ahead in the distance. This direction had dispelled any lingering doubts over their final destination – this was certainly no quiet sector of the front. Finally, after six hours, they had reached the little town of Corbie and gratefully threw themselves down to sleep. In the distance, the menacing sound of battle lingered long into the night.

By the following morning, all trace of the storm had passed. After a wash and breakfast, the Battalion set off again, only this time with the sun shining down. The march followed the course of the small River Ancre north-eastwards towards the celebrated town of

Albert. Situated only a mile or two behind the British trenches, it had been virtually in the front line since early in the war. Unfortunately, this had made it a frequent target for German artillery emplaced on the higher ground to the north. Over the months, frequent bombardments had driven out most of the inhabitants and shattered many buildings including the town's magnificent basilica with its famous golden statue of the Virgin Mary. Shelling had left her hanging at a perilous angle, and a legend had grown that whichever side finally sent the statue tumbling down would go on to lose the war. Fortunately (or perhaps unfortunately), on 31 August when the Jersey Company approached, she remained firmly, although precariously, in place.

It was during this march up to Albert that the truly awesome scale of the battle raging a few miles to the north had become obvious. On either side, there were immense arrays of camps, stores, workshops and field hospitals. Men, vehicles and guns choked the roads, some going towards the battlefield, and other returning from it. The almost continuous roar of artillery filled the air, the reverberations of exploding shells making the very ground tremble. None of the men marching towards the battlefield that morning could have had any doubt that the Battle of the Somme was a serious undertaking.

The British and French had originally conceived the Battle of the Somme as their primary war-winning effort of 1916. In scale at least, it was planned to be an unprecedented affair.

During the previous year, the Allies had attempted to breach the German defences several times – and failed on each occasion. The reason, some argued, was that each offensive had simply been too small in scale. By choosing to attack on too narrow a front, it allowed the Germans to first contain the assault, and then defeat it by rushing reinforcements from other unthreatened areas. Success, therefore, would only come when enough men, supported by enough guns, attacked the enemy across a broad enough section of the front. Such an attack would hopefully tear an irreparable breach in the German line, and allow an advance into the open countryside beyond. In 1915, for the British at least, the required number of men and guns had simply not been available. By the start of 1916, however, this situation was beginning to change.

At the beginning of 1916, the fruits of Lord Kitchener's far-sighted plan to raise a 'New Army' were starting to be realised. More and more British soldiers were arriving in France each month and taking their place in the trenches. When training and familiarisation was complete, these new divisions would be ready to take part in the planned 1916 offensive. The French had been delighted. Since the start of the war, their armies had carried the burden for most of the fighting and they were now wearing thin as a result. For the French generals, the great 1916 joint-offensive should start as soon as possible. However the British, under the leadership of General Sir Douglas Haig, had argued for more time. Haig knew that until recently most of his men had been civilians, so the more experience they could gain, the greater the chance of success. He also argued that more time would allow British industry to turn out enough of the heavy guns and shells needed to make success certain. In February, the Allies had sat down to thrash out a compromise.

That same month, while the British and French argued over timing, the Germans had moved with deadly purpose. Launching a massive assault on the eastern town of Verdun, they hoped to draw the French Army into battle there, and smash it with concentrated artillery. During the next four months, the fighting at Verdun had threatened to overwhelm the French defences. It was realised that if the planned Allied offensive did not start soon, they could reach breaking point. Haig agreed to set 1 July 1916 as the date, and as it was still to be a joint affair, the place chosen for the offensive was that part of the front where the British and French armies met. This was in the rolling country north of the River Somme.

On the morning of 1 July 1916, thousands of British and French soldiers had clambered out of their trenches and began to advance toward the German line. What happened next that day has become an infamous part of British history. The preceding seven-day bombardment, designed to smash the German defences and kill its defenders, had failed. Instead of the promised walkover, most of the advancing British soldiers discovered only intact barbed wire and resolute defenders. Many of the attackers, cut down in no man's land by machine guns and artillery, never even reached the German front line. Here and there, others had secured only a small foothold where they held out until bloodily ejected by the end of the day. By the time darkness mercifully came to put an end to the day's fighting, the number of British soldiers killed, wounded or captured had reached almost 60,000.

At only one location was there any appreciable British success to show for these dreadful losses. Adjacent to the more generally successful French attack in the south, British units had captured the village of Montauban and its surrounding fortifications. In the land behind lay the forbidding Bernafay and Trones Woods, now largely deserted as their defenders had scattered following the fall of Montauban. A little further off still sat the weakly-held villages of Guillemont and Ginchy, and behind them lay the longed-for open country. Despite the failures elsewhere, it seemed that a concerted effort here could result in a significant British success.

Yet it was not to be; the British acted too cautiously, and the Germans with professional haste. In the days that followed, the opportunity for a breakthrough at Montauban had quietly slipped away. The Battle of the Somme, however, continued. It became a slogging match, with each village, each wood and each bit of high ground only falling to set-piece, and invariably costly, assaults. The villages of Guillemont and Ginchy, so vulnerable in the first few days, remained firmly in German hands, and up until the beginning of September, all attempts to take them had failed. Reinforcements would be needed before the British Army could try again. It was time for the 16th (Irish) Division to enter the battle.

By 1 September 1916, the 16th (Irish) Division had completed its move from Loos and was assembling in reserve positions near the town of Albert. There its units waited for orders to move up and join the battle. One of those units was of course 7th RIR, and its attached Jersey Company. The march up from Corbie on 31 August had taken them as far as a former sandpit near the village of Meaulte. Here, two nervous days were passed in training, the men taking part in a series of attacks on practice trenches dug nearby, and rehearsing artillery cooperation techniques. Then, on 2 September, they had watched as the division's 47th Brigade left for the front. That evening, orders arrived for 48th Brigade to follow.

On the morning of 3 September, the men of the Jersey Company set off for the front line. Their winding route took them from the camp at Meaulte in a roughly north-easterly direction towards the Montauban ridge. Looking in that direction, a rising pall of smoke and dust thrown up by a thundering British artillery bombardment marked the battlefield. Dotted around it hung a number of huge sausage-shaped balloons, each tethered to the ground by a thick cable. Both sides regularly sent up these bizarre looking – and extremely vulnerable – observation platforms to seek targets across the enemy lines. On that day, however, there were only British ones in the sky. Allied aircraft had achieved air supremacy above the Somme battlefield; any German balloon daring to venture up soon risked being sent back to earth in flames. By midday, the Jerseymen had reached a site called Billon Farm, even though the motley collection of tents and rusting corrugated iron bore little resemblance by now to anything agricultural. After resting there, in the afternoon the march had continued, accompanied now by a light rain. That evening, just after 6.00 p.m., they trooped into the village of Carnoy.

Carnoy, or rather what remained of it, had become a staging post for the battlefield. Soldiers rested here, either on their way up to the front or when returning after having taken part in the fighting. At the start of the battle on 1 July, it was behind the British front line, yet it was close enough for persistent German shelling to have rendered it a shambles of broken buildings and shattered roads. Nonetheless, on the evening of 3 September 1916 the place was a hive of activity, and alive with tremendous news. A few miles away, around the village of Guillemont, it appeared that a great victory had been won.

For weeks, the German defenders of Guillemont had resisted every attempt to expel them. During July and August, they had steadfastly held their positions as the British edged closer and closer. Several direct assaults on the village had only resulted in bloody repulses. On the morning of 3 September, accompanied by a heavy and effective bombardment, the British had made another attempt. At its heart was the 47th Brigade of 16th (Irish) Division. In a tempestuous charge, the newly-arrived troops (which included the Guernsey Company of the 6th Royal Irish Regiment) had made the difference in the battle for the village. Surging forward, they braved the defensive fire and swept into the ruins. Stunned by the ferocity of the attack, the German defenders were overwhelmed. By the end of the day, Guillemont was finally in British hands – although the price of capture had been a high one. Waiting in Carnoy that evening, the Jerseymen watched as a steady stream of wounded from the 47th Brigade were carried or hobbled past. Up on the battlefield, many more remained lying were they fell.

Yet the capture of Guillemont did not mean an end to the fighting in this area. The British would need to consolidate their hard-won gains before the advance could continue. The Germans remained close by, meaning that there was the ever-present

threat of a counter-attack. Both sides needed fresh troops on the battlefield, to deal with
any eventuality. In the early hours of 4 September, orders had arrived in Carnoy for 7th
RIR to move closer to the front.

Stumbling forward through the night, the Jerseymen had marched north-east from
Carnoy towards the village of Montauban. Although movement under the cover of
darkness made sense, it meant a hellish trek that night through unfamiliar terrain,
scored by old trench lines and still laced with stands of barbed wire. With the rain
pouring down, they had finally struggled into Montauban, and then pushed on a
few hundred yards further on to nearby Bernafay Wood. The Battalion's orders were
to wait there for the day and be ready to support the units fighting further ahead.
Although it had the potential to provide shelter from observation, as they discovered
when the sun rose, Bernafay had become a wood in name only. Artillery fire had
blasted the trees, shattering trunks and stripping them of most foliage. It was also
a wood full of dead, with many only partly buried, leaving an appalling stench of
putrefaction.

Bernafay Wood, despite its conditions, did manage to provide sanctuary during the
daylight hours of 4 September. At 6.00 p.m., however, further orders had arrived to
move once again. The Battalion was to advance to Guillemont around a mile away
to the east. Its instructions were to take over the defence of the village. Two hours
later, with darkness descending, the men set off again. Skirting Trones Wood, they
struck out towards Guillemont. Soon, the grim consequences of previous fighting had
become shockingly evident as they made their way silently through the now deserted
battlefield:

> Here we beheld for the first time the awful and ghastly spectacle of an uncleared
> battlefield – absolute chaos and utter desolation everywhere. Shapeless masses of
> human beings lay strewn over the ground. The very air reeked with the smell of
> putrefying flesh and blood.
>
> Occasionally the flares in front would show up the grim horror of it all, then
> dwindle and die out, leaving us to pick our way through the abandoned material as
> best we could. Friend and enemy were all the same. Broken rifles, ammunition boxes,
> equipment, all bore testimony to the terrible wastage of war. Still we plodded on
> through the mud and stench.[1]

Although it is difficult to single out any part of the Somme battlefield as being more
exceptional than others, the area the Jersey Company was entering that night surely
deserves consideration as one of the worst. For weeks, Guillemont, and the nearby village
of Ginchy, had been thorns in the side of the British advance northwards. They also stood
on the junction of the attacking British and French armies and the continued presence
of enemy forces there had threatened to break the cohesion of any Allied advance. The
Germans knew this of course, and had been prepared to sacrifice men and material in
their defence. It resulted in some of the most intense and prolonged fighting of the whole

Battle of the Somme, all concentrated within a few square miles of land. The worst of it, as the Jerseymen would soon discover, had focused on the villages themselves.

Guillemont remained in the hands of men from 47th Brigade who had captured it so heroically two days previously. Understandably, they were now quite happy to hand over their prize to 7th RIR and hurry gratefully off towards the rear. Cautiously, the newly arrived men took up defensive positions. By now, a heavy rain had set in once more, adding its discomfort to the already tense atmosphere. Periodically, flares shot into the sky to descend slowly, illuminating the battlefield in a pale and eerie light. Here and there, a machine gun crackled, although in the darkness it was not possible to distinguish whether it was friend or foe firing. The Germans were known to be nearby, but where and in what strength could only be guessed. An enemy counter-attack under the cover of darkness remained a distinct possibility. Relief had only really come when the first signs of dawn appeared on the eastern horizon.

With morning, the full and terrible extent of the destruction visited on Guillemont during the battle became apparent:

> In the murky light of dawn we could just distinguish where the village had been. There was nothing of it to be seen but a heap of crumbled and distorted masonry. It is difficult to describe such a scene of wanton desolation. The whole area was nothing more or less than a wilderness of shell holes.[2]

There was little time to wonder. The purpose of sending 7th RIR to Guillemont was to ensure it remained in British hands. With the aid of some Royal Engineers, therefore, the men set about the day's work of consolidating and improving its defences.

Even in its ruinous state, the village had remained a valuable asset. In a war where advances were often measured in yards, the capture of any village was a towering achievement. Losing Guillemont to the enemy was unthinkable. More practically, roads, tracks, and trenches to and from the front line led through the village, rendering it a vital junction. Of course, the Germans knew this as well and so Guillemont would not be far from their thoughts in the days that followed. On 5 September, as German artillery fire began to increase in volume, the village started to receive some shells. Thankfully – on this day at least – casualties among the Jerseymen had remained light.

While the Jersey Company consolidated the defences of Guillemont, all around the situation remained somewhat confused. It was known that the Germans still held the nearby village of Ginchy, and were present in the some of the area's woods, but the state of their defences in between were uncertain, as were their intentions. On 5 September, with the news that the French Army had achieved a considerable success south of Guillemont, there was some hope that the Germans might be withdrawing from the area. The British commanders wanted more definite information, however, and so orders arrived for 7th RIR to send out a number of patrols. In the early hours of 6 September, men from the Jersey Company set out on one of them.

The patrol had headed eastward from Guillemont. Somewhere in the confusion of shell holes and abandoned trenches, it came up against manned German positions. Having found the enemy, the patrol moved in closer, possibly with the objective of taking some prisoners. Second Lieutenant Benjamin Merrin, one of the officers brought in to replace the departed Jersey officers, led men from his 2nd Platoon forward. Later recalling the confused fighting that followed, Merrin singled out two of the Jersey Company for special praise. Rifleman Arthur Champion from St Helier reportedly acted 'with heroic bravery to accomplish the task of getting information about the location of the enemy which three previous attempts by others had failed'.[3] And ex-fireman Corporal Harold Carver was named as 'one of the best in my platoon … He gave me valuable assistance in establishing the enemy position, which was the means of saving many other lives'.[4] Arthur Champion paid for his efforts with a bullet to the arm that resulted in it being amputated. Harold Carver, however, paid with his life.

Returning to Guillemont after the clash, the patrol had managed to bring back a number of wounded men, including Second Lieutenant Merrin. Others were less fortunate. Evidence suggests that along with Corporal Carver, the Jersey Company lost Sergeant Reginald Du Heaume and Riflemen Jean Blanchet and John Vibert that night.

The results of the patrol had indicated one thing at least: the Germans were clearly not withdrawing. From across this part of the front the indications were the same. Displaying their customary resilience and energy, the Germans had rapidly recovered from the defeat at Guillemont on 3 September. All talk of collapse or withdrawal quickly passed. For the British, attention turned to the village of Ginchy, and further set piece battles.

Ginchy lay about half a mile to the north-east of Guillemont. On the morning of 6 September, with it still firmly in German hands, the British 7th Division had started an attack on the village. The fighting would continue for most of the day.

In nearby Guillemont the men of Jersey Company, then holding positions on the northern edge of the village, would have been able to see the fighting. The rain had finally cleared and, despite an overcast sky, conditions were remarkably clear. It meant perfect observation for the German artillery officers waiting to direct fire in support of the defenders of Ginchy. In particular, they would plan to target the British rear areas in an attempt to disrupt the flow of supplies and reinforcements. Soon, the first shells began to fall on Guillemont.

Plunging into the ruins, the exploding shells threw up great clouds of brick dust and pulverised masonry. The air had soon filled with choking fumes and flying shards of red-hot shrapnel. For the Jerseymen, cowering in shell holes and shallow trenches, it was the start of a day of misery. Ordered to remain in this position, there was no escape from the carnage. Unable to fight back, they could only take the pounding, and pray that somehow the next shell missed them.

Perhaps mercifully, few details have emerged of exactly what happened in Guillemont on that terrible day, but the casualty figure alone is enough to paint a desperate picture. killed in action, the Jersey Company lost CSM William Marshall, Sergeant Harold

Reynolds, Corporal Edward Luce, Lance Corporals Jonathan Auffret and William Sweeney, and Riflemen John Carré, Charles Blampied, Charles Buttery, and Pierre Vasse. Scores of others were terribly wounded, including Sergeant Arthur Pirouet who would die in a casualty clearing station near the village of Heilly on 9 September. In terms of casualties at least, that Wednesday 6 September 1916 would thereafter remain as the worst day in the Jersey Company's history.

Conversely, amid the carnage, it was also one of great courage and heroics. As on most battlefields, when faced with death and destruction, instinctive bravery and self-sacrifice had come to the fore. Perhaps unsurprisingly, the man later singled out was CSM Jack Le Breton. In one selfless act, when shellfire trapped a group of wounded men in a temporary dressing station, he went immediately to their rescue. With little thought for his own safety, Le Breton had managed to pull three men from danger. He would be awarded the Medaille Militaire as a result.

By evening, the shelling finally eased, allowing Le Breton and the other dazed survivors to emerge from their holes and take in the situation. What they found left them aghast. If Guillemont was in a ruinous state already, the bombardment that day had pounded it further. An officer passing through the next day, noted to his amazement that:

> All former bombardments are eclipsed by the scene here … at Guillemont, it is almost literally true to say that not a brick or stone remains intact. Indeed, not a brick or a stone is to be seen, except where it has been churned up by a bursting shell. Not a tree stands. Not a square foot of surface has escaped mutilation. There is nothing but the mud and the gaping shell holes; a chaotic wilderness of shell holes, rim overlapping rim; and, in the bottom of many the bodies of the dead.[5]

Yet if the survivors thought they had endured enough by now, they were to be sorely disappointed. Despite the ordeal, there was no relief that night, or the next day. The 16th (Irish) Division would remain in this area there for at least a few more days. The attack on Ginchy by 7th Division had failed, leaving the distinct possibility of a German counter-attack from the area of that village. Guillemont still required to be strongly defended, while a further attack on Ginchy had to be planned. For this there would be more time to prepare. The 9 September was set as the date for the next attempt to capture Ginchy. The 16th (Irish) Division had been given the task of launching the attack.

Before the war, Ginchy had been a small and unremarkable village of less than 100 souls. They had lived a simple life, mostly earning a living from working the rich farmlands surrounding their homes. Little had changed here for generations – up until 1914, no one could see any reason why it would. That was until the German Army arrived.

By the end of 1914, the Germans were strongly entrenched in the area. The war of movement had ended, and now they were consolidating their gains by constructing lines of trenches across the countryside. Ginchy, together with neighbouring Guillemont, became part of a second line of defence; prepared in case the front line a few miles away near Montauban was lost. As a designated 'fortress village', Ginchy had been transformed by trenches, shelters, and barbed wire. In August and early September 1916, these preparations had proved their worth during several attempts to capture the village. For the British, Ginchy was proving a tough nut to crack. The 7th Division's attack on 6 September had been just the latest in a series of failed attempts.

Between the villages of Guillemont and Ginchy ran a narrow country road, sunken in places to a depth below the height of adjacent fields. On the evening of 7 September 1916, the British front line lay in the fields on either side, crossing the road roughly a third of the way up from Guillemont. After dark on the evening of 7 September, the remaining members of the Jersey Company had left Guillemont and silently set off up this road. In preparation for the forthcoming attack on Ginchy, 7th RIR was to take over the front-line trenches to the left of the road. On arrival, however, there was great dismay. What existed here was merely a series of shallow interlinked shell holes – the fighting had left little time to construct anything more substantial. It had meant a night of backbreaking digging in order to provide protection from German fire in the morning.

By sunrise, the toil had proved its worth. Exhausted, but now out of sight, the men settled down to pass the day. Those who could snatched some much needed sleep, while others nervously cleaned weapons or scribbled a few lines home. By now, the news was out that an attack on Ginchy was planned for the following day, and that 7th RIR was to be in the first wave. The prospect must have provoked mixed thoughts. On one hand, it meant that after nine months at the front, the men of the Jersey Company would finally get the chance to go 'over the top' and come face-to-face with their enemy. On the other, of course, all of them must have been aware that this was probably the most dangerous thing they would ever have to do. As a salutary reminder – if one was needed – the ground between their trench and the village was already strewn with the dead of previous attacks.

To improve the chances of survival, an order instructing 7th RIR to shorten the distance to Ginchy arrived. The night of 8 September was therefore spent digging a new set of advanced trenches, 200 yards closer to the village. It meant a second night of digging by the men. Yet, if it made crossing no man's land next day easier, no one begrudged the effort. By dawn, the work was complete. With the attack not scheduled to start until 4.45 p.m, the men settled down once more in the new trenches for some rest. Unfortunately, as they soon found out, not everyone was informed that they were there.

Just before dawn on 9 September, a steady British bombardment of Ginchy commenced. Tucked down in their newly dug positions, the men listened as shells whistled overhead before plunging into the German positions with a reverberating crash. Before long, however, it became apparent that not all the fire was on target. Somehow, a breakdown in communication had left elements of the British artillery unaware that the British front line had moved forward during the night. Consequently, British shells were sporadically falling on the newly advanced 7th RIR trenches. Despite requests to stop, the 'friendly fire' continued for much of the day. Soon, German artillery added its weight to the misery. Casualties had steadily increased.

By early afternoon, Lieutenant Colonel Francis, the Commanding Officer of 7th RIR, sent out an appeal for reinforcements. With the attack on Ginchy due to start in less than three hours time, the shelling had further reduced his Battalion until only 150 men remained. As a result, the 7th Royal Irish Fusiliers arrived some time later to provide support. It included a company of Guernseymen, and so the Channel Islands were to be well represented in the forthcoming attack. Under shelling from both sides, everyone had settled down to wait for zero hour.

At 4.45 p.m. on Saturday 9 September 1916, those members of the Jersey Company who remained clambered out of their trenches and stood for a moment on the parapet. Ahead, at the top of a gentle slope, lay their objective. On either side, summoned by the shrill blasts of officer's whistles, hundred of others stood and faced in the same direction. Just for a moment, the massed ranks hesitated; they had been waiting two days for this moment. Then, with a roar, the 16th (Irish) Division surged forward. The Battle of Ginchy had begun.

The plan that afternoon was relatively straightforward. A first wave, including 7th RIR, was to advance and capture most of the village. To suppress the German defences, a curtain of artillery shells, known as a 'creeping barrage', would land just in front of the attacking troops, and move forward at the pace of the advance. With Ginchy captured, a second wave would continue the advance beyond the village and secure a new defensive line several hundred yards to the east. Success depended on a number of factors, not least of which was how well the British preparatory bombardment had subdued the defenders' machine guns and artillery. If they remained intact, the chances of the attackers getting across no man's land were slim. Within a few paces of starting the advance, the signs had been ominous, as one man later recalled:

> We advanced at a steady walking pace, stumbling here and there, but going ever onward and upward … (A shell) landed in the midst of bunch of men about seventy yards away on my right. I have a most vivid recollection of seeing a tremendous burst of clay and earth go shooting up into the air – yes, and even parts of human bodies – and when the smoke cleared away there was nothing left. I shall never forget that horrifying spectacle as long as I live … I remember men lying in shell holes holding out their arms and beseeching water. I remember some men crawling about and coughing up blood, as they searched round for some place in which they could shelter until help could reach them.[6]

Fortunately – for the Jersey Company at least – the German shelling and machine gun fire was mostly concentrated on the units advancing on the Company's right. Approaching from the west of Ginchy, 7th RIR, closely followed by reinforcements from 7th Royal Irish Fusiliers, had closed on the village with few losses. In no time, they were through the outer defences and among the ruins of the village. What they found was a pitiful sight.

Days of shelling had reduced the once peaceful village to a bewildering chaos of shell holes, fallen trees and crushed masonry. Lying everywhere, were the contorted and mutilated remains of many of its defenders. Elsewhere, among the ruins, were pockets of shell-shocked survivors. The overriding priority for most of them had been to escape from their ordeal. Some were on their knees, shaking and crying, while others wandered aimlessly back and forth. Quickly rounded up, they were soon hurrying down the road to Guillemont alongside the British wounded.

Yet as the attackers further penetrated the ruins, it became clear that not all Germans were of the same mind. One stubborn group was holed up in a strongpoint built in the remains of a farmhouse. Armed with rifles and machine guns, they were soon inflicting British casualties. As the losses mounted, one of the British trench mortar teams accompanying the attack was called in to help. At short range, they had blasted the strongpoint. A successful infantry attack followed, during which recently-promoted Sergeant Charles Laugeard earned distinction, and received a bullet wound to the chest. For his bravery, the ex-policeman won the first Distinguished Conduct Medal, or DCM, for the Jersey Company. His citation recorded that the award was for 'the manner in which he led a certain important attack at [Ginchy], at the same time keeping up the supply of bombs and generally displaying great courage which, under the terrific conditions of the moment, was an almost superhuman task'.[7]

With the last defenders subdued, the whole of Ginchy was soon in British hands. The second wave of attackers arrived as planned, and had passed through to continue the advance beyond the village. Orders were for the first wave to remain in the village and consolidate the newly-won positions. Yet, with few officers left to hold them back (Lieutenant Colonel Francis had been temporarily incapacitated), and exhilarated by their victory, many 7th RIR men followed the advancing 8th and 9th Royal Dublin Fusiliers. Faced with little German resistance, this mixed force quickly swept on to and past their objective. Only with great difficulty were the men halted, and brought back to where they were originally supposed to halt. Not everyone, however, returned. Some men, isolated and outnumbered, were lost as the German's turned on their pursuers. One of them was Rifleman Steven Brint who was last seen in the enemy's trenches fighting against great odds.

Rifleman Brint was not the only one to lose his life that day. Among the many from 7th RIR killed were the Jersey Company's Lance Corporal Sid Olivery and Riflemen Harry Cauvain, Arthur Male, George Pearce and Dick Scott. Together with those lost on 6 September, it meant that twenty Jersey Company men had been killed in just three days. More than seventy others had been wounded.

The handful of survivors spent the remainder of 9 September in the ruins of Ginchy. Behind a hurriedly-established defensive perimeter, they waited nervously for an enemy counter-attack. In the end, none came; the Germans had had enough.

The tired victors celebrated with bread and sausage removed from the haversacks of dead Germans and waited for relief to arrive. On this day it did. The Battalion, along with the rest of 16th (Irish) Division, was a spent force. Just after midnight, a fresh battalion of Welsh Guards arrived to take over in Ginchy. By morning, the remnants of the Jersey Company were back in Carnoy, and the next day, after marching back to Meaulte, a convoy of trucks ferried the men to Corbie – from where they had set out twelve days earlier.

Behind them, the Battle of Somme rumbled remorselessly on. As with elsewhere, after losing Guillemont and Ginchy the Germans had regrouped in the next village, wood or line of trenches and prepared for another British attack. In the end, despite five months of fighting, the Allies would not achieve the planned breakthough – although they did inflict heavy casualties on the enemy. Yet the price of this limited success was a shockingly high one. When the fighting finally petered out in November 1916, 420,000 British soldiers had become casualties, alongside 200,000 French. German losses added perhaps 500,000 more to the shocking final tally.

For the Jersey Company, however, the battle was over. The surviving members would not return – they had done their bit, and had done it well. In a report on the attack on Ginchy, the commander of 48th Infantry Brigade wrote:

In conclusion I wish to express my extreme satisfaction at the spirit, courage, and determination displayed by all ranks during the operations … When it is remembered that the troops had been out in so-called trenches which were in reality merely shell holes, for five days and nights prior to the attack, during which period they were wet through by rain and did not have the chance of obtaining a hot meal, I submit that the highest credit is reflected on all ranks that the capture of Ginchy was effected under these adverse conditions, and the traditions of the Irish race were worthily upheld by these men of the New Armies.[8]

Brigadier General Ramsay may have forgotten to mention the Jerseymen (and Guernseymen) who fought alongside their Irish comrades specifically, but they had been there nonetheless. And the capture of Ginchy was indeed a remarkable achievement during a battle in which so many other attacks on fortress villages had ended in abject failure. The fact that it had come after the ordeal at Guillemont on 6 September further underlines the magnitude of the achievement. It is one that all Channel Islanders should be aware of and remember with pride.

Today, there is little to remind visitors to Guillemont and Ginchy of the terrible battles once fought there. A few memorials, including one to the 16th (Irish) Division next to the church at Guillemont, and the presence of a large Commonwealth War Grave Commission Cemetery on the road between Trones Wood and Guillemont are the only easily discernable clues. The cemetery is probably close to the route used by the Jersey Company in September 1916 to enter and leave the battle. To stand there today is a sobering experience. Looking out over the surrounding peaceful fields, it is almost impossible to contemplate the awful scenes of destruction and carnage witnessed by the men as they passed by.

Guillemont Road Cemetery also contains the grave of Rifleman John Vibert. His presence is the only physical evidence that the Jersey Company was ever here. No specific memorial exists in the area or back in Jersey. With the exception of Rifleman Vibert, and Sergeant Pirouet who lies at Heilly, no other named graves exist. The remains of the other eighteen Jerseymen were either never found, or subsequently lost. Today, they lie in one of the thousands of unknown graves that fill the Somme cemeteries, or indeed, remain buried somewhere under the earth of Guillemont and Ginchy.

Above: 1 The Town Battalion of the Militia is mobilised. (Société Jersiaise)

Above right: 2 Jersey's Lieutenant-Governor, Major General Rochfort, meeting with officers of the South Staffordshire Regiment. (Société Jersiaise)

Right: 3 Sir William Vernon, Bailiff of Jersey at the time of the First World War. (Société Jersiaise)

Below: 4 The volunteers receive gifts from the YMCA prior to their departure.

5 The West Battalion volunteers.

6 The final muster in St Helier's Royal Square on 2 March 1915.

7 The volunteers on the SS *Ibex* waiting for departure.

8 Major Stocker, the Jersey Company's original commanding officer.

Above left: 9 RSM Jack Le Breton, DSM MM. 'The Father of the Jersey Boys'. (St Helier Town Hall)

Above right: 10 CSM Christian D'Authreau, MM. Helped rebuild the Jersey Company after the Battle of the Somme. (St Helier Town Hall)

Left: 11 Sergeant Charles Laugeard, DCM, who died in the final battles. (St Helier Town Hall)

Above left: 12 Rifleman Frederick Gibbons, MM. He won the Jersey Company's first award for bravery. (St Helier Town Hall)

Above right: 13 Rifleman Jack Luce, MM, who won the cycle race on St Patrick's Day and a Military Medal at Frezenberg. (St Helier Town Hall)

Right: 14 Rifleman Jimmy Scoones, the Company butcher who found himself marching with helmet and bayonet to battle in November 1917.

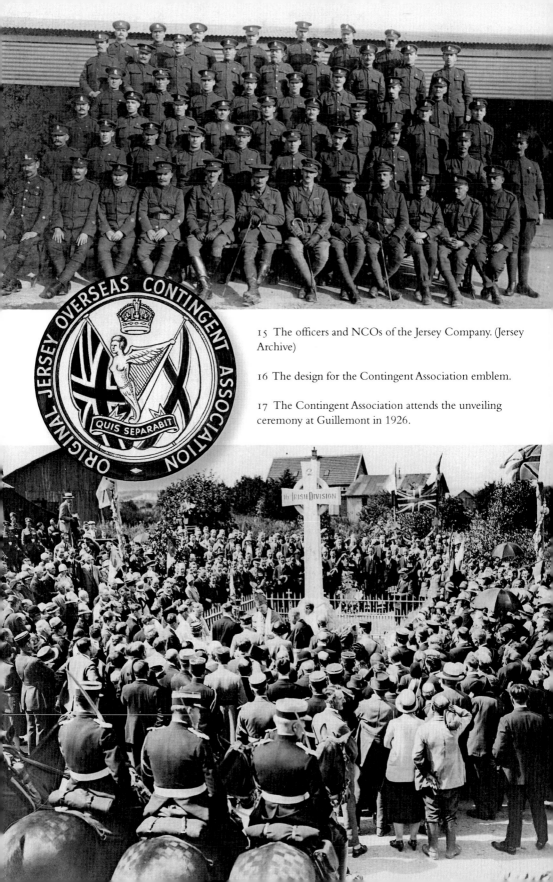

15 The officers and NCOs of the Jersey Company. (Jersey Archive)

16 The design for the Contingent Association emblem.

17 The Contingent Association attends the unveiling ceremony at Guillemont in 1926.

The defenders of
Guillemont return.

18 The last Contingent
Association reunion.
From left to right: Bert
Tostevin, Frank Dobin,
Arthur Durell, Sid Le
Monnier and Jack Luce,
MM. (*Jersey Evening
Post*)

Right: 19 Jimmy
Scoones in Grevillers
British Cemetery.

Far right: 20 Charles
Laugeard in Duhallow
ADS Cemetery.

21 The memorial to the 16th (Irish) Division in Guillemont today.

22 The fields between Guillemont and Ginchy today, from where the Jersey Company advanced to capture Ginchy in Spetember 1916.

Seven

Cold Front

There has been a great change in the old Company these last few weeks, and there are a great many faces we shall never see again.

Rifleman Harry Kent, Jersey Company RIR, October 1916

It would be difficult to describe the fate of neutral Belgium during the First World War as anything other than tragic. By the end of 1914, with its army beaten and the king driven from his capital, only a small triangle of land wedged between the French border and the English Channel remained outside of German occupation. Yet even this remaining fragment of sovereign territory would not avoid the conflict. Over the course of the next four years, both sides would engage in a more or less continuous and deadly struggle for its control. Central to this bitter battle was the historic small town of Ypres.

Ypres was no stranger to armed conflict. For hundreds of years the Flanders region had been in the so-called cockpit of Europe, repeatedly trampled over by the armies of ambitious warring nations. It had mostly survived these conflicts intact, however, and thrived during the years of peace that lay in between. Yet in October 1914 came the gravest challenge to date. The town lay in the path of advancing German armies, intent on pushing through the region and on to the Channel Coast beyond. The generals of Britain and France, however, had chosen Ypres as the place to stop that German advance.

The British Expeditionary Force had come to Belgium following the battles near Paris that had halted the German advance in September 1914. In October and November, it fought with extraordinary tenacity and valour to hold Ypres against repeated German attacks. At last, in December that year, with both sides exhausted, the fighting had ground to a standstill. The heroic defence had turned the town into a symbol of resistance for the British Army and Britain itself; Ypres had become 'sacred territory' – it was not to be given up at any cost. And there certainly would be a cost.

Ypres ended up at the base of a bulge, or salient, that protruded into the enemy lines surrounded on three sides by higher ground. From these vantage points, the enemy could maintain a ceaseless watch on all movement and bring lethal artillery fire on almost any point below. It was no wonder the 'Salient', as it quickly became known, was feared as one of the most dangerous sectors of the front. For the situation to change, the British would have to capture this high ground – a fact not lost on the Germans who heavily fortified their positions. Particular attention went on Messines Ridge, a kidney shaped stretch of low hills lying to the south of Ypres. Although less than 200 feet in height, it dominated the surrounding area. Both sides, therefore, saw the ridge as a site of great strategic importance. Messines Ridge was also destined to become a location of great significance to the Jersey Company. In September 1916, after their ordeal on the Somme battlefield, they had arrived in Belgium. Much of their next nine months would be spent looking up Messines Ridge.

Greatly weakened by the fighting at Guillemont and Ginchy, the 16th (Irish) Division had departed the Somme battlefield in mid-September 1916. Ordered north to Belgium for rest and refitting, it took over responsibility for a sector of the front facing Messines Ridge. There, its soldiers found themselves facing a most formidable set of defences.

Since capturing the ridge in late 1914, the Germans had gone to considerable lengths to ensure it remained in their hands. Complex trench systems, concrete bunkers and fields of barbed wire ran along its top and across the western face. The three villages on the crest of the ridge, St Eloi, Wytschaete and Messines, became important strongpoints, as did many of the abandoned farm buildings dotted along its flanks. Batteries of concealed artillery lay behind, and trench mortars lurked among the woods and copses crowding its folds and indents. By the time they had finished, Messines Ridge was one of the strongest positions on the Western Front.

The British, on the other hand, were left holding inferior positions along the bottom of the Ridge's western-facing slopes and out across the gently undulating stretch of land that lay behind. A high water table here had ruled out the construction of conventional trenches and dugouts. Instead, the defences lay for the most part above ground level, formed as breastworks using thick walls of sandbags, earth and other materials. This was not ideal as exposed to the ravages of weather and enemy fire, these artificial walls frequently sagged and collapsed. As the newly-arrived Jerseymen were soon to discover, just keeping the trenches intact was a job in itself.

On 23 September, just two days after arriving in Belgium, the Jersey Company had first entered these trenches. The location was a stretch of the front line below the German-held village of Wytschaete. After a brief handover from a departing Canadian battalion, they were on their own to take stock of the new surroundings.

Wytschaete itself was not actually visible from the British front line, the rise of the ridge and a swathe of trees concealing it from view. These woods, although thinned by shellfire, largely remained intact, and played an important part in the German defences. In front of the trenches occupied by Jersey Company lay two woods named Grand Bois and Petit Bois, and shell and mortar fire from them would be a continual source of harassment over the months to come. Here and there, signs of the ridge's former human occupants had been visible. Further up the ridge lay the imposing ruins of a hospice known to the British as the 'Red Chateau', while elsewhere the smashed remains of farm buildings were present. One group, called Maedelstede Farm, was particularly prominent, jutting out on a spur above the British lines. From it, the Germans had commanding views over the trenches below.

In these trenches, the men of 16th (Irish) Division had set to work soon after arrival, rebuilding, improving and reinforcing the defences in preparation for winter. Fortunately, German interference was minimal and casualties stayed low. This was just as well; after the recent fighting, the division could ill afford to lose many more men. All of its units were below strength by then and in desperate need of reinforcements. One of the most needy was the Jersey Company. 'There has been a great change in the old company these last few weeks,' Rifleman Harry Kent gloomily wrote early in October 1916, 'and there are a great many faces we shall never see again.'[1]

The Jersey Company taking up its new positions at Messines Ridge was certainly a much weakened band. Of the 200 men who had left Loos one month earlier, half had either been killed or seriously wounded in the fighting at Guillemont and Ginchy. Of the remainder, most seem to have ended up with some form of minor wound or injury. Anecdotal reports later claimed that only thirteen of the Jersey Company remained standing when 7th RIR returned from Ginchy on 10 September.

The number of men present did grow in the days and weeks that had immediately followed. Some men had missed the battle, having been deliberately kept out of the action in order to form a cadre on which to rebuild the Battalion in the event of heavy casualties. Others, only lightly wounded in the fighting, began returning to duty even before the Company departed for Belgium. 'From the Somme the men rested at Corbie for ten days,' Jack Le Breton noted, 'and the boys from hospital were glad to rejoin their friends.'[2] Nevertheless, at the start of October 1916, it seems unlikely that more than sixty or seventy Jerseymen were present in Belgium with 7th RIR. A larger number now lay in hospitals scattered across Britain and France. Wounded in the fighting at Guillemont and Ginchy, or during the months at Loos, they had been evacuated through the army's chain of treatment facilities.

During the First World War, the British Army had been quick to recognise the benefits of effective treatment for the wounded. As well as increasing the chance of recovery (and return to active service), it also greatly boosted a man's morale to know that if wounded he could expect medical care. One of the best ways of ensuring this care was to evacuate wounded soldiers from the battlefield as quickly as possible, and to send them to the appropriate level of medical facility. Fortunately for those wounded at Guillemont and Ginchy, there existed by then a comprehensive and well-established evacuation and treatment process.

It started at the Regimental Aid Post, or RAP. This was a makeshift facility established by Battalion Medical Officers as close as possible to the fighting to provide a first level of basic treatment. From the RAP, a wounded man was dispatched further back to an Advanced Dressing Station, or ADS, usually located in close proximity to the front lines. At the ADS, wounded men from a number of units were collected for further basic treatment and the first real assessment of the severity of their injuries. Depending on the nature of the wounds, the ADS would decide the evacuation priority, and the most suitable place to send the casualty next.

The usual location was a Casualty Clearing Station, or CCS. These were medical centres of significant size, manned by the Royal Army Medical Corps, or RAMC, and capable of dealing with up to 1,000 patients at a time. Some CCS' specialised in certain types of injury, treating mainly head injuries or stomach wounds for example. Others were more general, providing a range of surgical and non-surgical treatments. In some cases, the CCS was as far as the wounded man went – patched up, rested and fit again, they would return from there straight to their unit. Many others, however, required more significant treatment or convalescence than the CCS could provide, and so they were dispatched further down the chain. For these men, the ultimate destination was a Base Hospital in France, or one of the many hospitals in Britain used by the military during the war.

By September 1916, scores of Jersey Company men had already experienced the army's medical evacuation and treatment process. One of them was Sergeant Harry Ross. After initial treatment at a Regimental Aid Post and Advanced Dressing Station, he had found himself transported down the chain at a sometimes bewildering speed:

> Our stay at the C.C.S. was another short one. We slept but one night in the dormitory of a large school, and early next morning were told that a Red Cross train was waiting at the station to convey us to a base hospital. Motor ambulances were once more in attendance, and by 10 a.m. we were comfortably installed in a luxuriantly-fitted up corridor, which formerly belonged to the G.W.R.
>
> There ensued a journey of no less than 26 hours ... We went up the line to pick up more sick and wounded at several stations and then headed for the coast, although no-one on the train knew the exact destination until he had arrived at a certain point at nightfall. We had meals in the train – Maconochie (tinned stew) for dinner, bread and butter for tea, and a ham sandwich for breakfast, and the R.A.M.C. sisters and doctors treated us very kindly, supplying us with chocolate and cigarettes.[3]

The train had carried Ross and a number of other Jersey Company casualties to Etaples on the French coast. There, a former London bus transported them to the port where a hospital ship bound for Southampton waited. After reaching England, another train had taken the whole ship's complement of wounded on to Birmingham and a strange final leg of the journey:

> At the station was a fleet of privately-owned motor cars lent for the occasion with their prosperous-looking owners at the steering-wheel and the streets were lined with hundreds of women and children who cheered and yelled and shrieked as we drove by on our way to Dudley Road Hospital. We never dreamt of having such a reception did we four Jerseymen who had managed to get together in a car.[4]

And Birmingham was not the only location for Jersey Company wounded after the fighting in September 1916. From Southampton to Scotland, the men were found beds in hospitals up and down the length of the country. The nature and severity of their wounds varied. For many, the injuries meant an end to their military service, and the start of a lifetime of physical or mental suffering. The army would treat them as far as it could, after which they would return home to make the best of what was on offer there. Others, however, were more fortunate. Some were lucky enough to receive a much-longed-for 'Blighty wound', meaning an injury that was not life-threatening or likely to maim, but serious enough to send the man back to Britain, or 'Blighty' in the language of the troops. For these men, it was a spell in hospital, usually followed by a period of home leave.

Home leave was a regular feature of British soldiers' life during the First World War. It was granted to both convalescing wounded and men serving at the front and elsewhere. Allocated on a rota basis, most could expect to receive a week's leave once a year, although Jerseymen, having further to travel, may have managed to get ten days at a time. The prospect of home leave was a powerful morale booster. To escape the danger and squalor of the trenches even for a short while was an enticing prospect. Returning home, however, was often not as straightforward as it would seem. Some men felt a sense of guilt at leaving comrades behind. Others found it difficult to adjust to what now seemed like another world. Arriving in Birmingham on his way to hospital, Sergeant Harry Ross had experienced just such a feeling:

> How different the whole atmosphere to that of France. At the railway station … the unaccustomed glamour and the ceaseless turmoil of the people who hurried to and fro, seemed to weigh upon one's senses with all the oppression of a dream, and to the little knot of 'Jersey casualties' tutored by months of another life, the new world, with its strange sounds and unfamiliar shapes seemed quite an illusion.[5]

Like Ross, a steady stream of Jerseymen had found themselves returning to this unfamiliar world in the closing months of 1916. Whether recovering from wounds or direct from the trenches, home leave brought most of them back to Jersey at one time or another. Outwardly at least, to these men the island must have seemed little changed from that they left behind almost two years earlier in March 1915. Although casualties from the war were starting to affect many families, life in general went on much the same. In fact, some of the war-related issues under discussion two years earlier were again making the news.

In the closing months of 1916, the island had been arguing once more about whether to send its men off to war or not. In January 1916, the British Parliament had passed a ground-breaking new law. The Military Service Act allowed the government to call up into the armed forces all men between the ages of eighteen and forty-one. Conscription, as this process was termed, was by then the only realistic option for sustaining an army now numbering millions of men and committed to a war spanning half the globe.

This new law, however, did not automatically extend to the self-governing Crown Dependencies of Jersey, Guernsey and the Isle of Man. By constitution, they were free – in theory at least – to decide their own course of action. Yet to the governments on all three islands, not following suit at this time of grave national crisis was unthinkable; in no time, each had agreed to act.

In February 1916, the Isle of Man moved first. For expediency, and to affirm loyalty, the government there simply asked that Britain's conscription laws extend to its jurisdiction. Guernsey was next. Driven principally by the Lieutenant-Governor, Sir Reginald Hart, it had decided to disband that island's Militia and conscript the men released into a new local regiment. The Royal Guernsey Light Infantry would form in December 1916 and begin immediate preparations to send a battalion of infantry to the front. Jersey had been the last to decide. By July, however, a new law was in front of the States proposing a Military Service Act similar to that adopted in Britain. Similar that is, but not quite the same. The proposed legislation left a number of important controls in the hands of island government, rather than those of the military authorities. Unlike Guernsey, the Militia would remain in place for defence of the island. Furthermore, an automatic exemption from military service would exist for government employees. Most controversial of all, however, was the right to retain men on the island deemed necessary for 'important national work or on work essential to the needs of the island.'

To the independently-minded islanders, the proposed changes were perfectly reasonable. Recent demands from the British government for Jersey to increase its potato exports seemed to have left little choice. In the absence of French farm workers, and with so many island men now serving in the armed forces, farm labour was still needed to meet the demands for food.

The British authorities saw things differently. Politely, but firmly, they declined to accept Jersey's proposed new law. The defence of the island was now a British affair, it was stated, and British military authorities would decide who should stay and who should go. Additionally, Britain, not Jersey, would concern itself with ensuring sufficient men remained to carry out essential work such as farming. In October, Jersey tried again, this time by sending a delegation to London to argue the Island's case. Yet once more, Britain was in no mood for debate. Finally, in November, Jersey backed down and agreed to remove the contentious clauses. The way was clear for conscription to come into force on the island.

The new law came into existence in February 1917 – almost a year later than in Britain. At a stroke, the Jersey Militia law had ended; and with it almost a thousand years of history. Henceforth, all island men between the ages of eighteen and forty-one were effectively part of the British Army, and available for call-up as and when required. Not everyone would have to go of course. As in Britain, the new law provided a right of appeal, on the grounds of medical exemption or essential employment. In the island, there were special tribunals established to hear the claims of appellants and, in some cases, their legal representatives. Throughout the months that followed the law's introduction, they busied themselves hearing the first of many cases.

For some men, however, there was no choice. Without medical or essential employment grounds for appeal, they could only report for duty when the call-up papers arrived. Within days of passing the Military Service Act, the first batch of these had gone out, and the first conscripts were leaving to serve. The only question was to which regiment they would go.

For members of the Jersey Company arriving back on the island on home leave, the answer was obvious:

> While I was in France with the boys, we never got a draft from home. This naturally caused some comment amongst our Irish comrades. It seems a shame, and a crying one at that, that the splendid name the boys have made for themselves should become only a memory, which it certainly must do sooner or later. One cannot expect to go on without casualties. When the contingent was formed we were promised support, which I am sorry to say we did not get.[6]

The island's failure to raise a second company in the autumn of 1915 had clearly started a smouldering resentment among the Jerseymen already serving with 7th RIR. As the list of casualties grew throughout the summer of 1916, so too did the sense of frustration. 'Our Company is getting smaller every day,' complained one anonymous member in a letter to the *Evening Post*, 'I'm sure there must be still many able-bodied men who should be made to do a little bit more than swanking around the town.'[7] Yet apart from one half-hearted and unsuccessful attempt made by senior officers of the Militia in April that year, little had been done to persuade men to join the Jersey Company.

The casualties of Guillemont and Ginchy had of course profoundly exacerbated the situation. For the Jersey Company to return to anywhere near full strength after these losses a considerable injection of new recruits was vital. With the introduction of conscription in Jersey, it had seemed that this could now happen. In fact, the Jersey Company would only need a relatively small proportion of the men available in order to return to full strength. Yet it was not to be the case. Unlike Guernsey, which chose to form its own regiment, Jersey had decided simply to send its conscripts to the British Army. Logically, the British Army decided to send most to join existing English south coast regiments such as the Hampshire, Dorsetshire or Devonshire Regiments. Not one conscript ever went to the Royal Irish Rifles or ended up reinforcing the Jersey Company.

The full background as to why Jersey made this decision remains unclear today. The most likely reason is that given early in 1918 by the Bailiff, Sir William Vernon. Responding to a question in the States, he claimed that during the prolonged debate over the Military Service Act, the then Lieutenant-Governor, Major General Rochfort, had raised the question of forming a Jersey battalion. Rochfort's superiors in England had however decided against the idea. Their reasons were twofold: firstly, the practical difficulty of Jersey being too small to sustain a whole battalion; and secondly, the potential consequences of sending such a unit to the front.

The graphic consequence of sending units raised by small communities to war had become all too clear on the opening day of the Battle of the Somme. On 1 July 1916, many of the Pals battalions raised during the early days of the war had undertaken their first attack on enemy trenches. In many cases, the results were devastating. One well-known case was that of the so-called Accrington Pals. Within minutes of leaving their trenches that morning, 585 of the approximately 700 men had become casualties, including more than 200 dead. The result of so concentrated a loss on this small community had been understandably widespread and profound.

For the army, the conclusion had been clear: for the good of the country's moral, such community-based units should no longer be encouraged.

It seems, therefore, that Jersey did not receive permission to form its own battalion – or perhaps did not press for it. At this time, Major General Rochfort had been nearing the end of his tenure as Lieutenant-Governor and therefore unlikely to have been overly concerned with the formation of a Jersey regiment. Guernsey, on the other hand, who made its decision before the start of the Battle of the Somme, possessed a patriotic and zealous Lieutenant-Governor in the middle of his term.

With hindsight, Jersey's decision not to form its own battalion spared the island from the Accrington's fate. For Guernsey, its Royal Guernsey Light Infantry would fight a battle late in 1917 and another early in 1918 that would leave that island mourning over 200 dead on each occasion. Jersey's worst single battle had already passed when the Jersey Company lost twenty men killed in three days at Guillemont and Ginchy.

Whether the motivations for not forming a Jersey battalion also drove the authorities to decide not to reinforce the Jersey Company is unknown. It seems likely, however, that this was the case. To send young Jersey conscripts to join a 'Jersey Pals' unit no longer made any sense – to the army or the community as a whole.

The decision also made no sense to those men of the Jersey Company then occupying the trenches below Messines Ridge, but for different reasons. Confused, isolated and increasingly bitter, they viewed the decision not to send them reinforcements with growing anger. The message seemed to be becoming clear; from that time forward, they were effectively on their own.

While the debate over the Military Service Act had been rumbling on, there had been one man at least keen to leave Jersey and join the Jersey Company in Belgium. In the autumn of 1916, Major Stocker was looking forward to taking up his old command once more. Recovering from the pneumonia that had almost killed him in the summer, he had pressed the doctors and War Office for permission to return to active service. In November, it appeared the request had been granted. Despite his advancing years, he had received medical clearance to return for duty in the trenches.

A breakdown in communications, however, had led to a mistake. The War Office was adamant in fact that the forty-nine-year-old should not go back to the front; in its view, a man of that age was simply not suitable to lead a company in the present war. Yet somewhere in the system the message had been lost. At the start of December, and presumably much to the surprise of the Commanding Officer of 7th RIR, Major Stocker had arrived in Belgium to report for duty. It did not take long to sort out the mistake. Within days of arriving, Stocker was on his way back to Jersey, this time for good. His association with the Jersey Company was over – for the duration of the war at least.

Quite what the men then in Belgium made of this sudden arrival and departure is unknown. Presumably, however, Stocker's loss would have contributed to the growing sense of isolation from Jersey. Since July, the Jersey Company had been commanded by non-Jerseymen, with no effort made on the island to change this. More than this, Stocker had been such an important figurehead to the men of the Jersey Company – since the very beginning he had represented their interests in the army and at home. With his final departure, this link had been broken for good. From that point on, they would have to look to themselves for leadership, and representation, in the trials that still lay ahead.

Fortunately, there still remained a solid core of leadership within the Jersey Company. From the start, it had possessed a strong body of NCOs, and these men, or at least those remaining after Loos and the Battle of the Somme, then had a critical role to play. Chief among them was of course Jack Le Breton, although by October 1916, technically at least, he was no longer part of the Jersey Company. In August 1916, shortly before the 7th RIR departed from Loos, Le Breton had been promoted to Regimental Sergeant Major, or RSM. This new role, which was clearly in recognition of his performance with the Jersey Company, made him the highest NCO in the Battalion. It also took him away from his 'Jersey Boys' – something he had vowed never to let happen. So there had been some kind of compromise. Despite the change in role, Le Breton managed to remain closely associated with the Jerseymen in the months that followed – both at the front and at home. Under his guiding hand, the rebuilding of the Jersey Company had begun in the closing months of 1916.

The man who had initially replaced Le Breton in the position of Company Sergeant Major was Sergeant Thomas Whittle. His tenure was, however, only short; seriously wounded at Guillemont, he would never return to duty. The next candidate was thirty-two-year-old Christian D'Authreau, a much-respected Sergeant from St Helier who had previously been the senior NCO in 7th RIR's Machine Gun Section.

The other senior NCO position of Company Quarter-Master Sergeant had also changed. Since August 1915, Helier Bree had been in the role of CQMS, but in September 1916, he had moved to become the CSM for another of 7th RIR's companies. First appointed to take over was Sergeant Bertram Mallet, who left towards the end of the year to train as an officer. In his place, twenty-two-year-old Oscar Williams, a former probation officer who had been serving with the Battalion's Signal Section, became CQMS. Both he and CSM D'Authreau had quickly established the authority and stability needed in order to rebuild the Jersey Company back to at least a semblance of its former self.

For the positions of platoon sergeants and section corporals, there had also been a good selection of experienced men from whom to pick. The real problem of manpower shortage existed below those ranks, the obvious deficiency being the number of riflemen still serving with the Jersey Company. Even with the steady return of those previously wounded, and men who had been detached for other duties, it was a low number. By Christmas 1916, there may have been no more than 120 men still present with the Jersey Company in Belgium. With the near certainty that recruits would not be sent from Jersey, the chances of returning to full company strength of 230 had been remote.

If the island was not going to provide more men, the logical alternative was for 7th RIR to fill out the Jersey Company's depleted ranks with Irish recruits. It was, after all, part of an Irish battalion, and that battalion needed bringing up to strength in any case. But a problem had existed with this solution. By the autumn of 1916, it was not just the Jersey Company having difficulties with a lack of replacements. Recruitment for 7th RIR had virtually dried up also when the underlying 'Irish Problem' came to the surface in an unexpected and dramatic fashion.

On Easter Monday 1916, an Irish republican group had attempted to seize control of Dublin by force. Elsewhere in Ireland, there were smaller scale uprisings in support. The rebels demanded an independent Ireland, and had seen an opportunity to claim it with Britain then locked in an exhausting European war. Yet the various groups had lacked cohesion and also failed to capture the popular mood. The rebels in Dublin were soon isolated and left to face a reinforced British Army with considerably greater firepower. After just six days, the Easter Rising had ended, with its leaders dead, captured or on the run.

In defeat, however, the rebels gained far more than they had been able to achieve with the Rising. In the immediate aftermath – a harsh British response that included the swift execution of captured rebel leaders – there was a surge in nationalist and republican sentiment among the ordinary population. The result had been a further and severe decline in the rate of volunteering for the British Army. Moreover, as the British Government had not applied the Military Service Act to Ireland for fear of causing further unrest, the Irish regiments faced a real dilemma. Needing to rebuild after the losses on the Somme, there was even less of a guaranteed source of manpower to draw upon. It led to some drastic measures. A number of the 16th (Irish) Division's battalions were forced to amalgamate or even disband, with their replacements being Irish battalions then serving in other non-Irish infantry divisions. These measures, however, were only a short-term answer to the problem; if the 16th (Irish) Division was to survive, a longer-term solution was required. An obvious, though unwelcome option, was to draft in recruits from other parts of the UK.

At the end of 1916, for the Irish regiments and the Jersey Company, therefore, the dilemma had been the same. Bringing in non-natives to fill out the ranks would inevitably mean a watering down of identity, and a weakening of the 'esprit de corps' that had carried them to war in the first place. Yet by the winter of 1916/17, it was difficult to see any other option.

That winter turned out to be one of the coldest experienced in north-west Europe for more than thirty years. From December to February, Belgium had shivered under its icy grip. For men serving in the Messines Ridge sector it was a miserable time. One wrote home that:

> The weather had been and is 'arctic', with a biting wind, and the strain in the front line is considerable... The breastworks are in a horrible state, frozen hard as stone, the ground is white with snow, and the garrison stands four days and nights at a time, in the paralysing cold, without exercise, numbed, trench-mortared, and shelled.[8]

Yet one benefit of the bleak conditions was a lower level of enemy activity. During the Jersey Company's first five months at Messines, both sides seem to have contented themselves with worrying more about coping with the elements than killing each other. There were, of course, still threats. Snipers remained active, as did German artillery and trench mortars. The latter, launching projectiles known to the troops as 'rum jars' or 'flying pigs', were particularly fearsome in this sector. Often fired from the concealment of woods, they were capable of demolishing a whole stretch of trench and anyone in it.

Despite these threats, casualties in the Jersey Company had remained minimal during this period. Between October 1916 and February 1917, there were no fatalities and only a few wounded – a pointed contrast to the first five months at Loos where nine men had died, and scores more had suffered wounds. The harsh weather again took a toll on health, although it seems to a far lesser extent that in 1916. Possibly the men had been better prepared on this occasion. Illness, however, still claimed its victims. On 24 April 1917, twenty-two-year-old Sergeant Clarence Minchington would pass away at a hospital in the nearby French town of Hazebrouck.

Soon after arriving at Messines, 16th (Irish) Division had resumed the cyclic pattern of life already familiar from Loos. Its stretch of the front ran roughly from Vierstraat in the north to Spanbroekmolen in the south. Headquarters, and the divisional rest camps, were located in and around the village of Locre. It was here that the Jersey Company would spend most of its time when out of the trenches.

In Locre, there existed a curious atmosphere. Although the military dominated, numbers of civilian inhabitants lingered there including a group of nuns inhabiting a convent on the village outskirts. As it can be imagined, they took to the predominantly Irish Catholic soldiers in their midst very well. Nearby Locre, and providing shelter from the worst of the German long-range artillery, was the massive bulk of Kemmel Hill, or the Kemmelberg. This natural barrier and fortress lay opposite Messines Ridge, and being in British hands made an excellent observation point. On its lower slope, facing the German lines was the village of Kemmel, a location for many spells in Brigade Reserve. Leading away from there were the communication trenches stretching up to the front line. A pre-war route that was ominously named by the troops 'Suicide Road' ran between Kemmel and Wytschaete. Near the end of this road, as it began to climb the Messines Ridge, were the trenches in which the Jersey Company was to spend much of their front-line duty during the time there. It was there, in March 1917, that the war really caught up with the Jersey Company once more.

On 4 March 1917, twenty-one-year-old Rifleman Charles Parker was looking forward to his first home leave in months. He had already written his parents, telling them to expect him any day soon. That afternoon he had been resting in a dugout with a friend, Rifleman Winter Garde, when a German shell directly struck the shelter. By the time they managed to dig the two young Jerseymen out, both were dead. Coming after so many months without a loss, their deaths were felt deeply by the Company. Four days later, on 8 March, came an even greater shock.

The Jersey Company, along with one other, was holding the familiar stretch of trenches below Wytschaete at the time. Throughout the day, enemy shells had been landing intermittently on or near the trenches, although not in significant enough volume to cause any alarm. As darkness fell, however, the situation had suddenly changed. A heavy and sustained bombardment crashed down on the Jersey Company's positions. Under its ferocious weight, trench walls had sagged and collapsed, and dugouts had caved in. Desperately, the defenders sought whatever shelter they could, at the same time signalling frantically for a counter-bombardment. Then, after an hour, the enemy shelling of the British front-line trenches abruptly ceased – only to resume again almost immediately on positions further to the rear. Experience told those now trapped in the front line that a trench raid was imminent.

Out of the night three heavily-armed German trench-raiding parties loomed, each rapidly converging on a different spot in the British front line. One headed straight for the trenches held by the Jersey Company. The confusion caused by the bombardment meant there was little time for the defenders to organise a cohesive resistance. Swiftly, the Germans had leapt over parapet and into the trench. In the darkness, a frantic hand-to-hand struggle had ensued. With the officers out of action, it fell to a number of NCOs to organise resistance, one being CSM D'Authreau who was later awarded a Medaille Militaire for his endeavours. After about fifteen minutes, reinforcements arrived to drive the Germans out. The attack was over.

It had been a bad night for the British. The German intention had been to take prisoners, and in this, they were successful. At roll-call, 7th RIR found that twenty-five of its men were missing, presumed captured. Eight – Riflemen Edward Bastin, Harold Brochet, William Hughes, Sid Kerry, Charles Lafolley, Philip Laffoley, Alf Marett and William Whiteman – were from the Jersey Company. The remainder of their war would be passed within the confines of a German prisoner of war camp.

In addition to those lost as prisoners, the Battalion had also suffered numerous casualties included eight men killed. Among them was Rifleman George Picot from St Helier who had previously been wounded in July 1916. On the next day, the fatalities were increased by one when twenty-two-year-old Rifleman Clarence De Veulle died at a Casualty Clearing Station in the nearby French town of Bailleul.

Five days and four deaths – it was unwelcome reminder that winter was ending; having left Messines Ridge a quiet sector for some time now, the war was returning to Belgium with a vengeance.

Eight

Triumph and Tragedy

> There then occurred three attacks in 17 days, which can never be forgotten by those
> who survived. Ypres claimed more of our heroes than any other portion of the line.
> RSM Jack Le Breton, Jersey Company RIR, 1919

The final day of March 1917 had dawned gloriously bright and sunny in the Belgian
village of Locre. For the noisy crowd of soldiers gathering there, that morning's fine
weather was a welcome tonic. After six long months in the waterlogged trenches of
Messines Ridge, signs of an early spring were reason enough for celebration. On this
particular day, however, the fine conditions were not the only thing contributing to the
obviously excited atmosphere. As they shouldered rifles and packs, the men of the Jersey
Company knew that they had another reason to be cheerful. That morning, for the first
time in months, they were marching away from the front, rather than towards it.

The entire 48th Brigade of the 16th (Irish) Division had orders to report for training
at an army camp near the French town of St Omer. It was a much-welcome prospect for
the weary soldiers. For two weeks, they would be leaving behind the shattered, fearful
and deprived conditions of life at the front. In its place, there was the chance for two
weeks of decent living in the verdant and peaceful countryside of the Pas-De-Calais. It
was little wonder that curious onlookers had noted a particular swagger in the Brigade's
stride as it set off up the road to Bailleul behind massed pipes and drums.

The camp was a good distance away, alongside the picturesque village of Tournehem-
Sur-Hem. Here, and in the countryside around, the British Army had established
extensive training facilities. In no time at all the men fell into a daily routine. Mornings
had been devoted to military exercises, afternoons spent on some form of physical
exercise that included the staple diet of football, rugby and athletics. There was shooting
practice too, with the Jerseymen demonstrating that they had lost none of their prowess
as marksmen by winning first place in the Battalion competition. Over the final two
days, however, there was a distinct change in routine.

Engineers had laid out lines of simulated German trenches in a part of the camp.
With the entire Brigade assembled, a series of grand exercises took place practising
attacking these trenches repeatedly. There was great emphasis on learning new tactics,
particularly in working more closely with the artillery. Some of the painful and costly

lessons of Loos and the Somme had clearly been taken on board; the British Army were determined that things were going to be different in 1917. There was a genuine hope that the new tactics, together with new and improved weapons, would make the difference and lead to success on the Western Front.

But where would this success come? Scrutiny of the simulated German positions might have provided a clue. Laid out in the fields near Tournehem-Sur-Hem was a replication of the enemy trenches on Messines Ridge.

Messines Ridge had long been a feature in the thoughts of the British Commander-in-Chief, Field Marshal Sir Douglas Haig. As early as 1915, he had nurtured the idea of an offensive in Belgium, convinced that it was the place to defeat the Germans decisively and thus hasten the end of the war. Nevertheless, the plans and counsel of his French allies had held sway – and they had different priorities. That was until April 1917, after which the situation had begun to change.

For the Allies, the fourth year of the war had opened optimistically enough. Despite the disappointing end to the Somme offensive, in December at Verdun a French general had managed to win back much of the ground lost to the Germans during the first half of the year. Robert Nivelle was widely regarded as the rising star of the French Army. Early in 1917, this charismatic general convinced his colleagues and the politicians that he could repeat his Verdun success – but on a far grander scale. This time he proposed a massive French offensive on the German positions north of Paris, and promised to have the enemy on the run within days.

The British contribution to Nivelle's plan was to launch a diversionary attack around the town of Arras. It had started on 9 April, with notable success that included the Canadian Corps' capture of the formidable Vimy Ridge. Yet for the main French attack seven days later, the same was not the case. Forewarned, and fully prepared, the Germans had been waiting. Strongly entrenched in positions on the ridge, along which ran a road called the Chemin Des Dames, they met the French attack with devastating machine gun and artillery fire. With little or no progress in the days that followed, and growing numbers of casualties, French morale had plummeted. By early May, with their dreams of a swift end to the war in tatters, many French soldiers began to refuse returning to the front. The mutiny would soon spread to more than half the French Army.

While the French sought to regain control of their forces, the British Army had redoubled its efforts around Arras. There was little further success, however, other than to keep the Germans distracted. Furthermore, in assuming the lead role among the Allies, Haig was at last free to pursue his long-cherished offensive in Belgium, and decided that the first blow would fall on Messines Ridge. Yet unlocking German defences on the ridge would require something special. Fortunately for Haig, by the early summer of 1917, that something special was just about ready.

For two years British engineers had been working beneath the ridge, painstakingly tunnelling their way towards the German lines. Deep below selected strongpoints, chambers packed with explosives had been prepared and were primed for detonation.

Although this type of mine warfare was nothing new, the scale envisaged for Messines Ridge was unprecedented. These mines had also been prepared in great secrecy; when the moment came the intention was that their detonation would catch the unfortunate defenders above completely unaware.

Conscious of the need to deflect attention from the ailing French armies further south, Haig gave the orders for an attack on Messines Ridge. Completing the mines and amassing the artillery needed for the preliminary bombardment would take several weeks since many of the guns required were then in action at Arras. In the meantime, trench warfare in Belgium would have to continue as normal. Under gloomy skies, on 19 April the Jersey Company had returned once more to the depressingly familiar surrounding of Messines Ridge.

Although the terrain was familiar, one thing at least was changing. In preparation for the forthcoming offensive, 16th (Irish) Division was being strengthened at last. For some weeks, new men had been pouring into the Division, and more were coming. Many ended up in the ranks of 7th RIR. Few, however, were from Ireland – or for that matter from Jersey. To bring the Battalion back up to strength, drafts of mainly English conscripts were arriving instead. With little prospect of men from Ireland, there had been no real choice. Fresh-faced and nervous, they arrived in weekly batches. Some, of course, were sent to join the Jersey Company. Quite what these newcomers had made of their new posting is unknown, but there surely must have been some curiosity over these old hands with 'Jersey' on their shoulders, and an uncanny ability to talk the language of the natives. Quite what the Jerseymen made of their new comrades is also unknown. Yet what must have been clear was that everyone's life would now depend on how well they all worked together, and how quickly these newcomers learnt to handle life at the front. This was especially so given orders to adopt a more aggressive approach against the enemy on Messines Ridge.

British high command had decided that the Germans were to be kept distracted while preparations for the new offensive continued. For the men in the front line that meant one thing: trench raids.

Two days after returning from training, the first night-time patrol had gone out from the Jersey Company. Captain David Scollard, the officer appointed to command 'D' Company in October 1916, had led it and taken a small group into no man's land. In the darkness, however, the patrol had encountered the enemy and a firefight started. Only two men made it back to the British trenches, both badly wounded and unaware what had happened to the others. One of the missing, Rifleman George Willmett, was later confirmed as having been captured and was in a prisoner of war camp. The Captain was not so lucky; his body would eventually be found out in no man's land and brought back for burial at Kemmel.

A month later, another raid had led to even heavier losses for the Jersey Company. On the night of 22 May, Scollard's replacement, Lieutenant James Craig, took out a large patrol with orders to enter the enemy trenches opposite. Under the cover of darkness, the heavily armed group had set off. First into the enemy trenches was Corporal Ernest

Louis. The Corporal had acquired something of a reputation when it came to this kind of action. 'One of the finest men in the battalion', was how 7th RIR's Commanding Officer later described the twenty-two-year-old, 'always volunteered for every raid or dangerous enterprise.'[1] That night's raid, unfortunately, was his last. The German defenders reacted violently, firing wildly and hurling grenades at the attackers. There were heavy casualties among the raiding party, among them Corporal Louis who was killed. Another Jerseyman, Rifleman Arthur Bailey suffered severe wounds and would die three days later in a Casualty Clearing Station at Bailleul. A possible third victim was Rifleman Joseph Crenan, who having been evacuated to an English hospital, died of his wounds on 26 June 1917.

Another killed on the night of 22 May was Lance Corporal William Le Feuvre, one of the few members of the Militia's Medical Company to volunteer in 1914. Heedless of the risk, he had climbed out into the open to assist the returning men. A German bullet had killed the Lance Corporal as he tended to the wounded. They buried William Le Feuvre in the British war cemetery at Kemmel Chateau, nearby the graves of Riflemen Garde and Parker, the first Jerseymen to be killed in the trenches of Messines Ridge. Le Feuvre's burial, however, was to be the last there for the Jersey Company. A few days later, 7th RIR withdrew from the front line and moved back to Locre, to begin final preparations for its part in the imminent offensive. By then, the British bombardment heralding the start of the Battle of Messines Ridge had already roared into life.

The plan for attacking Messines Ridge assigned 16th (Irish) Division a key role. Its objective was to be the village of Wytschaete. The division's 47th and 49th Brigades had the task of storming the village. Once they succeeded, 48th Brigade would be committed to support a further advance to the German reserve line on the far side of the Ridge. The offensive was to start in the early hours of 7 June 1917.

It was a plan of attack that meant the Jersey Company would not take part in the initial assault, as the 7th RIR being part of 48th Brigade was in reserve. On the night of 6 June the men left Locre and moved to a position near a small copse called Rossignol Wood, some way behind the front line. The march up through the dark took place under conditions that were to be strictly observed. 'Whilst moving to assembly position and when finally in position, every care is to be taken to avoid arousing the suspicions of the enemy,' stated Battalion orders, 'smoking, striking of matches, flashing of torches and unnecessary talking are forbidden. All ranks will move as quietly as possible.'[2] The Germans were to be kept guessing as to the date and the time of the attack until the last possible minute.

All around, massed guns were remorselessly firing, pounding the enemy lines on the ridge in front. In the country between Rossignol Wood and the German positions, thousands of soldiers waited anxiously in the dark. Mindful of previous offensives, there were plenty of questions. Were the Germans waiting? Had the bombardment broken the defences? Would the mines make a difference? At just after 3.00 a.m. they started to find out when, with a roar that was reportedly heard as far away as London, the mines were detonated. Along the ridge, nineteen huge explosions sent towering pillars of fire – along with hundreds of German defenders – high into the sky.

Even before the debris had finished falling to the ground, the British assault troops were climbing out of their trenches and advancing across no man's land. On the 16th (Irish) Division's front, the commanders held their breath as the men cautiously approached the first German line. Yet the concern was unnecessary, the mines and bombardment had done their job well. Shredded barbed wire, smashed trenches, and dead or stunned defenders were all that remained. Sweeping through, the attack had swiftly converged on Wytschaete itself. Even there, German resistance was only sporadic; by 7.00 a.m., the village was in British hands.

Along the entire front of the attack, the objectives set had largely been achieved. At the end of that day, the whole of Messines Ridge was in British hands for the first time since 1914. Moreover, in comparison with previous offensives, British casualties were refreshingly low. The attack had been a triumph of preparation and planning.

News of the amazing victory must have come as great relief to those reserve units waiting to take their turn in the fighting. With Wytschaete and the German reserve positions taken, the Jersey Company had found its role on 7 June happily relegated to carrying forward water and munitions. On reaching Wytschaete, the reasons behind the German collapse became more obvious. The level of destruction was truly awesome. 'You can only just distinguish where the roads were,' wrote one man passing through at the time, and 'recognise what was the chief outstanding feature – the church – only by tracing its position from the map.'[3]

Enemy resistance remained weak in the days that followed. The main threat came from a few isolated pockets of German resistance on the ridge. One of these came to the attention of RSM Le Breton. An unknown number of Germans were found to be hiding in a deep dugout near Wytschaete. While others argued over the best way to get them out, the RSM calmly decided to go down personally and fetch them himself. A few minutes later, to widespread amazement, Le Breton had emerged with a German prisoner slung over his shoulder. After handing the man over, he went down again to collect another. This extraordinary act of bravery led to the award of a well-deserved Distinguished Conduct Medal, the second for the Jersey Company.

The assault on Messines Ridge had always been intended as the forerunner of a larger and far more ambitious offensive around Ypres itself. With his southern flank secured, Field Marshal Haig planned to break the German stranglehold on that key town. It was an attack he also was sure would hasten the end of the war. Haig believed that the German capacity to continue fighting was almost at an end. Worn down at the front by repeated Allied attacks, he had argued that its army was close to breaking point and, due to an Allied naval blockage, at home its civilians were ready to sue for peace. One more powerful blow, Haig reasoned, should be enough to bring about a complete collapse.

That blow, according to the Field Marshal's plans, would fall at Ypres. Several factors had influenced this choice. Firstly, it would keep German attention a long way from the wavering French armies in the south. Secondly, a key German railway supply line ran through Belgium just behind the enemy lines here. Cut it, and the entire German position in north-west France would be under threat. Thirdly – and perhaps most importantly from a British point of view – there was the chance of capturing the German-held ports of Zeebrugge and Ostend. From them, German submarines regularly emerged to menace the English Channel, threatening the vital supply routes to the Continent. Haig's plan envisaged an advance along the Belgian coast and an end to this threat.

For it to succeed, however, there would have to be a massive new build-up of men and materials. The guns that had helped blast the Germans off Messines Ridge had to be re-positioned and supplied with fresh stocks of ammunition. The troops, so meticulously prepared for the June battle, needed rest and re-training. New commanders were brought in and required time to understand the situation. It all had meant a considerable delay between the end of the Messines Ridge assault and the start of the next offensive, the date for that was set as 31 July 1917 – nearly two months later. Concerns that this delay was giving the Germans too much time to recover went unaddressed however.

Not that this bothered the men of the Jersey Company. For them it was back to the training camps of the Pas-De-Calais for an extended period of absence from the trenches. There must have been few complaints as the men finally left Messines, Kemmel and Locre for the last time on 13 June, and headed to a camp near the town of Hazebrouck. After a week there, they moved to a training camp near St Omer for the next four weeks. There, it would be a repeat of April's training routine and exercises. Finally, on 25 July, they moved again to a camp close to the Belgian town of Poperinghe.

Around Poperinghe, or 'Pop' as it was affectionately termed by the British soldiers, the remainder of 16th (Irish) Division was assembling. Several other divisions were gathering nearby. The roads around strained under the weight of dusty columns, as men and materials inexorably moved towards the front at Ypres a few miles to the east. It all could have left only one impression: Field Marshal Haig's forthcoming offensive was going to be on a huge scale.

Yet while every preparation was being made to ensure success, there was one factor Haig could not influence. The weather had the potential to play a crucial part in the forthcoming battle. The land around Ypres was mostly low-lying with a high water table. In peacetime, it managed to remain dry due to the presence of a complex system of drainage channels and ditches. By 1917, after three years of fighting, these systems had already sustained considerable damage. Further heavy bombardments, coinciding with any prolonged period of rain, would overwhelm the drainage and dissolve the countryside into a morass of water and mud. In the days leading up to the attack, British commanders would keep a nervous eye on the skies.

The Third Battle of Ypres, or Passchendaele as it later became widely known, started in the early hours of 31 July 1917. Following days of heavy bombardment, ten British divisions climbed out of their trenches just before dawn and stormed the German line on a broad arc in front of the town. To the north, a smaller French army had also attacked in support.

As at Messines in June, success that day had been immediate and dramatic. All along the front, German defences appeared to crumble before the advancing troops. Two key ridges had fallen, while an impressive haul of prisoners and guns was captured. By the close of that day, the attackers had penetrated the enemy line by as much as a mile in places. It seemed that Haig's convictions had been correct; the German Army looked a beaten force. Could the Allies now push on and finally break through its lines? There were certainly extra troops at hand if required.

The 16th (Irish) Division had remained in reserve during this first day of battle – the rapid advance having made its commitment to action unnecessary. The only movement for the Jersey Company was to occupy the old British front-line trenches around the tiny hamlet of Potijze shortly after the attack started. Ahead, another division had driven the German defenders back to their second line on the low Frezenberg ridge. Although resistance stiffened there, by the end of the day both Frezenberg itself, along with some of the surrounding German defences, had fallen. There, however, the fighting petered out – as it did across elsewhere along the front.

Despite the success of that first day, and the availability of fresh troops to push forward, the British plan required a pause to bring forward the artillery and ammunition needed to blast the next German line of defences into submission. This required time. In the summer of 1917, the capability that would allow for a battle of continuous movement was still lacking. The very bombardment that had ensured success on 31 July also served to churn up the ground over which the artillery needed to advance. It was a situation not helped by the weather. On the first day of the battle, it had started to rain. The worst fears of the planners were starting to be realised.

With no further plans to move forward, on 1 August, the Jersey Company had left the positions around Potijze and returned to the camp near Poperinghe under a steady drizzle. There they had remained until the evening of 7 August. By then, 16th (Irish) Division had been assigned responsibility for the newly-won British front line on the Frezenberg Ridge. Its battalions would take it in turn to hold the defences there while preparations continued for the next British push. Orders soon arrived for 7th RIR to move up to the front line.

The route up to the front took the Battalion through Ypres. It was a mournful sight. Three years of incessant shelling had reduced this once magnificent town to just the fragments of former buildings amid scattered piles of debris. The famous Cloth Hall and magnificent cathedral lay in ruins, their skeletal remains passed as the men marched across the town's main square. Hurrying swiftly through, the column struck out into the Ypres Salient under the cover of darkness.

Once outside the town, progress was painfully slow. The rain that had fallen on the first day of the offensive had more or less continued ever since. The landscape, already pock-marked and churned up by the heavy bombardment, was rapidly turning into an ocean of mud, deep enough in places to drown anyone unfortunate enough to fall in. As a consequence, movement had become restricted to roads and specially laid out track-ways. These fragile paths, which fanned out from Ypres to the front line like the spokes of a wheel, were heavy with traffic at night. The Germans knew this of course, and regularly shelled and machine gunned key routes to cause maximum damage and confusion. On the night of 7 August, they were particularly active as the Jersey Company approached Frezenberg.

Matters did not improve much on their arrival at the British positions around the ruins of Frezenberg. In fact, they worsened. The conditions encountered there by the Jersey Company were later claimed to be the worst of the entire war. 'Mud awful,' wrote one man serving there, 'no trenches, no shelter, no landmarks, and all movement by night … hell all the time!'[4] Shockingly, it was soon discovered that the British front line here was, in reality, a mere collection of linked shell holes, filled with vile-smelling liquid mud and offering scant protection against either German shelling, or the elements. The only shelters were a number of captured German concrete bunkers, but even these were deceptive. The Germans knew their locations of course, and they became the targets for artillery fire, leading to frequent casualties. On 8 August, the day after the Battalion's arrival, a shell had exploded among a group of runners waiting outside the bunker used as 7th RIR headquarters. Among the dead was nineteen-year-old Rifleman Arthur Gallie – the first of the Jersey Company to lose his life in the Salient.

During the next four days, 7th RIR suffered more than 200 casualties holding the line at Frezenberg – without ever seeing the enemy. Victims of artillery fire, sniping, mud and rain, their number added to the growing toll of the Ypres offensive. One was the Jersey Company's Rifleman George Laurens whose circumstances seem to epitomise the cruel nature of the fighting there.

At thirty-seven-years-old, Laurens was one of the older volunteers. In 1916, he had already had one narrow escape when a bullet passed through his steel helmet without causing serious injury. One year later, however, it was a different matter. Wounded on 7 or 8 August in a German bombardment somewhere on the route between Ypres and Frezenberg, Laurens had managed to crawl into a nearby dugout. There he lay for four days, before being finally discovered on 11 August and carried back to a Casualty Clearing Station near the village of Brandhoek. His condition was by then beyond help as an unknown nursing sister later explained in a letter to Lauren's parents:

44th C.C.S. B.E.F., 12/8/17

Dear Mr Laurens – Your son Rifleman G Laurens, 4161, of the 7th RIR was admitted yesterday very badly wounded in both legs and right arm. They had to amputate the right leg; but I regret to say that he died this morning at 2.40, never being sensible enough to talk coherently. He had been in a dug-out for four days when brought in; thus we felt his case was hopeless from the start.

Please accept my very sincere sympathy for your loss. All the patients in my ward are very, very ill but I'd like you to know that we did our very best for your son.

Believe me.[5]

Two days before Laurens died, 7th RIR had pulled back from Frezenberg and returned to a camp near Vlamertinghe. Those that had survived came back cold, wet and thoroughly shocked by their experience. Such was the Ypres Salient; it had been far from an ideal preparation for the Jersey Company's part in the next phase of the battle.

On 16 August 1917, the British offensive at Ypres recommenced. In common with the attack on 31 July, a heavy bombardment preceded a broad attack across the front, with the British objective being the capture of the next line of German defences. In contrast to 31 July, however, time and conditions had limited the preparations, with the bombardment less than extensive and many of the troops less than fresh. Yet expectations were high for this phase.

Unlike 31 July, and Messines Ridge before, the Jersey Company was to be part of the initial assault. From Frezenberg, 7th RIR had the objective of advancing towards the village of Zonnebeke, overrunning the German defences in between. The terrain over which it would attack was flat and largely featureless, with little if any natural cover on the battlefield. In the Battalion's sector only a raised embankment along which the Ypres-Roulers railway line had run before the war offered some protection – provided it was not in German hands.

The plan was for 7th RIR and 9th Royal Dublin Fusiliers to capture the first line of German defences some 500 yards to the east of Frezenberg. With this achieved, further elements of 48th Brigade would join in to continue the advance, with the objective being a strip of marshy ground marking the remains of small brook called the Hannebeek. The distance on the ground was not great, but the challenge was immense, for while British offensive capability had improved, so too had the level and sophistication of the German defences. By this stage of the war, many of the traditional German linear trench systems had been replaced by defences based on a series of interlinked strongpoints. In the Ypres Salient, these strongpoints were now constructed from concrete, and largely impervious to anything but direct artillery hits. Between Frezenberg and Zonnebeke lay a considerable number of these mini-fortresses, some concealed among the ruins of the area's pre-war farms. This made them difficult for the artillery to pinpoint and destroy, although for any advance to succeed it was important they were, a fact not lost on the men making the assault on 16 August.

On the evening preceding the attack, the Jersey Company made its way up to the front line in the dark. Once more, a steady drizzle fell, adding to the difficult conditions underfoot. With greatcoats and packs left behind as ordered, the men were soon cold and soaked to the skin. Keeping to the narrow road, they made their way towards Frezenberg. All around British artillery was putting on one last tremendous show, blazing away in the darkness to send shells to explode somewhere ahead and to light up the horizon. Worryingly, however, the enemy artillery also remained active. A shell hit the column soon after passing through the Menin Gate, causing confusion and several casualties. There was nothing for it, however, than to push on up the road.

The Jersey Company was to be in the centre of 7th RIR's opening attack. In the cold early morning darkness, the men waited nervously for the order to advance. Would the attack come as a surprise to the Germans, or would they be waiting? Success had come at Messines in June and at the start of this offensive on 31 July. Would Frezenberg be the same? With forty-five minutes to go, however, German shells began falling on their assembly positions causing numerous casualties. It seemed the element of surprise had already been lost.

At 4.45 a.m., as the first streaks of a grey dawn began to appear, whistles blew to signal the start of the attack. In front, the 'creeping barrage' began moving forward as the artillery lengthened its range. Gripping rifles, the men advanced towards the enemy. Everything now depended on whether or not the German strongpoints had survived the bombardment. Within minutes, the answer became known. From the ruins of one of the farms in front, a machine gun opened up. Several more soon joined in, while from the railway embankment others rattled into life, creating a deadly crossfire. The barrage had clearly failed; encased in concrete or protected by underground shelters, the German defenders remained a potent force in front of Frezenberg. The attackers were soon paying the price.

In the centre of 7th RIR's front, the advance had quickly faltered. Going to ground, some men of the Jersey Company attempted to work their way round the German defences, but with little success. All around, the field lay strewn with the dead and dying – there seemed little hope of any progress. Only in one place, was there a glimmer of hope.

On the Battalion's right flank, alongside the railway line, 'A' Company had managed to work its way forward, using the raised bank as protection. Seeing this, a number of Jersey Company men had made their way towards the embankment, bravely following the 'A' Company men forward towards the Hannebeek. Soon with the battalions on the right and left of 7th RIR stalled, this small party of men was the only element of 48th Brigade still advancing. Yet it was a futile cause. Isolated and without support, the attackers had soon become pinned down near the remains of the brook. With the rest of the Battalion held up, there was no way of assisting them. Still, the small group fought on into the afternoon, with slowly diminishing numbers and firepower. Only under the cover of darkness were a handful able to escape and return to British lines.

The rest, dead or wounded, remained behind. Among those killed were at least three Jersey Company men, Riflemen Bernie Jordan, Harold Gulliford and George Le Lievre. Also reported as killed was twenty-two-year-old Rifleman Edward Baillie, and his parents informed as such by letter a few days later. Yet in September another letter would arrive to say that in fact Baillie had been wounded and was now a German prisoner of war. Their elation was, however, tragically short-lived. Within days of hearing this astonishing news, another letter had arrived to announce that Edward Baillie had succumbed to his wounds on 20 September 1917.

Edward Baillie's parents were not the only ones mourning their losses after 16 August. The attack at Frezenberg had been a costly one for the Jersey Company. Sergeant's

Nelson Harding and Francis Baxter, and Riflemen Snowdon De La Haye, William Risebridger, Albert Wooton and James Vibert had all been killed. Scores of others fell wounded. It had been the worst day for the Jersey Company since Guillemont on 6 September 1916.

Yet if Frezenberg was one of the lowest points for the Jersey Company in terms of losses, in terms of bravery it ranks as the highest. During the course of the fighting there, no fewer than eight men would receive the Military Medal for bravery. Considering that during the whole course of the war, the Jersey Company only received fifteen of these highly prized awards, it is a measure of the achievement on that day that over half of them were won at Frezenberg.

Overall, 16 August 1917 was a day of mixed results for the British Army. In the north, around the village of Langemark, the attack had gone well, and a notable advance made. Elsewhere, however, there had been little success. Many divisions, including the 16th (Irish) Division, failed to make any progress in the face of determined enemy resistance. Despite Field Marshal Haig's optimistic assessment, it seemed the Germans were not on the verge of collapse after all. At Ypres, the British offensive had continued into the autumn. After the setbacks of August, new tactics led to smaller scale operations with an even greater reliance on a preceding bombardment to destroy the German defences before the infantry advanced. While successful, this intensive artillery pounding also served to worsen the conditions across the salient. The fighting during the final months of 1917 descended to new depths of misery, as mud became the defining factor of the battle. Finally, in November, the offensive spluttered to a halt around the village of Passchendaele – a name now synonymous with the whole battle, and the terrible suffering of the men who fought there.

After August, however, the Jersey Company had no further part to play at Ypres. On the day after the attack at Frezenberg, the 16th (Irish) Division left the front line and moved to the rear. The assault, and weeks that preceded it, had taken a grim toll. With losses of more than 4,000 men, the division, and its battalions, would need considerable rebuilding before it could take part in any further fighting. The question was, from where would the men come?

Nine

A Kick from the Trenches

It is the general opinion of the surviving members that we have been badly treated
by our fellow islanders … Are they going to stand by now and see the remnants go
without an attempt to keep them together?

RSM Jack D Le Breton, Jersey Company RIR, October 1917

It was in the middle of September 1917 that the news came through that everyone in
the 7th Royal Irish Rifles had been dreading. Their Battalion was to be disbanded.

Perhaps it was not totally unexpected. The recent fighting at Ypres had reduced 7th
RIR's strength to around 500, with no obvious source of new men to make up the
losses. With the continuing problem of raising recruits in Ireland following the Easter
Rising, other Irish battalions had already gone the same way. Nevertheless, for those
men having to suffer this fate, it was a painful and confusing moment. During the First
World War, a soldier's immediate loyalty was to his battalion. It was the focus of his sense
of identity and belonging, effectively being an extended family during one of the most
traumatic periods of his life. Now, that family was being torn away from the men of 7th
RIR, leaving them to face an uncertain future.

And none more so than those men who remained serving with the Jersey Company.
Over the course of the last two and half years, they had developed strong bonds with
their Irish counterparts. Through shared experience, good and bad, a deep sense of
camaraderie had developed. Indeed, as the support from home dwindled, the Jerseymen
seem to have drawn more strength from the relationship with their Battalion than from
their home island. Now, they not only faced the prospect of losing this relationship, but
also the probable loss of identity as a Jersey unit.

It felt like the final act of duplicity. Too long abandoned by their island, now
threatened with disbandment, it was time, some had decided, to make their feelings
known:

The Jersey contingent has not received any reinforcements of any kind since 1915, and
today we number about 100 all ranks. It has been quite forgotten, so much so that it is
on the eve of disbandment. Casualties have been replaced by men of all regiments, but
not one Jerseyman was sent to fill the gap.

[They have] let the Jersey contingent die out, with the result that today the boys in France are between the Devil and deep sea. They have the option to transfer within the division or be broken up. So much of them. The remnant will not forget this, and look with disgust on the island shirking in its duties. This is but a small kick from the boys, and their opinion of the shirkers left behind.[1]

Sergeant Alfred Marett, one of those who had left the island on the *SS Ibex* back in March 1915, had written the letter. Somehow escaping the military censors, it appeared among the columns of the *Evening Post* in early October 1917. Provocatively, it had the title 'A Kick from the Trenches'. In blunt fashion, it revealed the yawning gap that had sadly grown between the island and the men of 'Ours' since that memorable March morning two and half years earlier. On its own, the letter could do little to address this situation. Yet Sergeant Marett's 'kick from the trenches' was not alone. Others were being prepared. It was just the opening shot in a bitter battle for identity and recognition.

When the news came through on the fate of 7th RIR, the Battalion and its remaining Jerseymen had returned to France. After the mauling at Frezenberg in August, 16th (Irish) Division had left Belgium to rest and rebuild once again. The place chosen for this was a quiet stretch of the front in the countryside between the towns of Bapaume and Arras.

The train carrying the Jersey Company arrived at this new location on 21 August 1917. Accommodation was near the small village of Ervillers, in a bleak establishment of tents and wooden huts called Belfast Camp. It was located on the northern edge of the old Somme battlefields, and stark evidence of this earlier intense fighting lay all around. The twisted and rusting remains of old barbed wire surrounded the camp while abandoned fields were dotted with blackened skeletons of trees. Among them, noted one man, were hundreds of wooden crosses, where German and French dead who had fallen in previous fighting lay buried. Ironically, after three years the fighting was still raging only a few miles away.

The front line was actually about six miles away from Belfast Camp, in a north-easterly direction. On 4 September, following two weeks training and refitting, 7th RIR had gone into the trenches there for the first time. The approach march had been through the shattered villages of Saint Leger and Croisilles to the entrance of a mile-long communication trench, which led in turn to the front line around the village of Fontaine-Les-Croisilles. From there, peering through trench periscopes, the new arrivals could gaze for the first time across no man's land towards the infamous Hindenburg Line.

The origins of the Hindenburg Line had been the remorseless fighting of 1916, and the relentless toll it had taken on the German Army. Faced with the prospect of further Allied offensives the following year, the German generals had agreed a new, and altogether radical, strategy. If they had to suffer under the growing weight of Allied firepower and numbers, it would be better to do so in positions of their own choosing.

Better still if those positions could be prepared in advance, and built in such a way to minimise German casualties while inflicting maximum on the enemy. Furthermore, if the new line meant a shorter front, it would free up men to constitute a reserve force to mount counter-attacks against Allied advances.

At the end of 1916 therefore, some miles behind the existing front line, the Germans had laid out a new set of defences. Taking advantage of natural contours of the land, and using concrete and steel to buttress earthworks, new trenches were built along a seventy-mile stretch. In front lay vast fields of barbed wire, razor sharp and laid out to channel attackers into predetermined killing zones. Behind lay strongly fortified artillery positions, cunningly sited in order to present difficult targets for Allied guns. When complete, it was the most formidable defence system yet established, representing the final evolution in the art of trench warfare. The Germans called this new position the Siegfried Stellung; the British had nicknamed it the Hindenburg Line.

Early in 1917, the Germans had secretly withdrawn to this new line. As they did so, a policy of deliberate destruction had been adopted, leaving villages and farms wrecked, trees felled, and road and rail links destroyed. Many of the ruins were booby-trapped with concealed explosives to kill and maim the unwary, while wells were polluted to make life more difficult. After some initial elation, the Allies had advanced cautiously only to discover a wasteland left by the withdrawing Germans.

During the Battle of Arras in April and May 1917, the strength of the new German positions was tested. Yet several attempts to penetrate the defences had led only to bloody repulses, leaving just fragments of the German front-line trenches in British hands. It was at one of these locations that the Jersey Company had arrived in September 1917. To their dismay, the men found that the trenches and surrounding land remained littered with the grim evidence of the earlier battles. Evidence of the recent fighting lay everywhere. Scattered through the trenches were broken rifles, machine guns and mortars, while no man's land contained several disabled tanks and a large number of corpses. The bodies of the dead were not just out in the open; in some places, they had been used to repair breaches in the trench walls and then hastily covered by sandbags. Given these hellish conditions, it was fortunate both sides showed little desire to restart the fighting at Fontaine-Les-Croisilles. As a result, hostile activity was limited to occasional shelling and the usual sniper activity. Casualties were mercifully light.

Despite this, morale in the Battalion remained low, as the impact of the disbandment decision sunk in. Bitterly, men questioned why they were the ones chosen for this fate. Every one of them would have known of course about the recruitment problems in Ireland, but they had lived with this issue for some time. Some felt there were other motivations behind the decision. Rumours had been circulating that 7th RIR was being broken up for political reasons. As one of its officers later claimed, the Battalion had become unreliable because it was thought there were too many 'Sinn Feiners' in the ranks.

Sinn Fein had become the growing force in Irish politics following the unsuccessful Easter Rising. Staunchly anti-British and opposed to the war, it would soon become the leading party of the south. It also enjoyed increasing support from the communities in which battalions like 7th RIR had their roots. Some in authority had certainly thought this a cause for concern.

The performance of the southern Irish regiments, and the 16th (Irish) Division as a whole, had been put in the spotlight. The Easter Rising had raised old rifts over loyalty. Indeed, after the failure at Frezenberg, a number of British generals had been openly critical about the division, including the army commander at Ypres on 16 August, General Sir Hubert Gough, who believed the men had simply not tried hard enough. Of course, this criticism was later dismissed as unfounded – the failure on 16 August was not down to a lack of effort. Yet the slur, and the suspicion, remained. For the entire division the situation was becoming uncomfortable, particularly for the many men in its units who were not actually Irish. This included the Jersey Company. What direct impact these rumours had on them is unknown, or how it affected their relationship with the rest of the Battalion. What is clear, however, is that the rumours did nothing to improve the Jerseymen's resentment over their plight, and the growing determination to do something about it.

Following on from Sergeant Marett's letter, a second kick was on its way from the trenches. On 16 October 1917, a letter landed on the desk of Sir William Vernon, Bailiff of Jersey. In March 1915, Vernon had been one of those who had marched to the harbour with the volunteers in March 1915, and shook the hands of each and every man as they went on board. Promises had been made that day – and Sir William was about to be reminded of them:

Sir,

We, the undersigned, respectfully wish to bring this, our application to your notice for your consideration.

On the 7th February, 1915, we volunteered, and became attested as the Jersey Company, attached 7th Royal Irish Rifles, in which Battalion we formed 'D' Company. The Battalion is now for political and other reasons being disbanded. We therefore, as attached Jerseymen, claim to be returned to the Jersey Garrison Battalion to be re-drafted by the G.O.C. Channel Islands District at his discretion.

We were told on joining that we were to remain intact as Jersey's official representatives, and during our two years' service in France and Belgium we have done our very best to uphold the traditions of our island home as our record will prove by decorations and parchment awards. We are now to be broken up and posted to the 2nd Battalion Royal Irish Rifles, (Line Battalion) where we will eventually become separated and lost as a Company.

It is the general opinion of the surviving members that we have been badly treated by our fellow islanders in not feeding the Company and replacing casualties. Are they going to stand by now and see the remnants go without an attempt being made to keep them together? If this happens, the records we have made, the hardships we have suffered will, in the opinion of the members have been in vain, and the island will have no recognised body participating in this great struggle for democracy.

If we are to be left without an attempt being made, we claim the right to serve in battalions of our own selection. We respectfully desire you as our 'leading and most influential Jerseyman' to act without delay on our behalf and save the remnants of the finest and only company the Island has ever turned out.

We are ready and willing to fight on right down to the last man, but desire those at home do all they can to keep us as a company either at home or in some English division.[2]

Concluding with the appeal 'urgently waiting your reply', the letter was signed 'on behalf of the Jersey Company', by RSM Jack Le Breton. A further eleven of the surviving NCOs had also added their names.

Having read the letter, Vernon paused to consider its contents and implication. The demands were clear enough: the Jersey Company wanted to remain together as a unit, but believed it was their right to come back to Jersey now that 7th RIR was being disbanded. And the men were not saying they would not continue to fight – only that they wished to serve in a battalion of their own choosing. For the Bailiff, the implications of doing nothing in response were significant. Unlike the earlier correspondence from Sergeant Marett, or perhaps any other individually expressed discontent, the petition from RSM Le Breton and other NCOs carried too much weight to simply be ignored. Not that Sir William, who was certainly an honourable man, would have surely considered such an option. He had always thrived on the cultivated image of a 'man of the people' – the prospect of doing nothing to help this small but important group of islanders would have been unthinkable. If the highly regarded RSM Le Breton went public with the grievances, it was bound to lead to uncomfortable questions.

Vernon must have considered his options. On reflection, he would have known that the decision in 1916 to send Jersey conscripts directly to the British Army, rather than use them to form a Jersey Battalion, had ultimately sealed the fate of the Jersey Company. What he could not have foreseen, however, was the early disbandment of 7th RIR, and the resulting crisis for its Jersey members. Yet options now for action in the matter were strictly limited. After all, Jersey had long since abdicated any real ownership of its contingent – the men belonged wholly to the British Army; and the army was unlikely to allow a group of experienced soldiers to leave and go home. Still, he had to ask the question – if nothing else. Resolving to act, he sat down to draft a letter on the subject to the one man in Jersey who might be able to intervene.

Back in France, the time for intervention from home had been fast slipping away. RSM Le Breton's petition had been dispatched to Jersey on 12 October. Only the day before, he and the rest of the Jersey Company had faced a stark choice over their future.

On a cold afternoon, General Hickie, the current 16th (Irish) Division's commander, had stood in front of 7th RIR for the final time. In a few days, he announced, the

Battalion was to disband formally. Officers and men now had a choice: remain with the 16th (Irish) Division and join another one of its units, or transfer to the 2nd Battalion of the Royal Irish Rifles, which at that time was part of another division. It was a sad outcome, he concluded, but a necessary one in war. Offering his thanks for their splendid efforts during the past two and half years, he left them to ponder their future.

It was a not an easy choice. Staying with the 16th (Irish) Division meant the break-up of the Jersey Company, with its former members scattered among other battalions. Transferring to 2nd RIR – and into another division – meant an uncertain future with no guarantee the men would stay together as a unit when they arrived. They had one day to weigh up the options and decide. In the end, only a few men decided to stay and enter the ranks of another Irish regiment for the remainder of the war. Thus, a number of Jerseymen ended up serving in the Royal Dublin Fusiliers, the Royal Irish Fusiliers or the Royal Inniskilling Fusiliers. But the overwhelming majority of Jersey Company chose to leave 16th (Irish) Division and take their chances in the new battalion. This group numbered around 100 men by now. Together with 400 others from 7th RIR, they had just a short amount of time to prepare for the now imminent departure.

For those Jerseymen leaving 16th (Irish) Division at this time, there was at least one positive change to provide some comfort. After more than a year of being led by non-Jersey officers, there was a familiar face back in charge of the Jersey Company once more.

At the end of August 1917, Cyril Ogier, one of the six original Jersey officers, had returned to duty. The twenty-three-year-old son of an influential Jersey family had taken more than a year to recover from a severe wound received while at Loos. Now promoted to Captain, he had taken over command of 'D' Company, 7th RIR, soon after his return, much to the delight of the remaining Jersey Company men. Ogier had always been a popular as a platoon commander, and much respected by those he served with and led. His appointment at this time had a further benefit. Through his family, Ogier had good connections to the Jersey Establishment – hopefully, they could help further the appeal for support from home.

On 14 October 1917, Ogier paraded at Belfast Camp with the rest of the men leaving the 16th (Irish) Division. It was a fine morning, and a crowd including those leaving 7th RIR and staying behind had gathered to watch the departure. As the assembled band struck up a martial tune, barked orders called the parade to attention. To cheers, the 500 remaining men of 7th RIR marched out of the camp for the last time.

Leaving Ervillers behind, they had made the short march to the ruined town of Bapaume for the first night. The journey continued on foot the following morning, taking a meandering south-easterly course through the desolation of German demolitions and earlier battles. This route took the column near to the villages of Guillemont and Ginchy, by then curiously peaceful after the fighting had moved on. A thick growth of scrubby grass and weeds covered the site, hiding the ruins and crumbling trenches that had been the location of such suffering less than a year before.

Yet the battle had not been completely forgotten. Already erected on the roadside between the former villages was a rough wooden cross to commemorate the sacrifices of the 16th (Irish) Division. But it was not a place for celebration yet. Shouldering packs, the marching soldiers had hurried by.

At around 3.00 p.m. on 15 October, they arrived at the village of Ytres. Their camp was under the trees of a copse known as 'Little Wood' that lay only a short distance away. Here at least, the surrounding countryside was less devastated, although many of the buildings showed signs of recent damage. After a night's rest, the men paraded the next day for an inspection by the officer commanding their new division.

The 36th (Ulster) Division was also from Ireland. There, however, the similarities with their former unit largely ended. At the outbreak of war, the 36th (Ulster) Division had been formed in the north of Ireland, in the province of Ulster. Fiercely loyal to Britain, and largely Protestant, Ulstermen had flocked to the colours, quickly filling the new division's ranks. Three years on, although some of the old fire may have gone, it remained for the most part staunchly loyalist. Unsurprisingly, the largely southern Irish Catholic men of 7th RIR were going to experience some difficulties settling in. There was going to be time to do this, however, as the 36th (Ulster) Division was in reserve at that time, resting and refitting away from the front line. Furthermore, the 2nd RIR, which they were to join, was not due to arrive until mid-November. The men could look forward to a three week period of training, labour duties and church parades.

Before this could start, there was a further sad occasion marking the demise of 7th RIR to endure. Lieutenant Colonel Francis, the Battalion's Commanding Officer since early in 1916, was leaving to take command of a brigade. In a ceremony on 18 October, the Battalion had lined up for an address from this much-respected officer for a final time before sending him off with three rousing cheers. For the Jersey Company in particular, it was yet another blow. Francis had been a strong friend and supporter from the start, recognising the Jerseymen's contribution and their value to the Battalion. With his departure, the wait for news from home became even more anxious.

On 22 October, there was an opportunity to discover what was happening in Jersey. Captain Ogier was returning to the island on home leave. Agreeing to find out what he could, and press the case for the men to be allowed to go home, Ogier had departed with the cheery promise to do everything possible.

As Captain Ogier would find out, back in Jersey RSM Le Breton's petition had led to a flurry of official meetings and correspondence on the subject of the Jersey Company. On receipt of Le Breton's letter, Sir William Vernon had immediately written to the one person who may have been able to do something about the situation. Jersey's new Lieutenant-Governor, Major General Sir Alexander Wilson, was responsible for all military matters on the island. Although his command did not extend to Jerseymen serving overseas in the army, Vernon asked Wilson to bring his influence to bear in this matter.

Explaining the background to the men's situation, in a letter to the Lieutenant-Governor he wrote that 'they are ready and willing to fight right down to the last man, but do not wish to be simply merged, as is now proposed to be done into another Irish Regiment.' What they most want, he explained, is to return to Jersey as part of the garrison. Or, if that is not possible to at least be allowed to serve in an English regiment of their own selection. 'May I', he concluded, 'ask whether anything can be done in order to gratify the very natural desire of these brave fellows who enlisted from sheer patriotism long before compulsory service came in, and who have done and are doing their duty so well and so fully.'[3]

Vernon had also pointed out that it was Major General Rochfort, the Lieutenant-Governor in 1914, who had been very much behind the original decision to raise a Jersey contingent. Could his successor do anything to support the men now? Despite having no connection with the Jersey Company, Major General Wilson had agreed to try. The options were few however. With no direct responsibility for the Jersey volunteers, the Lieutenant-Governor could only forward their request to the War Office for consideration. Nothing more, he explained, could happen until it had considered the matter. Everyone would just have to wait on the outcome.

Captain Ogier returned to France with this news. Although nothing definite had been decided, the eagerly waiting Jerseymen had taken it as a positive sign. A few days later, this belief strengthened when a letter arrived directly from the Bailiff to explain the situation. Writing home to his wife on 11 November, Rifleman Jimmy Scoones, the former island footballer, certainly thought things were looking up:

> Now my dear Alice here's a bit of news for you. Today the R.S.M. had a letter from home telling him that they are doing their best to get us home, and he said it would come off as they have sent up to the War Office and the answer might come any day. If we can't come back, they have got to send out the ones from home to keep us up to two-hundred strong. And he said that as they have not got the men to do that, we will get to come home.[4]

By the time of Scoones' letter, however, among the Jersey Company there was a growing sense of anxiety over how long it was all taking. Not only was the 2nd RIR expected to arrive at Ytres imminently, meaning a final end to 7th RIR, more worryingly, there were clear indications that 36th (Ulster) Division was being prepared to take part in another major battle. The obvious signs of a new British offensive were all around. More and more fresh troops were arriving; the number of artillery batteries in the area grew daily; all around huge stockpiles of ammunition gathered. Yet most significant of all were the tanks. Unloaded from trains in great secrecy and then parked under the canopies of woods, 471 of these latest weapons of war had clearly been gathered there for a purpose. The reason was soon to become clear.

The Battle of Cambrai was to be the final, but arguably most important, British offensive of 1917. It was also one of the defining moments of the war. For the first time, the tactics were markedly different to what had previously been used, in that there was to be no lengthy bombardment to soften-up the German defences, no mines being detonated to signal the start, and no lines of exposed infantry marching slowly towards the enemy. Most importantly, there would be tanks.

The British had first used tanks in September 1916 during the Battle of the Somme. The results had been mostly disappointing. Far from being the war-winning weapon envisaged, these early versions had proved too unwieldy, too unreliable, and too few. Nevertheless, in 1917 they had featured in all of the British offensives to date, although on each occasion they had largely failed to live up to the promise. By October that year, there were many with serious doubts as to whether these crawling leviathans had any future at all on a modern battlefield.

Yet supporters of the tank continued to champion its cause. Pointing to the positives in their limited deployment to date, they had argued that given the right machines, the right conditions, and – most of all – the right numbers, tanks could be instrumental in breaking through even the strongest of enemy positions. To back these claims, the supporters put forward their plan for a limited offensive to breach one of the strongest parts of the Hindenburg Line and capture the German-held city of Cambrai. In virtually every respect, this latest plan was different. The offensive was to be a surprise, as there would be no preliminary bombardment to warn the enemy. The artillery would only start firing when the attack began, and then only at carefully chosen and marked targets. From the air, squadrons of planes would cooperate closely with the ground forces, bombing enemy strongpoints, and disrupting counter-attacks. Most importantly the tanks would lead the way, rather than operate in a supporting role. In unprecedented numbers, they would spearhead the offensive, while the infantry were to follow on behind to consolidate the captured positions. It was a ground-breaking proposition; remarkably, in mid-October, it was given the go ahead.

By this time, the massive British offensive at Ypres was toiling to its unsatisfactory conclusion. With no prospect of a decisive victory, and few limited territorial gains in return for lengthy casualty lists, Field Marshal Sir Douglas Haig was facing mounting criticism from home. The British Commander-in-Chief needed something to deflect it. A limited offensive, such as the one proposed for Cambrai, could be just the thing. On 13 October 1917 therefore, Haig had given the plan his approval, setting the challenging target of 20 November for the start. It meant the units taking part had less than six weeks to prepare. These were ambitious timescales – particularly given that with less than a week to go, some units were still arriving in the area.

One of the worst prepared for the forthcoming battle was undoubtedly the 2nd Battalion, Royal Irish Rifles. Up until the start of November, it had been miles away serving with the 25th Division near the town of Bethune. It only arrived at Ytres on 14 November – six days before the offensive was due to start. In that brief period, it had to absorb 500 new faces from the 7th RIR, including 100 or so Jerseymen hoping to hear at any minute the news they were going home. It was far from an auspicious prospect.

The 2nd Battalion of the Royal Irish Rifles was a 'Regular Army' unit, one of the two normally provided by the Regiment in peacetime. As such, it had been in the war since the beginning, and had gained an excellent fighting reputation. By then, however, like most other Irish battalions, it too was short of men, with little prospect of finding them at home. Amalgamation with another battalion was the answer, and as the senior unit, 2nd RIR would keep its identity. This took place on the very day 2nd RIR arrived in the camp at Ytres. By evening of 14 November 1917, the 7th Battalion of the Royal Irish Rifles had officially ceased to exist.

For the men of Jersey Company, the plan for amalgamation meant they at least remained together because the 500 men of 7th RIR transferred to their corresponding companies in 2nd RIR. Thus, the Jerseymen of 'D' Company 7th RIR became members of 'D' Company of 2nd RIR. There were, however, shortcomings. Within the ranks of 2nd RIR, there was no room for each man to resume his previous duties. One, for example, was Rifleman Jimmy Scoones. As a butcher by trade, he had served as part of the catering section in 7th RIR, putting his skills to good use. Yet within 2nd RIR, there was no place for another butcher.

On 19 November, Rifleman Scoones found himself amongst the ranks of the infantry once more, marching with helmet and rifle towards the front line. His hope, and those of the rest of the Jersey Company, to get back home before the latest offensive, had come to nothing. The War Office had considered the information passed on to them by Jersey's Lieutenant-Governor, but had been unable to decide the matter. Only the Commander-in-Chief of the British Army on the Western Front could agree to such a request. And Field Marshal Haig was far too busy at this time to consider the fate of 100 Jersey volunteers. His mind was focused on the latest British attempt to break through the German defences.

Just after dawn on 20 November 1917, the early morning peace in the countryside before Cambrai was shattered as over 1,000 British guns roared into life. From hundreds of concealed positions they unleashed a targeted bombardment of ferocious intensity onto unsuspecting German defences. While the stunned defenders cowered in their bunkers, hundreds of British tanks crawled out of the mist towards them. Moving at their top speed of four miles an hour, the thirty-ton monsters crossed no man's land and approached the Hindenburg Line. Crashing easily through the barbed wire belts they pushed through to the first line of German defences, with the British infantry following in their wake. Upon reaching the trenches, some tanks dropped in the specially constructed bundles of wood, or fascines, they had been carrying to form bridges, and, passing over, pressed on. Others turned to drive parallel to the trenches, spraying cannon and machine gun fire at any startled defenders who dared to emerge. Soon, a huge swathe of the first line defences of the Hindenburg Line was in British hands, and the tanks were pressing on to the second. Soon it too fell to the same tactics, as did the third line a short while later. It was an achievement on an unprecedented scale. At one of its strongest points, the previously unassailable Hindenburg Line had been broken and the tanks were rolling on into the open country beyond.

In Britain, there was great euphoria at the news. On the day following the opening of the offensive, church bells rang out across the country in celebration for the first time since the war had begun. After more than three years of fighting, and so many false dawns, there was at last a real hope of victory. The curse of trench warfare appeared to have been broken.

Yet the elation was premature. Despite the spectacular success of the first day, on the battlefield at Cambrai there were some worrying signs. Although there had been an improvement in the mechanical reliability and capability of the tanks, large numbers had still broken down or ended up ditched. What's more, here and there along the front, small pockets of German resistance had held up the advance, using artillery to destroy the tanks as they had approached. These factors had conspired to leave only half the number of tanks available at the start of the offensive ready to resume the attack on the second day.

Nevertheless, on 21 November the British advance continued, closing in on the objective, Cambrai. Yet with German resistance toughening there, and elsewhere along the front, the going was becoming harder. By nightfall, however, the fighting had reached the outskirts of the city. If the British had enough men available, one final push seemed enough to win through and secure victory. The problem was that by then fresh troops were in short supply. With the offensive only ever planned to be a limited affair, there were few reserves available to support the original attacking formations. Those that were, however, were to be committed on the third day of the battle.

One of the battalions in reserve during the first two days of fighting had been 2nd RIR. After absorbing the men of 7th RIR on 14 November, it had remained at Ytres for a few days while reorganisation was completed. On 20 November, when the battle started, 2nd RIR was stationed at the village the Hermies, just behind the original front line. With no part to play in the initial fighting, it moved up behind the advance, spending a wet and numbingly cold night in the old British front-line trenches. During the next day, the Battalion had moved northwards towards the village of Moeuvres, which remained stubbornly in enemy hands.

By the third day of the offensive, the continued German presence at Moeuvres, and in nearby Bourlon Wood, presented a considerable problem for the British. Situated on the flank of the thrust towards Cambrai, they needed capturing if the advance was to resume. During 22 November, 36th (Ulster) Division has tried, and failed, to take Moeuvres; on the next day, it would have to try again. Taking part this time would be 2nd RIR and its attached Jerseymen.

The little village of Moeuvres lay in a shallow valley running northwards from the main Bapaume to Cambrai road. The Germans had made it part of the Hindenburg Line, strongly fortifying both the village and the surrounding high ground. On the morning of 23 November, the 36th (Ulster) Division planned to attack both. Failure to take the high ground on the previous day left troops who had entered the village exposed to cross-fire and the threat of counter-attack. With the additional men of 2nd RIR available, the hope was to prevent this situation occurring again.

The bombardment of Moeuvres started at 9.00 a.m. on 23 November. Leading the attack on the village itself was the 12th Battalion of the Royal Irish Rifles. Advancing without tank support at 10.30 a.m., its men made steady progress up the valley towards

Moeuvres, while on either flank, other units attempted to clear the Germans from the surrounding high ground. Initially, there was encouraging success, but by 2.00 p.m., the attack on the village was showing signs of tiring. Sent forward to help were the fresh troops of 2nd RIR.

Most of the Battalion went to support the 12th RIR's assault on the village, which by now had succeeded in reaching the ruins. 'D' Company, with its Jersey contingent, had orders to attack a trench to the west of the Moeuvres, and work their way through to clear the high ground on that side. Soon, most of the village was in British hands, but to the west and east, the advance stalled. Despite its efforts, 'D' Company was unable to overcome stubborn German resistance, losing a number of men in the attempt. With dusk starting to fall, and considerable German reserves massing for an obvious counter-attack, the only remaining option was to order a retreat. By the end of the day, 2nd RIR was back where it had started the day.

The price of failure had been a high one. In total, 2nd RIR lost twenty-four men killed and just over 100 wounded. Among the dead were the Jersey Company's Lance Corporal Albert Le Feuvre and Riflemen Reginald Mauger and Joseph Moy. Among the wounded was Rifleman Jimmy Scoones. Having exchanged his butcher's knife for a bayonet, Scoones had taken part on the assault at Moeuvres. Gravely wounded in the chest, he ended up in a Casualty Clearing Station at the village of Grevillers. There, on 24 November, he died of his wounds. The letter of hope written just two weeks earlier turned out to be his last.

A few days after the failed attack on Moeuvres, the entire British offensive had petered out. In the end, the town of Cambrai had remained firmly in German hands. All that the British were left with was an awkward salient thrust deeply into the enemy line. After such a brilliant start, the result was immensely disappointing, both at the front and for those at home in Britain. On the positive side – and there were many positives from the battle – the British had at least demonstrated that the trench stalemate could be broken. They had at last brought together what ultimately was to prove the war-winning formula of weapons and tactics. On this occasion, however, there were too few reserves to hand and the tanks still suffered with reliability problems. They also were not fast enough to exploit any breakthough. In the offensive at Cambrai, this was supposed to have been the role of the cavalry, but they arrived too late to make a difference, being stopped by German bullets when an opportunity did arise.

Compounding the British shortcomings was the performance of the German Army. Notwithstanding the five dreadful months of casualties in the fighting at Ypres, it remained unbeaten and full of fight. In the face of the unexpected British offensive at Cambrai, it had shown remarkable resilience and character. Despite the initial heavy losses and considerable confusion, within a few days the Germans were fighting back. As the Jerseymen found out at Moeuvres, by 23 November, the enemy was capable of not only holding on, but launching counter-attacks as well.

Following the attack on Moeuvres, 2nd RIR had not taken any further part in the fighting, spending the last few days of the battle in reserve around the village of Hermies.

With the British decision to halt the offensive, 36th (Ulster) Division was ordered into reserve. On 29 November, 2nd RIR had marched back to Ytres, to board a train for the village of Simencourt south of the French town of Arras. There, in a rest camp, the tired and dishevelled men settled down for a well-earned rest. Unfortunately, it would not last for long.

As the British offensive had wound down, with great secrecy, the German commanders planned a major counter-offensive. The failed thrust on Cambrai had left a deep salient pushed into their lines; by attacking on either side, they hoped to pinch it out, and capture the thousands of British soldiers holding its tip. What's more, like the British before them, the Germans planned to use new weapons and tactics to ensure success.

Surprise was to be the key factor once again. Quietly and unnoticed, masses of German artillery and substantial infantry formations had moved into place. For the German attack however, with the exception of a few captured British examples, tanks were not part of the plan. In their place, the intention was to breach the British defences using groups of specially trained infantry, or stormtroops. Bypassing strongpoints, these heavily armed soldiers were trained to rapidly penetrate the enemy defences and push on towards the rear. Conventional infantry followed to consolidate and widen any breach, while the stormtroops drove forward again. On 30 November 1917, these new troops and tactics were put to the test for the first time on the Western Front.

Under the cover of a fortuitous early morning mist, the German counter-offensive at Cambrai had commenced. In common with the British attack ten days earlier, there had been immediate and striking success. South of Cambrai, the German attackers had torn a great hole in the British defences, and recaptured much of the ground lost a few days before. Turning north, the Germans hoped to complete the victory by sweeping behind the British troops around Cambrai. Standing in the way, however, were a few resolute British battalions. Among them was the 1st Battalion of the Royal Guernsey Light Infantry.

The Royal Guernsey Light Infantry had formed in Guernsey in 1916 when conscription had come into force. Its first real action had been in the opening attack of the Battle of Cambrai where, as part of the 29th Division, it had taken part in the attack and capture of the village of Marcoing. Remaining in the area during the days that followed, on 30 November it had hastily deployed with a number of others to halt the suprise German advance. For three days the Guernseymen valiantly resisted a number of heavy and sustained attacks, eventually helping gain the time needed for the British position to stabilise. But the price paid was a high one. By the end of the battle, the 1st RGLI had suffered over 500 casualties – enough to affect nearly every family in that island.

While the Guernseymen were fighting and dying in Marcoing, the outcome of the battle remained far from certain. For several days, the Germans continued in their attempt to break through the British lines, and cut off the salient. In response, the British rushed men and tanks back to the battlefield to help stem the onslaught. Among them were the tired men of 2nd RIR.

On 2 December, three days after the German counter-offensive started, the Jersey Company had arrived back at the front near Cambrai. Such was the rush to get them back there had been no time to organise transport. If the mood had been dark when the order arrived to abandon the rest camp, the thirty-mile march in wintry conditions could hardly have helped lighten it. Fortunately, by the time 2nd RIR returned, the worst of the crisis was over. Like the British before them, the Germans had been unable to sustain their offensive after a few days of fighting. A lack of reserves, together with the heroic defences of places such as Marcoing, had helped slow and eventually halt its momentum. The Germans too needed time to improve their capabilities and build up strength before trying again.

On 4 December, 2nd RIR went into the front-line trenches south of Cambrai on high ground overlooking the village of La Vacquerie. By then, the winter had set in, leaving the whole area covered in a thick blanket of snow. These conditions, together with a state of general exhaustion on both sides, limited the prospect of any further large-scale fighting in the area. Activity was limited to strengthening defences and sending out patrols to probe enemy positions. One of these patrols resulted in Jersey Company's final death of 1917. On 10 December, Corporal Archibald Weeks had been severely wounded while out in no man's land. Carried back by his brother Robert, the twenty-two-year-old, who in happier times had been one of the Company's pipers, died at a Casualty Clearing Station near the village of Rocquigny.

Four days after the loss of Corporal Weeks, 2nd RIR received orders to leave the front line. The crisis caused by the German counter-attack was over, and the 36th (Ulster) Division was to resume its period of rest and refitting. This time the location was near the French town of Doullens, in a camp next to the small village of Warlincourt. To everyone's great elation, it was learned that they would be spending Christmas there.

There was further good news for the remaining members of the Jersey Company. With the fighting at Cambrai finally over, it appears that Field Marshal Haig had found time to consider their request for a transfer home or to an English regiment. Unsurprisingly, the former was out of the question; even a small number of trained and experienced soldiers could not be lost on garrison duty. Haig, however, had looked favourably on the request for a transfer to another front-line regiment. The request could be considered if a suitable opportunity arose.

With spirits understandably higher, the Jersey Company survivors had settled down for their third Christmas at the front.

Ten

The Tigers

Many amongst us are now tired. To those I would say that victory will belong to the side which holds out the longest...

Field Marshal Sir Douglas Haig, Order of the Day, April 1918.

At the start of 1918, the British Army's Hampshire Regiment could look back with some pride on a long and illustrious history of service. With a lineage stretching back to 1702, it had seen action in most of the wars fought by the British Army since that date. These included a number of Indian campaigns during which the Regiment earned the unofficial title of the 'Tigers'. At the outbreak of war in 1914, it had set out to uphold that proud nickname. During the course of the next four years, the Tigers fought with distinction in virtually every theatre served by the British Army. By the First World War's end, it would have sent more than ten battalions for active service overseas, many of which contained a fair number of Jerseymen.

The proximity of the county of Hampshire to the island made it a natural choice for many young islanders seeking a military career. Over the years, the Regiment had welcomed many Jerseymen into its ranks. In February 1917, with the advent of conscription, the numbers involved rose considerably. When the British Army looked for somewhere to send its new Jersey recruits, the Hampshire Regiment was a natural choice for their training and eventual service overseas.

The British Army made another decision late in 1917 that would further cement the bond between the island and the Tigers. With the agreement that the surviving members of the Jersey Company could leave the Royal Irish Rifles, a new home was required for them. The one offered by the army was the Hampshire Regiment.

On 6 January 1918, in the French village of Gentelles, the Jersey Company had paraded as part of the Royal Irish Rifles for the very last time. There must have been a certain amount of emotion, and trepidation, associated with the occasion. Despite recent unhappiness, the Royal Irish Rifles had been their home by then for nearly three years. Yet with a brisk salute and firm handshakes for those remaining behind, the association ended. Ahead now, for most of the surviving Jerseymen, was a future with the 2nd Battalion of the Hampshire Regiment.

The 2nd Hants, as it shall be referred to from this point forward, had been one of the British Army's regular units at war's outbreak and fought more or less continuously since. Its most recent battle had also been at Cambrai in November 1917, fighting alongside the men of the Royal Guernsey Light Infantry as part of the renowned 29th Division. This action had taken a heavy toll however. On 9 January 1918, when the Jerseymen arrived, 2nd Hants was in reserve, still resting and refitting near St Omer after the losses of this latest campaign.

Most of the surviving Jersey Company men had chosen to transfer from 2nd RIR to 2nd Hants. The first group of sixty, led by Captain Cyril Ogier, arrived in January, with a further nine arriving in ones and twos during the weeks that followed. Although small in number, all were experienced soldiers, and two-year veterans of trench warfare. This would have made them most welcome; reinforcement drafts at this stage of the war usually consisted of eighteen-year-old boys, and family men approaching the age of forty. The newly arrived Jerseymen also included a number of highly experienced NCOs, including CSM Christian D'Authreau and CSM Helier Bree. One man, however, was conspicuous in his absence – the inspirational figure of RSM Jack Le Breton was no longer on the scene.

Le Breton had been struggling with his eyesight for some time. In the closing months of 1917, with the vision in one eye practically gone, the military authorities had decided that enough was enough. Despite strong protests, the order had come for the RSM to leave the front and move to a training role with a home-based battalion. His departure was a sorrowful moment for all. Only a few months before, while on leave in Jersey, he had reiterated his intention to remain with the Jersey Company to the very end. 'I left Jersey with the Jersey boys,' he had pledged, 'and if I am spared, I intend to come back with them.' Yet it was not to be; what remained of 'his boys' would have to go on without him.

During January 1918, those that did remain were swiftly incorporated into 2nd Hants – mostly as Privates now, rather than Riflemen. On joining the Battalion, Captain Ogier was given command of 'Z' Company (the Hampshire Regiment choosing to name its companies 'W', 'X', 'Y' and 'Z', rather than the Royal Irish Rifles' 'A', 'B', 'C' and 'D'). The rest of the men formed a single 'Jersey Platoon', which presumably was allocated to Ogier's command. What is not clear is whether any transfer of recently conscripted Jerseymen into 'Z' Company took place, in order to give it a wider Jersey identity. It seems unlikely however. By this stage of the war, the romantic ideal of small community-linked units had long since vanished. For good reasons, the army would not particularly have wanted to resurrect them.

Any romantic ideal associated with gallantly holding the Belgium town of Ypres against the German invader had also long gone by this time. The Ypres Salient was by now just another part of the front – and an exceptionally unappealing one. The battles of the last three years, and particularly the fighting in the final months of 1917, had turned it into a wasteland of death and destruction. So there must have been little joy among the newly-arrived Jerseymen to discover that the Ypres Salient would once again be their destination. On 18 January, nine days after the Jersey Company's arrival, 2nd Hants left for the front line there.

The location was to be the Goudberg sector in the tip of Salient, near to the infamous village of Passchendaele. It was a miserable spot, as one man gloomily recorded at the time:

> No one who had not seen this sector at the beginning of 1918, after the continuous fighting and bombardments of the previous summer and autumn, can conceive the scene of appalling desolation and destruction which the countryside afforded. It was almost an impossibility to dig trenches in that water-logged ground, so that approaches to the front line could only be made over duck-board tracks, many of which were fully visible to the enemy and in consequence by day were scarcely usable, and by night were under constant artillery and machine-gun fire.[2]

For the newly-arrived Jerseymen, the location and conditions had a depressingly familiar feel. The battlefield at Frezenberg, with its nightmarish memories of August 1917, was only a few miles away to the south. The only positive difference in January 1918 was that the level of military activity was considerably lower now that the British offensive was over. Yet even this would soon unfortunately be changing.

For the remainder of January, and much of February and March, 2nd Hants had remained near Ypres. Duties alternated between holding the front line and labouring duties working on a new line of defences then under construction close to the town itself. Right across the Western Front at this time the British were adding depth and complexity to their trench lines. There was a sense of nervousness in the air; a German offensive seemed likely in the next few months. For their part, the German played up the concerns as the weeks went by with increased shelling and strong trench raids.

On 11 March, after days of shelling and machine gun fire, 2nd Hants had to repel a major and very bruising German trench raid. Two days later, a heavy barrage of gas shells deluged the Battalion's positions, leaving forty-two men wounded and six dead. Among them was the first member of the Jersey Company killed since they had joined the Hampshire Regiment. At forty-two-years-old, Private Edward McLeod was the oldest of the Jersey Company to die when he passed away at an Australian Casualty Clearing Station from the effects of the gas.

A few days after the fatal gas attack, 2nd Hants had moved back to the town of Poperinghe for a rest – much to the delight of the men. 'The change was very pleasant', recorded the Battalion War Diary, 'and the men welcomed the cafés, estaminets and cinemas.'[3] The first signs of spring also helped lift the spirits. Yet on 21 March, the mood began to change. News has begun filtering through of another major offensive starting in France. Yet unlike most of those that had preceded it during the war, it was the German Army on the attack on this occasion. Even more disturbingly, unlike most of those earlier offensives, the Germans seemed to found the formula to break the deadlock of the trenches.

As the year 1918 started, there had been grounds for German optimism. On the eastern front, Imperial Russia, weakened by defeat in battle and revolutionary turmoil at home, had finally withdrawn from the war. In the Italy too, the Germans and their Austro-Hungarian allies had won a significant victory, employing new leaders and tactics to drive the Italian Army back to the gates of Venice. For the first time since 1914, Germany could focus most of its forces solely on the Western Front. After three years of stalemate, it seemed the German Army might have the means to win a decisive victory. For the Germans, that victory had to come soon.

Even as Russia was leaving the war, a new force was entering. Provoked by aggressive diplomatic and naval tactics, America had at last sided with the Allies and declared war on Germany. Given time, its manpower and industrial capacity would inevitably tip the balance of strength in favour of the Allies – and the Germans knew this. But America had entered the war in April 1917 with a small peacetime army and industry unprepared for wartime manufacturing. It would not really be in a position to contribute decisively until mid-1918 at the earliest.

Recognising this, the Germans had attacked on 21 March 1918 near the French town of St Quentin. At 5.00 a.m. that morning, a barrage of unprecedented fury crashed down on the British front line there, signalling the start of a five hour pounding. When it lifted, German troops had advanced using the stormtroop tactics tested at Cambrai. Helped by a thick early morning mist, they pushed quickly through advanced British positions, and on towards the main line of defence. By the end of the day, much of this was in German hands and the British Army was in full retreat back towards the River Somme.

At last, it seemed that one side had finally succeeded in really achieving the elusive breakthrough. For the next five days, the Germans drove the Allies back towards the city of Amiens, their relentless advance appearing to be unstoppable. In that moment of crisis, there was even talk among Allied leaders of falling back for a final defence of the Channel Ports and the French capital. Fortunately, wiser counsel had prevailed. The decision was taken to make a stand in front of Amiens, and British, French and Australian troops rushed to that city's defence. It was one of the decisive moments of the war. The Germans, tired and stretched after their unprecedented advance, encountered a thin but determined line of defenders around the village of Villers-Bretonneux. The fighting raged there for several days. Finally, unable to find a way through, the German assault slackened and then ceased. The Allies had won the battle for Amiens.

Any cause for celebration was premature. On 9 April, four days after fighting stopped near Amiens, the Germans struck again. The location this time was Flanders, near the British held town of Armentieres. With the defences weakened by the need to send troops to the fighting around Amiens, the Germans again achieved early success. Breaking through, they headed for the key supply hubs of Hazebrouck and Bailleul, and the Channel coast beyond. In desperation, the British began to rush units from other parts of the front to stem the advance. These would include the 29th Division.

The Jersey Company had remained in Belgium while these dramatic events had unfolded to the south. Yet news of the fighting had certainly filtered through – sometimes in the strangest of ways. On a number of occasions, enemy planes swooped low over the British trenches to drop bundles of newspapers containing details of German successes. Whether these were fully believed or not, it would have made worrying reading. After all the years of fighting and sacrifice, it seemed that for a time there was a real prospect of the Allies losing the war.

For the surviving members of the Jersey Company it must have been an anxious time. News of the Allied victory at Amiens had brought some relief, although the overall situation remained uncertain. For a few days, there must have been a hope that they had been lucky enough to avoid the battles in the south. That was up until 10 April, and the order to move to the French town of Bailleul to face the latest German offensive.

For 2nd Hants, the journey from Belgium to Bailleul was a short one. From Poperinghe, a fleet of former London buses ferried the Battalion the short distance to Bailleul where they disembarked. By mid-afternoon, the men were moving smartly to take up positions in the countryside to the east. All around, however, the situation was chaotic. The roads around Bailleul were choked with civilian refugees from the fighting, fleeing westward with whatever pitiful possessions they could carry. Among them were small knots of British soldiers, mostly bewildered and leaderless, intent on putting as much distance as possible between themselves and the enemy. To the east, the sky was filled with clouds of acrid black smoke. Towns and villages were burning – set on fire by German shells or by the deliberate destruction of British supply dumps. For men schooled only in the art of trench warfare, this was all something new. The German offensives meant that an open style of warfare had returned for the first time since 1914. The men were going to have to quickly learn new ways of fighting.

Captain Ogier's 'Z' Company was despatched to the tiny village of La Creche with orders to take up defensive positions there. The remainder of 2nd Hants were deployed nearby. The Germans were believed to have reached Steenwerck, a short distance away across the railway line that ran between Bailleul and Armentieres. As dusk fell, their presence was confirmed when shells began to fall on the Battalion's positions, killing one man. Private Harry Richards from St Helier had been wounded twice before, first at Loos in 1916 and then at Frezenberg the following year. Outside the village of La Creche on 10 April 1918, his luck finally ran out.

During the next day, German fire intensified. Casualties began rising significantly as the shells and machine gun fire caught men in lightly constructed defences. Nevertheless, the Battalion repulsed a strong German attack in the early evening, and managed to do the same on the following day.

The success was short lived. On 13 April, with adjacent units giving way under pressure, the only option for 2nd Hants was to retreat or risk being cut off by the German advance. At the start of 14 April, the entire British line had fallen back on Bailleul, with the Battalion taking up position on a winding ridge to the east of the town called the Ravensberg, or Ravelsberg in some accounts. There, 2nd Hants would make its stand.

The general situation around Bailleul, and elsewhere in the area, was critical. The Allied line was holding – but only just. If it gave way, the entire British position in Belgium – and indeed in the war – was under grave threat. Field Marshal Haig, in a remarkably frank and emotive Order of the Day on 11 April 1918, had appealed to the troops to hold fast:

> Many amongst us are now tired. To those I would say that victory will belong to the side which holds out the longest … There is no other course open to us but to fight it out! Every position must be held to the last man: there must be no retirement. With our backs to the wall, and believing in the justice of our cause, each one of us must fight on to the end.

Up on the Ravensberg Ridge, the men of the Jersey Company did just that. On 14 April, massed German attacks were unable to make progress in the face of resolute British defence. Three days later, another powerful assault was also held, with Captain Ogier singled out for special praise in the Battalion's War Diary:

> At 5.00p.m. the enemy again attacked, Captain Ogier who commanded the two support companies Y and Z forestalled a wavering in the front line by advancing his company and meeting the enemy in the front line. This action undoubtedly saved a breach in the line.
>
> Throughout operations Captain Ogier has greatly distinguished himself showing great powers of command and initiative. Unfortunately the services of this gallant officer will not be available in the near future as he received a bullet wound in his leg. He did not leave his company however till all was settled and dusk had fallen.[3]

For his actions that day, Ogier was to receive the Military Cross – one of the highest awards for bravery in the First World War. Yet the wounds he had sustained meant the end of his service with the Jersey Company. With his departure, the last of the original Jersey officers was now gone.

The fighting around Bailleul in April 1918 had also taken its toll of other ranks. 'When the remnants of the Company joined the Hampshires they were formed into a Jersey Platoon,' noted Harry Perks on 21 April, 'but now there were scarcely enough of them to form a Jersey Section.'[4] Although there had been no further deaths, there were a considerable number of men wounded, and one, Private John Keast, had been captured and made a prisoner of war. Once again, the war had bitten deep into the Jersey Company.

The only consolation was that the German offensive in Flanders, as at Amiens before, was finally running out of steam. But it remained a tight affair – Bailleul itself would eventually fall, along with Messines Ridge, Mount Kemmel and Locre to the north.

The British and French had held firm elsewhere, however, and forced the advance to a halt. The German generals then decided to turn their attention elsewhere. For the tired men of 2nd Hants, a semblance of normality could return.

At the end of April's fighting, the 29th Division took over a stretch of the front near the French town of Hazebrouck. There it would stay during May and most of June. As in the earlier part of 1918, it remained a period of nervous activity. The British were on the alert for further enemy offensives; the Germans wanted to maintain an aggressive posture here in the north. Small scale actions prevailed, leading to small scale losses that were painful nonetheless. One such action on 15 June at a location known as 'Fantasay Farm' claimed the life of Private Clarence Dorkins, at nineteen-years-old the youngest of the Jersey Company to die in action. Two days later, in the same area, shelling killed Privates Walter Hopkins and Chrles Fox, and possibly wounded Private Edward Machon at the same time. He would die in a Casualty Clearing Station at St Omer on 30 June.

The deaths of these four men came only days before 2nd Hants left the Hazebrouck area for a rest and training camp at the rear. Lumbres, near St Omer, was the location for another of the many army facilities dotting the Pas-de-Calais. There, during July, rebuilding and retraining had started with the aim of bringing the Battalion back up to strength and prepared for battles yet to come. It was obvious the nature of warfare was changing once more, and skills largely unused since 1914 now needed relearning. The German breakthroughs, and subsequent Allied counter-attacks, had driven the fighting out of the trenches and into the open once more. The Allies were determined to keep it there.

In August, 2nd Hants returned to Hazebrouck for another spell at the front there. By then the British were starting to push the Germans, seeking to drive them from the territory lost in April. It was a tough assignment; German determination to give up ground only after a fight led to a steady stream of casualties. Fighting near the village of Merris on 11 August led to the death of Private St Elmo Le Breton, one of the most renowned snipers in the Jersey Company. On 4 September, as 2nd Hants re-entered Belgium once more, Sergeant Osmand Touzel died in the push towards the important 'Hill 63' near Ploegsteert.

The day after Touzel's death, 2nd Hants left the front line once more for a camp in the rear. There, the Battalion was to begin preparations for an important forthcoming offensive. The tide of the war was turning. While the Jersey Company had been fighting its actions in the north that summer, momentous events further south had given the Allies the advantage. There were grand plans to exploit it.

With the failure of their April offensive in Flanders, at the end of May the Germans had looked elsewhere for victory. A growing American presence gave them little choice. The location this time had been the French positions to the east of Paris. On 27 May, a massive German assault struck unsuspecting French forces in the region of the Chemin Des Dames, and quickly rolled them back. Caught up in the advance were also a number of British divisions that had been sent south to recuperate after the recent fighting. They too were swept out of the way, as the Germans drove a deep bulge into the Allied line, and crossed the Marne River to threaten Paris itself. For a third time in as many months, the Germans seemed on the verge of victory.

Once again in the moment of crisis the Allies had considered retreat and a last ditch defence of the French capital. Yet once again, the Allied armies, now under the firm direction of Generalissimo Ferdinand Foch, rallied and the German offensive had stalled. Subsequent German attacks near Compiègne and on either side of the French city of Reims were unable to restart the advance. By now, the Germans had played their final card.

On 18 July, a secretly-assembled French and American force counter-attacked near Compiègne to send the surprised Germans reeling back. Then, on 8 August, a British Army under the command of General Sir Henry Rawlinson launched an offensive at Amiens. Before the day ended, Rawlinson had won a landmark victory. The battle succeeded in driving the Germans back over fifteen miles, and resulted in the capture of 30,000 German soldiers and 400 artillery pieces. Finally, after four long years of fighting, it seemed the Allies had managed to assemble and unleash a war-winning formula of guns, tanks, planes and infantry.

Over the next few weeks, they used it to drive back the exhausted and increasingly disillusioned Germans. By the middle of September, the line from which the Germans had originally launched their attack of in March 1918 had been reached, and the British were facing the formidable Hindenburg Line once more. There, despite the recent victories, Field Marshal Haig had paused. To assist with the assault on the Hindenburg Line, simultaneous Allied offensives would be launched to the north and south. One would be in Belgium, where a combined force of British, French and Belgian troops would open an offensive in front of Ypres. The date set was the 28 September. One of the formations scheduled to lead this assault was the 29th Division.

On 28 September 1918, at 5.30 a.m., British artillery all around Ypres opened up to herald the opening of the new offensive. Waiting tensely to the south-east of the town, near the village of Zillebeke, were 2nd Hants, with its attached Jerseymen now probably down to less than fifty in number. Behind the German front line, lay the strongpoints known as Stirling Castle, Glencorse Wood and Inverness Copse. During the 1917 offensive there, they had only fallen after heavy fighting and considerable loss. Nervously, the men of 29th Division wondered if it would be the same in September 1918.

After a while, the curtain of shell fire descending on German positions began to roll forward in what the 29th Division history described as a 'perfect' barrage. It was the signal for the infantry to advance, and cautiously, the men pushed toward the enemy line. In contrast to the previous year, resistance turned out to be mercifully weak. Under the intense artillery barrage, the German defences had crumbled. All along the front, it was largely the same story. At last, it appeared that the enemy's willingness to continue the fight was finally ebbing away. Having put so much into its earlier offensives, the German Army by then had no answer for Allied superiority in numbers, material and tactics. The war, while not yet over, looked to be moving towards its conclusion at last.

For the opening attack on 28 September, 2nd Hants had been in reserve, ready to move forward and to provide support as required. But no calls came during the morning, as the 29th Division sliced through the previously resolute lines of defence. By afternoon, the village of Gheluvelt and its important surrounding high ground had fallen. After that, 2nd Hants had moved up to take the lead in the advance that continued along the strategic Menin Road. By the end of that day, members of the Battalion were further forward in the Ypres Salient than any British soldier had been since November 1914. The cost for 2nd Hants had been four dead, two missing and thirty wounded – a remarkably low figure when contrasted with previous battles. Regrettably, for the Jersey Company, one of those killed was twenty-five-year-old Private William Johns.

During the next two days, the British advance had resumed. Heavy rain and stiffening resistance meant that the pace on 29 September slowed in comparison to the previous day, but progress continued nonetheless. On 30 September, after taking the village of Kruiseke, 2nd Hants pressed forward to the outskirts of Gheluwe, a large village strongly held by the Germans. After initial British patrols were driven back, a set piece attack involving several battalions, including 2nd Hants, was planned for the morning of 2 October.

Two of the Battalion's companies were to attack the village directly, while 'Z' Company with its remaining Jerseymen would follow up and consolidate. The fourth company remained in reserve. At 6.30a.m. that morning, British guns began targeting the village, using a mix of high-explosives and smoke shells to mask the attack. Half an hour later the assault began.

Called to action, the men of 'Z' Company worked their way forward towards the strongly defended cemetery on the east side of the village. A gallant rush cleared this position, capturing prisoners and two machine guns. But in the village itself, the attack stalled. The Battalion's War Diary noted that, 'throughout the morning the German machine gunners had proved obstinate and continued firing until surrounded'[5]. Indeed, counter-attacks were soon driving 2nd Hants and the other battalions back.

Although casualties from that day's fighting were fortunately light, the Jersey Company had suffered once more. Private Ernest Gosselin was a married man with four children back home in St Helier when he fell in the fighting at Gheluwe. Tragically, his family initially heard that he was missing, but believed wounded and captured by the Germans. Hope remained for another five months before the tragic news that he was actually dead finally came through.

The other man to lose his life that day was Sergeant Charles Laugeard, a former police officer from St Helier. His story is particularly poignant. Laugeard had a fine reputation because of his wartime achievements. Joining the Jersey Company as a Rifleman, he quickly rose to the rank of Sergeant through outstanding service. Wounded in the attack on Ginchy in September 1916, Laugeard had won the Distinguished Conduct Medal for bravery in the same action. In October 1917, he survived injuries resulting from a prematurely exploding hand grenade whilst serving as a military instructor in Ireland. On his recovery, he returned to the Jersey Company, now with the Hampshire Regiment, and had taken part in the fighting throughout 1918. Just before his death, the Sergeant had returned to Jersey and married Lillian, the widow of another serving police officer killed in action in 1917. With Laugeard's death on 2 October, she was widowed by the war for a second time.

Perhaps most tragic of all, however, was that these two deaths had occurred so close to the end of the war. They were to be the Jersey Company's last losses in action. Peace was now only a few weeks away.

For 2nd Hants, two weeks of rest had followed the fighting at Gheluwe. When the Battalion did return to the front, the Allied advance in Belgium had reached the villages of Moorsele and Gullegem on the outskirts of the large town of Courtrai. There, between 14 October and 19 October, the Battalion took part in a series of attacks driving the Germans further east. In one of them on 14 October, Lance Corporal Harold Battam won the Military Medal for leading his section forward to capture a German machine gun. It was to be last award for bravery won by the Jersey Company. The fighting at Courtrai also proved to be the last of its battles. On 19 October, 2nd Hants was relieved and marched back to rest at the village of Staceghem.

By 11 November, 2nd Hants had returned to the front and was preparing to advance once more. At 10.00 a.m. that morning, however, an officer on a horse brought tremendous news. An armistice ending the war had been signed.

At 11.00 a.m. on 11 November 1918, the First World War finally ended. With its armies in retreat and revolution breaking out at home, Germany had finally conceded defeat and asked the Allies for an armistice to end the fighting. In a railway carriage near the French city of Compiègne, the armistice was signed. After four years of conflict, in Belgium, and everywhere along the Western Front, peace could reign once more.

Eleven

Till the Last Man

The contingent was a purposeful band; the flower of the population who had set out to their duty to King and country. It was high adventure; it made island history; it brought lustre to their homeland. It also brought a good modicum of personal sorrows.

General Sir James Steele, Former Commander of the Jersey Company, 1965

News of the armistice arrived in Jersey on the same day that it came into force in France and Belgium. Although speculation had been rife for a number of days, the official announcement on 11 November had been the signal for a spontaneous outbreak of noisy celebration.

In St Helier, people left their homes and places of work to pour out onto the streets. Church bells were soon ringing out across the town, while from the harbour came the brazen sound of blasting ship's horns. Bunting – not seen for years – appeared in great quantities, and before long it bedecked buildings across the town in red, white and blue. To the cheers of the crowd, the signal station on Fort Regent high above St Helier quickly ran up the same colours; while from its masts' flags proclaimed an end to the war. The festivities went on all day and into the night. It was as though, as one newspaper claimed, 'simultaneously the whole town seemed to awaken as if from a lethargy[1].'

Yet the war's end also brought the terrible toll it had exacted sharply into focus. Even in the midst of the celebrations, tragic news of those men killed and wounded in the final days of the war continued to arrive. In due course, a more sombre and respectful atmosphere rightly displaced the initial mood of jubilation. The cost of victory had been a prohibitively high one; respectfully, Jersey set about the task of commemorating its fallen, and ensuring their sacrifice was not forgotten.

Away from the Island, many of those who had fought for victory and managed to survive were also anxious to not be forgotten. As volunteers or conscripts, they had signed up for the duration of the war – now that it was over most of them simply wanted to return home. The British government and army, however, were not necessarily in a hurry to let them leave. Demobilisation – the act of returning soldiers to civilian life – needed careful management. Simply releasing millions of men into the community could result in all manner of problems. What's more, although the fighting may have now been over, there remained military duties to complete. In fact, as the dust settled on the armistice, the last members of the Jersey Company found themselves marching further away from their island, rather back than towards it.

Under the terms of the recently-signed armistice, Germany had been given just one month to withdraw its army from France, Belgium and Luxembourg. It also had to give up the disputed provinces of Alsace and Lorraine, taken from France forty-seven earlier. Furthermore, pending the signing of a final peace settlement, the Allies would establish a number of military zones of occupation in Germany's Rhineland. The purpose of these was to prevent the defeated enemy reorganising behind the great river and posing a threat once more. In mid-November 1918, a newly formed British Army of Occupation set off to garrison them. One of the units chosen to lead the way was the 29th Division.

Since the armistice, 2nd Hants had been waiting in Belgium around thirty miles from Brussels, near the village of Lessines. On 18 November, it was time to move once more, this time on the march to Germany. Within the Battalion was the last remnant of the Jersey Company, now perhaps twenty men strong. For the next three weeks, this small band marched eastward, first through a welcoming, cheering Belgium, and then into an unreceptive, sullen Germany. The weather *en route* had been atrocious, dampening any initial spirit of excitement they may have felt as a conquering army. Finally, on 9 December, they reached the great Rhine city of Cologne and pushed on over the river for a few miles before halting. The 29th Division had reached the end of its road; the victorious British Army had advanced as far as it was going to in this war, and with that, the job of occupation began.

For the occupying soldiers, any lingering excitement present on arrival in Germany had quickly faded away. Their life on guard was a tedious one, still subject to military rules and regulations and restricted by a rigid code of anti-fraternisation. Most were soon longing to go home.

A number of the Jersey Company men felt they certainly had a special case for an early release. In early December, they wrote an open letter to the *Evening Post* to press their claim:

> Dear Sir
>
> Would you kindly insert this letter in your widely circulated paper on behalf of the Jersey boys who are left of the Jersey contingent? We are thinking something should be done to get us back to Jersey, after what we have gone through. And as we all want to get back as soon as possible. No one seems to care now what becomes of us. It is time someone looked into the matter....[2]

Some felt the delay was yet further evidence of the island reneging on its promises to the volunteers. 'We were given to understand on joining,' wrote Corporal Harry Perks, 'that immediately the fighting was finished we were to be returned to our homes...'[3]

Unfortunately, for Corporal Perks, and the other Jersey Company men with 2nd Hants in Germany or elsewhere with the army, no immediate help was forthcoming. Having long since given up any control over its contingent, the island's authorities could not now intervene on their behalf. The Jerseymen remained under the control of the British Army; they would just have to wait for demobilisation like everyone else.

Yet while the serving soldiers grumbled about their fate, within weeks of the war ending one group of former Jersey Company men had returned to the island. With the end of the war, the thousands of prisoners of war in Germany had been released and sent home. In December 1918, those members of the Jersey Company captured at Messines Ridge, Frezenberg, or in the final year of fighting, had arrived back on the island for a heroes' welcome. Despite the deprived conditions of their captivity, their families were relieved to find them largely in good health.

The same was not necessarily true for another group of returned former Jersey Company men. During the course of the war, around 100 of the volunteers had suffered a serious wound or injury. Unable to resume active service, they had been cared for by the army until well enough for discharge back to civilian life. By December 1918, many of them had returned home to Jersey. Some bore obvious physical evidence of their experience, having lost limbs or sight, or been left terribly scarred in some way. Others appeared less obviously affected, yet remained debilitated nonetheless by the effects of gas, shell shock or exposure. In the years to come, the war would continue to take its toll on these men, with most experiencing continued ill-health and, in many cases, a premature death.

The war had also continued to take its toll on former Jersey Company men during 1918. In May that year, Rifleman Louis Le Claire died while with Royal Irish Rifles Depot Battalion and former Rifleman Frank Lunn had been killed in action while serving as a Lieutenant in the King's Liverpool Regiment. In October, ex-CSM Thomas Whittle died in Jersey having been discharged following wounding at Guillemont in September 1916. Finally, in November Private Peter Bonny, by then serving with the Royal Engineers, died of illness in France. When Private William Remy died in a train crash near Amiens early in 1919, the total number of Jersey Company men who had lost their life since March 1915 reached eighty. This number meant that a shocking 25 per cent of the 326 men who joined the Jersey Company had died during or immediately after the war. The corresponding figure for Jersey as a whole was around 15 per cent, while that for Britain was 13 per cent.

Rational reasons can of course be found for this disproportionately high number of deaths among members of the Jersey Company. As a small unit from the same community more or less continuously at the front for three years, it was bound to run the risk of casualties that were higher than average. Furthermore, without any reinforcements, the original group of volunteers had to bear all of the losses. Yet while these reasons can explain the high losses, a further, less rational factor may have also contributed.

From its very beginning, the Jersey Company had something to prove. A difficult start, followed by a questionable future and finally a sense of abandonment may have contributed to its members trying that bit harder. Fiercely proud of their small unit, and the island they represented, the men may have felt the need to risk more in order to demonstrate their commitment and bravery. Certainly, the haul of medals won by Jersey Company members suggests a higher than average performance. By the end of the war, they had won two Military Crosses, two Distinguished Conduct Medals, two French Medaille Militaire, one Belgian Croix De Guerre and no less than fifteen Military Medals. It meant that 7 per cent of the Jersey Company won a medal for bravery, compared to 3 per cent for the island as a whole.

The Jersey Company had also won a great deal of admiration among those with whom they had served during the war. Throughout their time in Ireland, in England and at the front, they had consistently received glowing reports from superiors and peers. One letter, written at the end of the war by their former 7th RIR Commanding Officer, Lieutenant Colonel Francis, summed these feelings up:

> Sir,
>
> Now that the war is over, I should like to bring to your notice the splendid services rendered by the Company of Jerseymen attached to the 7th Battalion, Royal Irish Rifles. As commanding officer of that Battalion during that period, I wish to express my admiration and appreciation of the behaviour and devotion to duty of the Jersey Company.
>
> At the Battle of the Somme, at Wytschaete and at Ypres, as well as for long periods in the trenches, they bore themselves as brave, well-disciplined soldiers who will be remembered with affection by all who had the honour to serve with them.[4]

At a special sitting of the States of Jersey in July 1919, this letter was read out. The States had convened on that occasion to pass a special act acknowledging the contribution made by Jersey's servicemen during the course of war. To their credit, the politicians singled out the Jersey Company for a special mention:

> The States have unanimously and with acclamation decided to pass an Act recording their gratitude to the officers, non-commissioned officers and men of the Jersey contingent who, as soon as permission was granted, offered their services for the fighting forces... The States note with pride the flattering eulogies which the services of the contingent and of other Jerseymen on service have constantly evoked...[5]

Perhaps it was a belated act of support; something the Jersey Company could have done more with in the dark days of 1917.

It was not until well into 1919 that most of the remaining members of the Jersey Company returned to Jersey. In ones and twos, they had arrived alongside the quays of St Helier's harbour and stepped ashore. Four years had passed since they had left from the same place, and the difference was marked. There were no bands or dignitaries on this occasion, or cheering crowds with waving banners. As they landed, some perhaps cast wistful glances across to the New North Quay from where they had departed so magnificently in March 1915, and reflected how different things were now.

Jersey as a whole, in fact, was a different place to that they had left four years earlier. Much may have looked the same, but the war had deeply affected the small island community, and it would go on doing so in the years to come.

The most obvious sign was the impact on the island's male population. Jersey had sent more than 6,000 men to fight in overseas in the British armed forces, and over 2,000 more in those of the French. Furthermore, hundreds of sons of Jersey families had joined the armies of Australia, Canada, New Zealand and South Africa, and seen active service across the world. Official figures put the number of those who died at 862 in the British and Dominion forces, and 264 in the French. Yet even these grim figures are undoubtedly too low. Recent research puts the number of Jerseymen killed by the First World War in excess of 1,200.[6] The number of men wounded would have been many times that figure. Yet if the most immediate and outward sign of the impact on Jersey was the casualty list of dead and wounded, below the surface more subtle effects were taking shape. One of the most important was the changing role of women.

The war had forced island society to reconsider traditional attitudes on the role of women. With so many men taken to serve in the armed forces, the only option in many cases had been to use women to fill the gaps left in the workforce. As the war progressed, the island's shops, offices, transportation and even some farms turned to women as their prime source of labour. Furthermore, in their own right, a number of women had left the island to work in Britain's munitions industry, or to serve as nurses for both military and civilian patients. Even in the home, wives and daughters had needed carry out the household duties so long the preserve of men. These changes – almost unimaginable prior to the war – could not be turned back in 1919. In that year, women in Jersey became entitled to vote for the first time. Four years later, in 1924, they became eligible to stand for the States.

The war has also changed another bastion of Jersey society for good. The Jersey Militia, so much an integral part of pre-war island life, somehow seemed less relevant now that the conflict had ended. In the new world of tanks, submarines and aeroplanes, the value of a part-time lightly armed force was questionable. After some debate, however, the Militia was reconstituted in 1921, although by then reduced to a single infantry battalion – initially under the command of the Jersey Company's Lieutenant Colonel Stocker. Eight years later, in 1929, it changed again, this time to an all-voluntary service and consisted of a company of only 260 men – less than one tenth of the number available in 1914.

The immediate aftermath of the war also saw a rise in unemployment and social unease as the returning soldiers attempted to fit back into island life. The thousands of demobilised men needed work, and the authorities had attempted to create jobs wherever possible. Yet in the austere post-war world, it has simply not been possible to provide something for everyone. Many disillusioned ex-soldiers were forced to seek handouts in order to make ends meet. To help, a number of ex-servicemen organisations had soon sprung up. One of the earliest formed was the Original Jersey Overseas Contingent Association.

A number of former Jersey Company NCOs conceived the idea of a Contingent Association. Formed in 1919, it offered not only a chance to socialise with former comrades-in-arms once more, but also practical and financial support. Within the governing rules its purpose had been enshrined: it would exist for the 'good comradeship and mutual benefit' of the members. In a bold resolution, it was agreed the association would continue 'till the last man'. Meetings were held quarterly, with an Annual General Meeting held each November to coincide with the newly established Armistice Day commemorations.

To lead the Contingent Association, many of the men who had led the Jersey Company during the war came forward. Colonel Stocker was the Honorary President, ex-CQMS Oscar Williams the President. Ex-RSM Jack Le Breton, Ex-CSM Helier Bree and ex-CSM Chris D'Authreau also had committee roles. Under this auspicious and respected leadership, the association had thrived. As well as the regular meetings, the membership took pride of place on the island's annual Armistice Day commemoration ceremonies. Overseas visits were also organised. The first major one came in 1926 when Lieutenant Colonel Stocker led a delegation to the unveiling of memorials to the 16th (Irish) Division in Guillemont and Wytschaete.

For Stocker in particular, the Contingent Association appears to have been his opportunity to remain active in the welfare of his former charges. During the years that followed the war, he took a special interest in the men and their families, together with the relatives of the fallen. Deeply affected by his wartime experiences, Stocker clearly felt obligated to the men he had led away from the island in 1915, especially in view of how many had not returned – and of those still dying.

The war had continued to claim its victims long after the guns had fallen silent. Thousands on the island harboured the scars of old wounds, the legacy of gas and the trauma of shell-shock. They continued to suffer, periodically or continuously, and for some it meant an early death. Among them were a number of former Jersey Company men, including the man who in 1918 had led them into the Hampshire Regiment. Cyril Ogier had been wounded three times in the course of the war, the last time being in April 1918 during the fighting near Bailleul. The ex-Captain never fully recovered, and his subsequent years were passed in hospitals and nursing homes. Despite care, and several operations, Ogier had continued to suffer chronic head pains due to his wounds. By 1937, this continued ill-health proved too much, and in April he died aged just forty-three. At his funeral in Jersey, the Contingent Association provided an honour guard to escort the coffin of their popular former commander to his final resting place.

In 1939, war broke out in Europe once again. Despite the claim that the Great War had been the war to end all wars, Britain (and Jersey) found itself in conflict with Germany once more. Contrary to many predictions, however, the Second World War bore little resemblance to the First.

When the Germans attacked France and Belgium (and Holland for good measure) in May 1940 there was to be no miraculous victory on the Marne, no last ditch defence outside Amiens. Within six weeks, France, Belgium and Holland were beaten, and Britain bundled back across the Channel from Dunkirk. This was not destined to be a war in the trenches: tanks, aircraft and rapidly increasing mechanisation had seen to that.

By the end of June 1940, the German Army had reached the French coast opposite the Channel Islands. Recognising the futility of trying to defend Jersey in the face of an overwhelmingly superior force, the British ordered the island demilitarised and the 200 or so men of the Jersey Militia left for England. Unlike their forebears, however, they would never see action as a united unit; the lesson of community-based units remained from the last war. There was to be no Jersey Company in this second great conflict of the twentieth century.

On 28 June, German planes had bombed and machine-gunned Jersey and Guernsey. Three days later, on 1 July 1940, a disarmed and unprotected Jersey surrendered and allowed German troops to begin an occupation. For those left behind in Jersey, there would be five long years of occupation to endure. It was to be a traumatic and humiliating time. For the ex-servicemen of the First World War among the population it must have also been a time of great bitterness. Having endured the horrors of the trenches and watched comrades die in the name of freedom, seeing a German military band marching through the streets of St Helier would have been a devastating blow.

Someone who felt it especially deeply was Colonel Stocker. Not only were the Germans on his island, but early in the occupation they had forced him from his home which overlooked a strategically important bay. Undaunted, he continued to work for the welfare of ex-soldiers – although the death of his wife Louisa in February 1941 had drained much his remaining enthusiasm and energy. Perhaps her passing lay heavily on his mind when he left the offices of the British Legion in St Helier's Hill Street on the afternoon of 27 May 1941. Stepping into the road, a passing car hit the seventy-five-year-old and knocked him down. Never regaining consciousness, Stocker died that evening at the island's General Hospital. Ironically, the driver of the car was a German soldier.

Walter Stocker's death was deeply felt on the island. His service with the Militia, the Jersey Company, and post-war as president of numerous clubs and associations, had made him a well-known and popular figure. A huge crowd assembled for his funeral at St Helier's Town Church, the Germans being remarkably (yet perhaps understandably) benevolent towards the gathering. They had even allowed Stocker's coffin to be draped with a British flag for its journey to St Saviour's churchyard. The Jersey Company was strongly represented with fifty ex-members present. At the graveyard, four ex-NCOs under Jack Le Breton bore their former commander's coffin to its final resting place. It was their final act of homage for a man so highly esteemed by those that he led.

Jersey endured German occupation for five long years. Bypassed and isolated by the Allied occupation of the nearby French coast, islanders had to wait until the very end of the war in Europe for their liberation. Yet when the joyous feelings of regained freedom had subsided, they found their island changed forever by this latest war. Massive concrete walls and bunkers now ringed the coast; many buildings had been damaged or demolished; leafy valleys had tunnels blasted into their sides. The people of the island had changed too. Confinements, deportations, isolation and near-starvation had left a deep and collective sense of trauma. It was understandable then that the Second World War became the defining moment on the island's modern history. The sacrifices of the First World War – while not quite forgotten – had been overshadowed forever.

Nevertheless, and perhaps due to this change, the Contingent Association was reformed with a renewed vigour at the end of the Second World War. Much of the drive came then from some of the Jersey Company's younger members. In particular, from ex-Rifleman Arthur Durell, a veteran of both the Royal Irish Rifles and the Hampshire Regiment, who became the Association's President. One of his first steps was to re-establish links with the Jersey Company's old regiment – although technically at least, it no longer existed.

The years following the First World War had witnessed tremendous upheavals in Ireland. They led to the partitioning of the country, into the Irish Republic and the separate country of Northern Ireland. The change meant the disbandment of many of the old Irish regiments of the British Army, including the Royal Dublin Fusiliers and Royal Irish Regiment. The Royal Irish Rifles remained, but in reflection of the changes, had been renamed the Royal Ulster Rifles. Nevertheless, the regiment and its veterans associations warmly welcomed their former comrades-in-arms from Jersey.

Through the connection, the former Jersey Company members were reunited with one of their old commanding officers. Captain James Steele, who had taken over when Stocker had fallen ill in July 1916, was by then a retired Major General in the British Army. In the 1950s and 1960s, he visited Jersey on numerous occasions to be present at the Contingent Association's annual dinner. During one visit, in 1961, the General had unveiled a small plaque at the parish church of Grouville commemorating the Jersey Company. In a speech, Steele summed up what he thought of his former soldiers. They were 'a purposeful band,' he stated, 'the flower of the population who had set out to do their duty to their king and country. It was high adventure; it made island history; it brought lustre to their homeland. It also brought a good modicum of personal sorrows'.[7]

By the late 1970s, time had almost caught up on this purposeful band. Most, including ex-RSM Jack Le Breton had passed away by then. Le Breton had died in 1970, aged eighty-six, by then awarded an MBE for his services to the island to go with his medals for bravery. In November 1979, the last five surviving former Jersey Company members agreed to hold a final reunion dinner. In the presence of the island's Bailiff and other dignitaries, the Contingent Association was formerly brought to an end.

It was not quite the end. During the next few years the dwindling little group of survivors were fêted at specially arranged lunches and events. It was almost as though the island's government was trying to put right the injustices of so many years before. Yet it could not go on forever. With the death of Arthur Durell in 1988, only the 'last man' remained.

Ex-Sergeant Bert Tostevin had left Jersey with Jersey Company in March 1915 as a young man of twenty. He had enjoyed the delights of an Irish summer in County Cork, endured the monotony of Aldershot, and learned the lessons in the trenches of Loos. He had been wounded there in June, and again at Guillemont/Ginchy in September of that year. Recovering, he was hit once more during the terrible fighting at Frezenberg in August 1917. Finally, during the advance to victory in October 1918, he received his fourth and final wound of the war. He seems to have made a remarkable recovery from them all.

In January 1995, Bert Tostevin reached the remarkable age of 100. A few days later, he died. After eighty years in existence, the final page in the story of the Jersey Company had been written.

The Proudest Day in Our History?

Sergeant Charles Laugeard, DCM, today lies buried in a British war cemetery on the outskirts of the Belgium town of Ypres, or Ieper as it is now called. He is in good company; more than 1,000 other fallen soldiers rest with him in this oasis of beauty and tranquillity, sandwiched between a gently flowing canal and a busy main road. For a visitor today, it is impossible to imagine the same place on that day more than ninety years ago when Sergeant Laugeard was first brought here. The dugouts, wire, shell craters and trenches have all long since been cleared or filled in.

The same is true for virtually all of the old Western Front. For the most part, the only tangible evidence that it ever existed is the ribbon of memorials and cemeteries that follow its former course. Like the one in which Sergeant Laugeard lies, the Commonwealth War Graves Commission maintains these cemeteries in wonderful condition, honouring in perpetuity the memory of those they hold. In some lie the fallen of the Jersey Company, with the largest concentrations understandably being around Loos, Kemmel and Ypres. Other members are to be found elsewhere in France and Belgium, and in Ireland, England, Germany and Jersey. An almost equal number of the Jersey Company dead are to be found only as names carved into the panels of the great memorials to the missing of the Somme, Ypres and Cambrai; the violence and confusion of battle having denied them the dignity of a marked grave. On neither grave nor panel, however, is there any indication that these men were once members of the Jersey Company. They rest today under the names or badges of the Royal Irish Rifles or Hampshire Regiment or one of the other units to whom they eventually were attached.

In March 1915, the *Evening Post* described the departure of the Jersey Company as the proudest day in our history. Yet, at the time of writing, there is little to recall that event, or the deeds that followed, or even the Jersey Company itself. The names of the Jersey Company fallen do appear individually on the island's roll of honour, while many are also inscribed on the parish and community memorials erected directly after the war. The parish church of Grouville has a memorial tablet that commemorates those who served in 'D' Company, 7th Battalion Royal Irish Rifles, and a book of remembrance that contains most of their names. To its absolute credit, this parish also continues to hold an annual dinner around Remembrance Day to honour the memory of the volunteers. Both the tablet and dinner are legacies of the last President of the Contingent Association, Arthur Durell, and his long association with the parish, and long may both continue.

Elsewhere on the island, Jersey's First World War is largely forgotten. Due honour is of course given to its dead, but in contrast to the Second World War which continues to this day to inspire new memorials and ceremonies, the deeds of the earlier conflict are forgotten. Perhaps this is for the best; the last of those who lived in that time will soon be gone, while those who left Jersey to fight in the First World War are no longer with us. Yet it seems a shame we only commemorate their memory, and not the deeds and actions of their youth.

Could this book be the start of a resurrection?

Endnotes

Chapter One

1   Men Whom I Have Known, *Evening Post*, 6 January 1914
2   The Shadow of a Great War, *Evening Post*, 30 July 1914
3   The Mobilisation, *Evening Post*, 31 July 1914
4   The War, *Evening Post*, 3 August 1914
5   How Jersey Stands, *Evening Post*, 5 August 1914

Chapter Two

1   The Duty of Citizenship, *Evening Post*, 14 September 1914
2   Armchair Reflections, *Morning News*, 17 September 1914
3   D/AP/R/13/37, Jersey Archive
4   D/AP/R/13/37, Jersey Archive
5   Will the Militia Go to the Front, *Morning News*, 7 October 1914
6   Soldiers & Sailors Club at Prince of Wales Rooms, *Evening Post*, 5 October 1914
7   Notes and Queries, *Evening Post*, 15 October 1914
8   Jersey's Chance, *Morning News*, 5 December 1914
9   The States, *Evening Post*, 15 December 1914
10   The States, *Evening Post*, 15 December 1914
11   A Jersey Girl's Appeal, *Morning News*, 9 December 1914
12   Editorial, *Evening Post*, 20 December 1914
13   'To Strike a Blow for the World's Freedom', *Evening Post*, 7 December 1914
14   Guernsey's Volunteers, *Evening Post*, 15 January 1915
15   Editorial, *Evening Post*, 6 January 1915
16   Departure of the Jersey Contingent, *Morning News*, 2 March 1915
17   The Proudest Day in Our History, *Evening Post*, 2 March 1915
18   *Ibid.*

Chapter Three

1   With the Jersey Boys in Ireland, *Morning News*, 3 June 1915
2   Interesting Letters from the Jersey Contingent, *Evening Post*, 8 March 1915
3   *Ibid.*
4   *Ibid.*
5   The Jersey Contingent, *Morning News*, 19 March 1915
6   Analysis based on evaluation of available records. These include information held by the Jersey and National Archives, Commonwealth War Grave Commission, National Census, *Evening Post* and *Morning News*.
7   The Camp Flag for the Jersey Contingent, *Evening Post*, 12 March 1915
8   Our Lads in Ireland, *Morning News*, 5 April 1915

9   General Sir James Steele, *60th Anniversary of the Original Jersey Overseas Contingent Association* (Royal Ulster Rifles Museum Library, File M143)
10   Our Lads in Ireland, *Morning News*, 5 April 1915
11   *Ibid.*
12   *Ibid.*
13   Our Lads in Ireland, *Morning News*, 3 April 1915
14   With the Jersey Boys in Ireland, *Morning News*, 13 July 1915
15   Letter, *Evening Post*, 17 December 1915
16   With the Jersey Boys in Ireland, *Morning News*, 13 July 1915
17   With the Jersey Boys in Ireland, *Morning News*, 11 August 1915
18   General's High Praise of Jersey Company, *Evening Post*, 12 August 1915

Chapter Four
1   General's High Praise of Jersey Company, *Evening Post*, 13 August 1915
2   Jersey and its Contingent, *Morning News*, 13 August 1915
3   *Ibid.*
4   *Morning News*, April 10 1915
5   Opening of Recruitment Rally in Jersey, *Evening Post,* 6 October 1915
6   Author's analysis of newspaper reports on recruitment results in October and November 1915
7   An Appeal From Ireland, *Evening Post*, August 12 1915
8   Author's analysis based on official island and national records, memorial lists and newspaper reports. See Appendix One for details.
9   With the Jersey Boys, *Morning News*, 21 September 1915
10   *Ibid.*
11   With the Jersey Boys, *Morning News*, 13 October 1915
12   *Ibid.*
13   With the Jersey Boys, *Morning News*, 29 October 1915
14   With the Jersey Boys, *Morning News*, 4 January 1916
15   *Morning News*, 3 December 1915
17   Jersey's Gift to the Jersey Contingent, *Morning News*, 20 December 1915
18   Letter, *The Evening Post*, 21 January 1916
19   With the Jersey Boys, *Morning News*, 4 January 1916

Chapter Five
1   With Our Jersey Boys, *Morning News*, 25 January 1916
2   With Our Jersey Boys, *Morning News*, 18 February 1916
3   With Our Jersey Boys, *Morning News*, 25 January 1916
4   With Our Jersey Boys, *Morning News* 27 January 1916
5   With the Jersey Contingent, *Evening Post*, 17 February 1916
6   *Ibid.*
7   Armchair Reflections, *Morning News*, 11 January 1916
8   With Our Jersey Boys, *Morning News*, 14 March 1916
9   *Ibid.*
10   The Late L.B. Hibbs, *Evening Post*, 27 March 1916
11   MN Readers and the Jersey Boys, *Morning News*, 12 April 1916
12   National Archive, WO95/1972 48th Brigade HQ, December 1915 – December 1916

Chapter Six
1   Walker, G.A.C, *The Book of the 7th Royal Inniskilling Fusiliers. From Tipperary to Ypres,* Page 66. (The Naval & Military Press [www,naval-military-press.com])
2   *Ibid.*

3   Letter, *Evening Post*, November 8, 1916
4   *Ibid.*
5   Fielding, R. *War Letters to a Wife: France and Flanders, 1915-1919*, Page 70(Spellmount, 2001)
6   Houseman L, *War Letters from a Fallen Englishman*, Page 168 (1930)
7   Presentation to a Jersey Police Constable DCM, *Evening Post*, 2 January 1917. (Note: the actual report names the village as Givenchy, but this clearly is a mistake in that the Jersey Company never fought near this town.)
8   National Archive, WO95/1975 War Diary 7th Royal Irish Rifles

Chapter Seven
1   With the Jersey Company, *Evening Post*, 10 October 1916
2   States of the Island of Jersey, Roll of Honour 1914-1919,1919
3   With Our Jersey Boys, *Morning News*, 1 May 1916
4   Ibid.
5   With Our Jersey Boys, *Morning News*, 29 April 1916
6   From One of the Jersey Boys, *Evening Post*, 24 October 1916
7   A Call From the Trenches, *Evening Post*, 27 July 1916
8   Fielding, R. *War Letters to a Wife: France and Flanders, 1915-1919*, Page 94 (Spellmount, 2001)

Chapter Eight
1   The Roll of Honour, *Evening Post*, 31 May 1917
2   National Archive, WO95/1975 War Diary 7th Royal Irish Rifles
3   Fielding, R. *War Letters to a Wife: France and Flanders, 1915-1919*, Page 117(Spellmount, 2001)
4   Papers of A.E. Glanville, 2nd Royal Dublin Fusiliers, Copyright Imperial War Museum
5   The Roll of Honour, *Evening Post*, 20 August 1917

Chapter Nine
1   Hear All Sides, *Evening Post*, 5 October 1917
2   The Jersey Company, RIR, *Evening Post,* 15 January 1918
3   The Jersey Company, RIR*, Evening Post,* 15 January 1918
4   Letters of C.J. Scoones, Authors collection

Chapter Ten
1   Honouring the Brave, *Evening Post*, 24 September 1917
2   Stair Gillon, *The Story of the 29th Division*, Page 185 (The Naval & Military Press [www.naval-miliary-press.com])
3   *WO95/2308 War Diary 2nd Hampshire Regiment,* National Archive
4   *WO95/2308 War Diary 2nd Hampshire Regiment,* National Archive
5   Great Town Hall Reception for Local Heroes, *Evening Post*, 22 April 1918
6   *WO95/2308 War Diary 2nd Hampshire Regiment,* National Archive

Chapter Eleven
1   The Armistice, *Evening Post*, 11 November 1918
2   The Original Jersey Co. and Demobilisation, *Evening Post*, 11 December 1918
3   Jersey Contingent and Mobilisation, *Evening Post*, 13 January 1919
4   The States, *Evening Post*, 14 July 1919
5   *Ibid.*
6   Channel Island Great War Study Group (www.greatwarci.net)
7   Overseas Contingent Celebrate Golden Jubilee, *Evening Post*, 3 March 1965

Appendix A

Roll of Service

Compiling a complete and accurate list of all the men who served in the Jersey Company is a not a straightforward matter. Other than some individual records held at the National Archive in Kew, no formal military documentation of the membership exists today. This leaves those lists and rolls of service compiled in Jersey during or after the war as the primary sources of information. These, however, contain a number of obvious errors and omissions. A book of remembrance created by the Contingent Association in the 1960s, for example, mostly excludes the men who volunteered but never served in France and Belgium. Among them are the three who died in Ireland of natural causes – which surely ranks as an injustice. Furthermore, in each there are variations on spelling, rank, date of enlistment, etc.

The creation of this appendix comes from an analysis of all available records and lists together with some interpretation and conclusion based on a cross-reference of the data. Invariably, however, it will continue to include both omissions and errors, although both are hopefully minimal. For this, there is an unreserved apology given, especially to any living relatives of the men.

The nature of print invariably means that information published can never be fully withdrawn. To compensate for any errata, therefore, a website exists that contains not only the most up-to-date Jersey Company roll of service, but also further detailed information on each of the volunteers where known. Readers can find this at www.thejerseypals.com.

KEY OF ABBREVIATIONS FOR FOLLOWING TABLE

Rank						Medals	
Rfn	Rifleman	L Sgt	Lance Sergeant	2nd Lt	Second Lieutenant	MM	Military Medal
Drum	Drummer	Sgt	Sergeant			MedM	Medaille Militaire
Bugl	Bugler	CQMS	Company Quartermaster Sergeant	Lt	Lieutenant	CDeG	Croix De Guerre
L Cpl	Lance Corporal			Cap	Captain	DCM	Distinguished Conduct Medal
Cpl	Corporal	CSM	Company Sergeant Major	Maj	Major	MC	Military Cross

† = Died during the course of the war, or immediately after. Rank shown is that reached by the end of 1915.

Name	Rank	Month joined	RIR number	Hants number	Bravery awards
Ahier, Clarence	Rfn	Feb 1915	4058(?)		
Andrews, Ernest	Rfn	Feb 1915	4057		
Arnold, Henry	Rfn	Feb 1915	4059		
Aubert, Albert	Rfn	Feb 1915	4056		
† Auffret, John	Rfn	Mar 1915	4821		
† Bailey, Arthur	Rfn	Feb 1915	4064		
† Baillie, Edward	Rfn	Feb 1915	4066		
Balston, Thomas	Rfn	Feb 1915	4354	29960	
Banks, Henry	Rfn	Jul 1915	4060		
Banks, Robert	Rfn	Jul 1915	8074		
Banks, William	Rfn	Jul 1915	8079		
† Bartlett, Charles	L Cpl	Feb 1915	4068		
Bastin, Edward	Rfn	Aug 1915	8704		
Baton, John	Rfn	Jul 1915	8389		
Battam, Harold	Rfn	Aug 1915	8681	29957	MM
Battam, John	Rfn	Feb 1915	4065	29956	
† Baxter, Francis	L Cpl	Feb 1915	4062		
Bertram, Ernest	Rfn	Feb 1915	4063		
Best, William	Rfn	Aug 1915	8703		
Bevis, Arthur	L Cpl	Feb 1915	4367		
Biddlecombe, George	Rfn	Feb 1915	4238		
Binet, Roy	Cpl	Feb 1915	4073		MC
† Blampied, Charles G.	Rfn	Feb 1915	4071		
† Blampied, Charles W.	Rfn	Feb 1915	4372		
Blampied, Sidney	Rfn	Jul 1915	8075		MM
Blanchard, John	Rfn	Feb 1915	4352		
† Blanchet, Jean	Rfn	Aug 1915	8385		
Bliault, Sylvan	Rfn	Jul 1915	8042	25670	
Boeshat, Joseph	Rfn	Feb 1915	4353		
Boleat, John	Rfn	Feb 1915	4244		
† Bonny, Peter	Rfn	Feb 1915	4366		
Boulaire, Eugene	Rfn	Feb 1915	4241		
Boulaire, Jonathan	Rfn	Feb 1915	4240		
Bourke, Thomas	Rfn	Jun 1915	7547		
Bowditch, Leonard	Rfn	Feb 1915	4072	29958	
Brassel, Ernest	Rfn	Feb 1915	4074	29961	
† Bree, Arthur	Rfn	Feb 1915	4070		
Bree, Helier	CQMS	Feb 1915	4069	31138	MM, CDeG
Bree, John	Rfn	Jul 1915	8081		
Brée, William	Rfn	Jul 1915	4243		
† Brint, Stephen	Rfn	Jul 1915	8089		
Brisset, Peter	Rfn	Feb 1915	4239		MM
Brochet, Harold	Rfn	Jul 1915	8083		
Buesnel, Clement	Rfn	Feb 1915	4067		
Butters, John	Rfn	Feb 1915	4061		
† Buttery, Charles	Rfn	Jun 1915	7563		
Carpenter, Henry	Rfn	Feb 1915	4081		
† Carré, John	Rfn	Feb 1915	4356		

Name	Rank	Month joined	RIR number	Hants number	Bravery awards
Carter, William	Rfn	Feb 1915	4089	29962	
† Carver, Harold	L Cpl	Feb 1915	4090		
Cashel, James	Rfn	Feb 1915	4355		MM
Cauchard, Philip	Rfn	Feb 1915	4246	29963	
† Cauvain, Harry	Rfn	Feb 1915	4080		
Cawley, Francis	Rfn	Jul 1915	8056		
Champion, Arthur	Rfn	Feb 1915	4079		
Coles, John	L Cpl	Feb 1915	4084		
Collis, Frederick	Rfn	Aug 1915	8829		
Connell, John	Rfn	Feb 1915	4247	29964	
Coombs, Amice	Rfn	Feb 1915	4078		
Coombs, Henry	Rfn	Feb 1915	4088	29966	
Coombs, Herbert	Rfn	Feb 1915	4077	30019	
Coombs, Percy	L Cpl	Feb 1915	4083		
Cooper, Charles	Rfn	Feb 1915	4076		
Corbel, Philip	Rfn	Feb 1915	4075		
Cornick, Arthur	Rfn	Jul 1915	8109		
Cotillard, Peter	Rfn	Feb 1915	4245		
Coutanche, William	Sgt	Feb 1915	4087	29965	
† Crenan, Joseph	Rfn	Jul 1915	9469		
Crocker, Adophus	CQMS	Feb 1915	4082		
Cullen, Joseph	L Cpl	Feb 1915	4085		MM
D'Authreau, Christian	Sgt	Feb 1915	4091	30028	MedM
Dauvin, Alfred	Rfn	Aug 1915	8708		
Dawe, John	Dmr	Feb 1915	4093	29969	
De Bourcier, Francis	Rfn	Jun 1915	7565		
De Gruchy, Philip S.	Rfn	Feb 1915	4095	30042	
De Gruchy, Philip W.	Rfn	Jun 1915	7569	29972	
De Gruchy, William	Rfn	Feb 1915	4096	29968	MM
† De La Haye, Snowdon	Rfn	Feb 1915	4382		
† De La Lande, Arthur	Rfn	Feb 1915	4099		
De La Perrelle, Herbert	L Sgt	Feb 1915	4100		
† De Veulle, Clarence	Rfn	Feb 1915	4097		
Delanoe, Louis	Rfn	Feb 1915	4098		
Dickson, Thomas	2nd Lt	Feb 1915			
Dobin, Arthur	Rfn	Feb 1915	4375		
Dobin, Frank	Rfn	May 1915	6692		
Dobin, George	Rfn	Feb 1915	4374	29967	
† Dorkins, Clarence	Rfn	Jul 1915	8062	29971	
Drouin, Frank	Rfn	Feb 1915	4094	29970	MM
Du Feu, Henry	Rfn	Feb 1915	4102		
† Du Heaume, Reginald	Sgt	Feb 1915	4351		
Dupré, Francis	Rfn	Feb 1915	4101	29974	
Durell, Arthur	Rfn	May 1915	6693	29973	
Eraut, George	Rfn	Feb 1915	4104		
Eveleigh, Edward	Rfn	Feb 1915	4103		
Fennessey, Joseph	Rfn	Feb 1915	4107		
Filer, Albert	L Cpl	Feb 1915	4105		
Finch, Richard	Rfn	Feb 1915	4368	29975	

Name	Rank	Month joined	RIR number	Hants number	Bravery awards
Finch, Thomas	Rfn	Feb 1915	4820		
Finnegan, Alex	L Cpl	Feb 1915	4106		
† Fox, Charles	Drum	Feb 1915	4109	29976	
Fox, George	Bugl	Feb 1915	4108		
Freeman, Alfred	Rfn	Jul 1915	8049		
Gale, Harry	Rfn	Feb 1915	4115		
Gallichan, A.	Rfn				
Gallichan, John	Rfn	Feb 1915	4123		
† Gallie, Alfred	Rfn	Feb 1915	4114		
† Gallie, Arthur	Rfn	Feb 1915	4125		
† Garde, Winter	Rfn	Jul 1915	8073		
Garner, George	Rfn	Feb 1915	4371		
Geary, Arthur	Rfn	Feb 1915	4121	29977	
Geary, John	Rfn	Feb 1915	4122		
Gibbons, Frederick	Rfn	Feb 1915	4112		MM
Gibbons, Wallace	Rfn	Feb 1915	4120		
Giffard, Edward	Rfn	Feb 1915	4231	28741	MM
† Gionta, Joseph	Rfn	Aug 1915	8701		
Godfray, Francis	Rfn	Feb 1915	4119		
Godrich, Clarence	Rfn	Feb 1915	4113	29980	
Gold, Peter	Rfn	Jul 1915	8064		
Gordon, Alfred	Rfn	Feb 1915	4118		
Gosling, Thomas	Sgt	Jul 1915	4111	29979	
† Gosselin, Ernest	Rfn	Feb 1915	4117	29978	
† Gregory, Oscar	Rfn	Feb 1915	4116		
Guillet, Harry	Rfn	Feb 1915	4124		
† Gulliford, Harold	Rfn	Feb 1915	4110		
Hacquoil, Stephen	Rfn	Feb 1915	4126	29985	
Haines, William	Rfn	Feb 1915	4128		
Hamon, Thomas	Rfn	Feb 1915	4226		
† Harding, Nelson	Sgt	Feb 1915	4232		
Herbert, Eugène	Rfn	Feb 1915	4248		
† Hervé, William	Rfn	Apr 1915	4822		
Herviou, John	Rfn	Feb 1915	1025		
† Hibbs, Laurence	2nd Lt	Feb 1915			
Hibbs, William	Rfn	Feb 1915	4127	29981	
Hingston, Alfred	Rfn	Aug 1915	8702		
Honeycombe, Samuel	Rfn	Aug 1915	8705		
† Hopkins, Walter	Rfn	Feb 1915	4131	29982	
Horman, James	Bugl	Feb 1915	4130		
Houguet, Philip	Rfn	Feb 1915	4227	30023	
Hoyles, George	L Cpl	Feb 1915	4129	29987	MM
Huchet, Albert	Rfn	Feb 1915	4376		
Hughes, William	Rfn	Sep 1915	8682		
† Jeffreys, Ernest	L Cpl	Feb 1915	4228		
Jehan, Albert	Rfn	Feb 1915	4826	30031	
Jehan, Alfred	Rfn	Jul 1915	8072		
Jesty, William	Rfn	Jul 1915	8058		
† Johns, William	Rfn	Feb 1915	4136	29989	

Name	Rank	Month joined	RIR number	Hants number	Bravery awards
† Johnson, George	Capt	Feb 1915			
Jones, William	Rfn	Feb 1915	4135	29986	
† Jordan, Bernard	Rfn	Jul 1915	8050		
Journeaux, Clarence	Rfn	Feb 1915	4132	29988	
Journeaux, Henry	Bugl	Feb 1915	4133		MM
Journeaux, Wilfred	Rfn	Feb 1915	4134		
Keast, John	Rfn	Feb 1915	4140	29992	
Kent, Henry	Rfn	Feb 1915	4139		
Kerry, Sidney	Rfn	Feb 1915	4138		
Kessell, Cyril	Rfn	Feb 1915	4137	29990	
Labon, John	Rfn	Feb 1915	4357	29997	
Laffoley, Arthur	Rfn	May 1915	6688	28747	
Laffoley, James	Rfn	Feb 1915	4827		
Laffoley, Philip	L Cpl	Feb 1915	4142		
Lafolley, Charles	Rfn	Feb 1915	4387(?)		
Larbalestier, Morris	Rfn	Feb 1915	4157		
† Laugeard, Charles	L Cpl	Feb 1915	4163	28461	DCM
Laugée, Alfred	Rfn	Feb 1915	4162	29996	
† Laurens, William (George)	Rfn	Feb 1915	4161		
Laurent, Marcel	Rfn	Mar 1915	4823		
Le Boutillier, Francis	Rfn	Feb 1915	4160		
Le Breton, Adrian	Rfn	May 1915	6687		
Le Breton, John	CSM	Feb 1915	4145		DCM/ MedM
† Le Breton, St Elmo	Rfn	Feb 1915	4230	29998	
† Le Claire, Louis	Rfn	Dec 1915 (?)	10180		
Le Cocq, Clarence	Rfn	Feb 1915	4159		
† Le Feuvre, Albert	L Cpl	Feb 1915	4155		
Le Feuvre, J.	Rfn	Feb 1915	4143	29995	
† Le Feuvre, William	Rfn	Feb 1915	4158		
Le Geyt, Abraham	Rfn	Jul 1915	8388		
Le Geyt, Henry	Sgt	Feb 1915	4146		
Le Gresley, Ernest	Rfn	Feb 1915	4151		
Le Lievre, Francis	Rfn	Feb 1915	4150	29993	
† Le Lievre, George	Rfn	Feb 1915	4149		
Le Lievre, Walter	Rfn	Jul 1915	8071		
Le Monnier, Charles	Rfn	Feb 1915	4377	29999	
Le Monnier, Sydney	Rfn	Jul 1915	8082		
Le Piez, Leon	Rfn	Feb 1915	4817		
Le Provost, John	Rfn	Feb 1915	4148		
Le Quelenec, Charles	Rfn	Feb 1915	4141		
Le Riche, Francis	L Sgt	Feb 1915	4144		
Le Rue, John	Rfn	Jul 1915	8060		
Le Sueur, Charles	Rfn	Jul 1915	8051		
Le Sueur, Charles	Rfn	Feb 1915	4164		
Le Tourneur, Jack	Rfn	Jul 1915	8046	30000	
Le Vaillant, William	Rfn	Feb 1915	4370(?)		
Le Vesconte, Stanley	Rfn	Feb 1915	4229		
Lewis, Arthur	Rfn	Feb 1915	4156		

Name	Rank	Month joined	RIR number	Hants number	Bravery awards
L'Homme, Peter	Rfn	Feb 1915	4147		
† Louis, Ernest	Rfn	Feb 1915	4373		
Lozouet, Louis	Rfn	Feb 1915	4154	30025	
Lucas, Frank	Rfn	Feb 1915	4153		
† Luce, Edward	L Cpl	Feb 1915	4365		
Luce, John	Rfn	Feb 1915	4152	29994	MM
† Lunn, Frank	Rfn	Jul 1915	8387		
Macfarlane, Henry	Rfn	Mar 1915	4824		
† Machon, Edward	Rfn	Feb 1915	4242	30004	
† Male, Arthur	Rfn	Feb 1915	4174		
Mallet, Alfred	Rfn	Feb 1915	4172		
Mallet, Arthur	Rfn	Jul 1915	8059		
Mallet, Bertram	L Cpl	Feb 1915	4175	30003	
† Mallet, Charles	Rfn	May 1915	6690		
Mangan, Lawrence	Rfn	Feb 1915	4179		
Marais, Philip	Rfn	Feb 1915	4173	30005	
Marett, Alfred J.	Rfn	Feb 1915	4252		
Marett, Alfred J.	Rfn	Feb 1915	4253		
Marett, John	Cpl	Feb 1915	4167		
Marrett, Edwin	Rfn	Feb 1915	4166		
Marshall, Albert	L Cpl	Feb 1915	4171		
Marshall, Reginald	Rfn	Aug 1915	8706		
† Marshall, William	Sgt	Feb 1915	4168		
† Martin, Walter	Rfn	Feb 1915	4170		
Matson, Alfred	Rfn	Jul 1915	8052		
† Mauger, Reginald	Rfn	Feb 1915	9493		
McCarthy, Michael	L Cpl	Feb 1915	4176		
McClinton, Edward	Rfn	Feb 1915	4177		
McDermott, Francis	Sgt	Aug 1915(?)	3669		
McDermott, Frederick	Drum	Feb 1915	4165		
† McLeod, Edward	Rfn	Jul 1915	8076	30007	
† Minchington, Clarence	L Cpl	Feb 1915	4364		
Moisan, Alfred	L Cpl	Feb 1915	4250		
Monet, Edwin	Rfn	Jul 1915	8386		
Morcel, Alfred	Rfn	Feb 1915	4251		
Morin, Albert	Rfn	Jul 1915	8066		
Morrissey, John	Rfn	Jul 1915	8063		
Mortimer, Frederick	L Cpl	Feb 1915	4169		
Mourant, George	L Cpl	Feb 1915	4249		
† Moy, Joseph	Rfn	Feb 1915	4359		
Moyse, James	Rfn	Feb 1915	4369		
Moyse, Stanley	Cpl	Feb 1915	4092		
Nerac, Francis	Rfn	Feb 1915	4180	30008	
Neville, William	Rfn	Jun 1915	7566		
Nicolle, Cyril	Lt	Feb 1915	–		
Noel, Edwin	L Cpl	Feb 1915	4224		
Noel, George	Rfn	Jul 1915	8053		
Norris, Harold	Rfn	Jul 1915	8067	30009	
Ogier, Cyril	Lt	Feb 1915	–		MC

Name	Rank	Month joined	RIR number	Hants number	Bravery awards
† Olivery, Sidney	Rfn	Feb 1915	4233		
Olsen, Owen	L Cpl	Feb 1915	4360		
Pallot, Abraham	Rfn	Jul 1915	8077		
Pallot, Charles	Rfn	Feb 1915	8069		
Pallot, John	Rfn	Feb 1915	4378		
† Parker, Charles	Rfn	Jul 1915	8054		
† Pearce, George	Rfn	Feb 1915	4185		
† Pennec, Alfred	Rfn	Feb 1915	4235		
Perks, Harry	Rfn	Feb 1915	4236	30010	MM
† Picot, George	Rfn	Feb 1915	4184		
† Pirouet, Arthur	Cpl	Feb 1915	4234		
Poignard, Francis	Sgt	Feb 1915	4181		
Price, Joseph	Rfn	Feb 1915	4183		
Prigent, Augustin	Rfn	Feb 1915	4182	30011	
Quant, William	Rfn	Jul 1915	8068		
Ralph, William	Rfn	Feb 1915	4193	30015	
Randall, Lawrence	Rfn	Jun 1915	7246		
† Remy, William	Rfn	Jul 1915	8065		
Renouf, William	Rfn	Aug 1915	8396		
† Reynolds, Harold	L Sgt	Feb 1915	4187		
† Richards, Albert	Rfn	Feb 1915	4192		
† Richards, Harry	Rfn	Feb 1915	4186	30012	
Richmond, Thomas	Rfn	May 1915	6689		
Richomme, Albert	Rfn	Feb 1915	4191		
Risebridger, Charles	Rfn	May 1915	6691	30013	
† Risebridger, William	Rfn	Feb 1915	4361		
Robert, Roberts	Rfn	Jul 1915	8078		
Roche, Arthur	L Cpl	Jun 1915	7564		
Rodger, James	Rfn	Feb 1915	4189		
† Rogers, Arthur	Rfn	Feb 1915	4194		
Romeril, Henry	Rfn	Feb 1915	4190		
Ronxin, Jean	Rfn	Feb 1915	4362		
Ross, Harry	L Sgt	Feb 1915	4188		
Rowe, Henry	Rfn	Feb 1915	4818		
Ruellan, Peter	Rfn	Aug 1915	8418		
Salain, Emile	Rfn	Feb 1915	4202	30016	
Sansom, Stanley	L Sgt	Feb 1915	4195		
† Scoones, Christopher	Rfn	Feb 1915	4201		
† Scott, Dick	Rfn	Feb 1915	4198		
Shackell, Alfred	Rfn	Apr 1915	4825		
Sohier, Phillip	Rfn	Jul 1915	9739		
Sorel, Francis	Rfn	Feb 1915	4200		
St George, Edward	Rfn	Feb 1915	4199		
Stephens, Albert	Rfn	Jul 1915	8061		
Stivey, Albert	Rfn	Feb 1915	4197		
Stocker, Walter	Maj	Feb 1915	–		
Stott, Percy	L Cpl	Feb 1915	4237		
† Sweeney, William	L Cpl	Feb 1915	4196		
Thelland, William	CSM	Jul 1915	8045		

Name	Rank	Month joined	RIR number	Hants number	Bravery awards
Thomas, Harry	Rfn	Jul 1915	9481		
Torode, Cyril	Rfn	Aug 1915	8707	30018	
Tostevin, Herbert	L Cpl	Feb 1915	4205		
† Touzel, Osmand	L Cpl	Feb 1915	4206	30017	
Trenchard, Samuel	Bugl	Feb 1915	4204		
† Turner, Francis	Sgt	Feb 1915	4203		
Vade, Cyril	Rfn	Jun 1915	7245		
† Vallois, Ernest	Rfn	Feb 1915	4211		
† Vasse, Pierre	Rfn	Feb 1915	4210		
Vautier, Clarence	Rfn	Feb 1915	4209		
Vautier, Francis	Rfn	Feb 1915	4207		
Vautier, Frank	L Cpl	Feb 1915	4208		
Veron, Ernest	Rfn	Jul 1915	8070		
† Vibert, James	Rfn	Feb 1915	4380		
† Vibert, John	Rfn	Feb 1915	4363		
Vickers, Harold	Rfn	Aug 1915	8527		
Vickers, Joseph	Rfn	Feb 1915	4212	30020	MM
Walters, Charles	Rfn	Feb 1915	4819		
† Warren, William	Rfn	Feb 1915	4221		
Watton, Francis	L Cpl	Feb 1915	4225	30030	
† Weeks, Archibald	Bugl	Feb 1915	4215		
Weeks, Robert	Rfn	Aug 1915	8556		
† West, William	Rfn	Feb 1915	4220		
Wherry, Harry	Rfn	Jul 1915	8048		
Whiteman, William	Rfn	Feb 1915	4219		
† Whittle, Thomas	Sgt	Feb 1915	4214		
Wickers, Edwin	Rfn	Feb 1915	4218		
Wickers, George	Rfn	Feb 1915	4217		
Williams, Oscar	L Cpl	Feb 1915	4213		
Williams, Stanley	L Cpl	Feb 1915	4223		
Willmott, George	Rfn	Feb 1915	4222		
Winter, John	Rfn	Feb 1915	4379		
† Wooton, Albert	L Cpl	Feb 1915	4216		
Wooton, William	Rfn	Jul 1915	8127		

Appendix B

Roll of Honour

Eighty members of the Jersey Company died during the war or in the months immediately following. For further details on the cemeteries or memorials listed, visit the website of the Commonwealth War Graves Commission (www.cwgc.org).

Date	Name	Cemetery / Memorial
11 May 1915	Richards, Albert	Buttevant (St John) Churchyard, Ireland
23 Jul 1915	Blampied, Charles W.	Ballyhooly (Christchurch) Church of Ireland Cemetery
14 Nov 1915	Hervé, William	Ballykinlar (St Joseph's) Roman Catholic Cemetery
21 Mar 1916	Hibbs, Laurence	Lapugnoy Military Cemetery, France
1 Apr 1916	Johnson, George	Vermelles British Cemetery, France
16 Apr 1916	Bree, Arthur	Loos Memorial, France
20 Apr 1916	Vallois, Ernest	Bethune Town Cemetery, France
14 May 1916	Mallet, Charles	Bois-Carré Military Cemetery, Haisnes, France
14 May 1916	West, William	Bois-Carré Military Cemetery, Haisnes, France
17 May 1916	Rogers, Arthur	Bois-Carré Military Cemetery, Haisnes, France
18 May 1916	Turner, Francis	Bethune Town Cemetery, France
19 May 1916	De La Lande, Arthur	Mont-a-l'Abbe New Cemetery, Jersey
12 Jun 1916	Warren, William	Dud Corner Cemetery, Loos, France
16 Jun 1916	Bartlett, Charles	St Patrick's Cemetery, Loos, France
28 Jul 1916	Pennec, Alfred	Bois-Carré Military Cemetery, Haisnes, France
30 Jul 1916	Martin, Walter	Caterpillar Valley Cemetery, France
1 Aug 1916	Jeffreys, Ernest	Bois-Carré Military Cemetery, Haisnes, France
6 Sep 1916	Auffret, John	Thiepval Memorial, France
6 Sep 1916	Blampied, Charles G	Thiepval Memorial, France
6 Sep 1916	Blanchet, Jean	Thiepval Memorial, France
6 Sep 1916	Buttery, Charles	Thiepval Memorial, France
6 Sep 1916	Carré, John	Thiepval Memorial, France
6 Sep 1916	Carver, Harold	Thiepval Memorial, France
6 Sep 1916	Du Heaume, Reginald	Thiepval Memorial, France
6 Sep 1916	Luce, Edward	Thiepval Memorial, France
6 Sep 1916	Marshall, William	Thiepval Memorial, France
6 Sep 1916	Reynolds, Harold	Thiepval Memorial, France
6 Sep 1916	Sweeney, William	Thiepval Memorial, France
6 Sep 1916	Vasse, Pierre	Thiepval Memorial, France

Date	Name	Cemetery / Memorial
6 Sep 1916	Vibert, John	Guillemont Road Cemetery, France
9 Sep 1916	Brint, Stephen	Thiepval Memorial, France
9 Sep 1916	Cauvain, Harry	Thiepval Memorial, France
9 Sep 1916	Male, Arthur	Thiepval Memorial, France
9 Sep 1916	Olivery, Sidney	Thiepval Memorial, France
9 Sep 1916	Pearce, George	Thiepval Memorial, France
9 Sep 1916	Pirouet, Arthur	Heilly Station Cemetery, Mericourt-L'Abbe, France
9 Sep 1916	Scott, Dick	Thiepval Memorial, France
4 Mar 1917	Garde, Winter	Kemmel Chateau Military Cemetery, Belgium
4 Mar 1917	Parker, Charles	Kemmel Chateau Military Cemetery, Belgium
8 Mar 1917	Picot, George	Kemmel Chateau Military Cemetery, Belgium
9 Mar 1917	De Veulle, Clarence	Bailleul Communal Cemetery Extension (Nord), France
24 Apr 1917	Minchington, Clarence	Hazebrouck Communal Cemetery, France
22 May 1917	Le Feuvre, William	Kemmel Chateau Military Cemetery, Belgium
22 May 1917	Louis, Ernest	Kemmel Chateau Military Cemetery, Belgium
26 May 1917	Bailey, Arthur	Bailleul Communal Cemetery Extension (Nord), France
26 Jun 1917	Crenan, Joseph	Almorah Cemetery, Jersey
8 Aug 1917	Gallie, Arthur	Ypres (Menin Gate) Memorial, Belgium
12 Aug 1917	Laurens, William (George)	Brandhoek New Military Cemetery, Belgium
16 Aug 1917	Baxter, Francis	Tyne Cot Memorial, Belgium
16 Aug 1917	De La Haye, Snowdon	Tyne Cot Memorial, Belgium
16 Aug 1917	Gulliford, Harold	Tyne Cot Memorial, Belgium
16 Aug 1917	Harding, Nelson	Tyne Cot Memorial, Belgium
16 Aug 1917	Jordan, Bernard	Tyne Cot Memorial, Belgium
16 Aug 1917	Le Lievre, George	Tyne Cot Memorial, Belgium
16 Aug 1917	Risebridger, William	Tyne Cot Memorial, Belgium
16 Aug 1917	Vibert, James	Tyne Cot Memorial, Belgium
16 Aug 1917	Wooton, Albert	Tyne Cot Memorial, Belgium
20 Sep 1917	Baillie, Edward	Hamburg Cemetery, Germany
23 Nov 1917	Le Feuvre, Albert	Cambrai Memorial, France
23 Nov 1917	Mauger, Reginald	Cambrai Memorial, France
23 Nov 1917	Moy, Joseph	Cambrai Memorial, France
24 Nov 1917	Scoones, Christopher	Grevillers British Cemetery, France
6 Dec 1917	Gregory, Oscar	Birmingham (Handsworth) Cemetery, England
10 Dec 1917	Weeks, Archibald	Rocquigny-Equancourt Road British Cemetery, France
13 Mar 1918	McLeod, Edward	Nine Elms British Cemetery, Belgium
10 Apr 1918	Richards, Harry	Ploegsteert Memorial, Belgium
6 May 1918	Le Claire, Louis	Almorah Cemetery, Jersey
31 May 1918	Lunn, Frank	Couin New British Cemetery, France
15 Jun 1918	Dorkins, Clarence	Ebblingham Military Cemetery, France
17 Jun 1918	Fox, Charles	Cinq Rues British Cemetery, France
17 Jun 1918	Hopkins, Walter	Ploegsteert Memorial, Belgium
30 Jun 1918	Machon, Edward	Longueness (St Omer) Souvenir Cemetery, France
11 Aug 1918	Le Breton, St Elmo	Ploegsteert Memorial, Belgium
4 Sep 1918	Touzel, Osmand	Strand Military Cemetery, Belgium
28 Sep 1918	Johns, William	Hooge Crater Cemetery, Belgium

Date	Name	Cemetery / Memorial
1 Oct 1918	Gosselin, Ernest	Tyne Cot Memorial, Belgium
2 Oct 1918	Laugeard, Charles	Duhallow ADS Cemetery, Belgium
31 Oct 1918	Whittle, Thomas	Jersey
27 Nov 1918	Bonny, Peter	St Andre Communal Cemetery, France
5 Mar 1919	Remy, William	Blargies Communal Cemetery, France

Sources and Recommended Further Reading

Periodicals and Official Records

Newspapers

Evening Post
Morning News

National Archive: War Diaries

WO 95/1972: 48th Brigade HQ, December 1915 – December 1916
WO 95/1973: 48th Brigade HQ, January 1917 – April 1918
WO 95/1975: 7th Royal Irish Rifles
WO 95/2502: 2nd Royal Irish Rifles
WO 95/2308: 2nd Hampshires

Channel Islands History

Syvret, Marguerite and Stevens, Joan, *Balleine's History of Jersey* (Phillimore & Co. Ltd., 1981)
Parks, Edwin, *Diex Aïx: God Help Us. The Guernseymen Who Marched Away 1914-1918*
    (Guernsey Museums & Galleries, 1992)

Specific Military History

Denman, Terence, *Ireland's Unknown Soldiers: The 16th (Irish) Division in the Great War* (Irish
    Academic Press Ltd, 1992)
Cooper Walker, G A, *The Book of the Seventh Service Battalion The Royal Irish Fusiliers From
    Tipperary to Ypres* (The Naval & Military Press Ltd)
Fielding, Rowland, *War Letters to a Wife* (Spellmount Ltd, 2001)
O'Rahilly, Alfred, *The Padre of Trench Street* (Diggory Press, 2005)
Falls, Cyril, *The History of the First Seven Battalions: The Royal Irish Rifles* (The Naval & Military
    Press Ltd)
Gillon, Stair, *The Story of the 29th Division: A Record of Gallant Deeds* (The Naval & Military
    Press Ltd)

General Military History

Taylor, A.J.P., *The First World War* (Penguin Books 1966)

Holmes, Richard, *Tommy: The British Soldier on the Western Front 1914-1918* (Harper Perennial, 2005)

Sheffield, Gary, *The Somme* (Cassell, 2003)

Passingham, Ian, *Pillars of Fire: The Battle of Messines Ridge June 1917* (Sutton Publishing Ltd, 1998)

Steel, Nigel and Hart, Peter, *Passchendaele: The Sacrificial Ground* (Cassell, 2000)

Cooper, Bryan, *The Ironclads of Cambrai* (Pan Books Ltd, 1970)

Toland, John, *No Man's Land: The Story of 1918* (Eyre Methuen, 1980)

Index